ROB KEARNEY

NO HIDING

ROB KEARNEY

NO HIDING

WITH DAVID WALSH

Reach Sport

www.reachsport.com

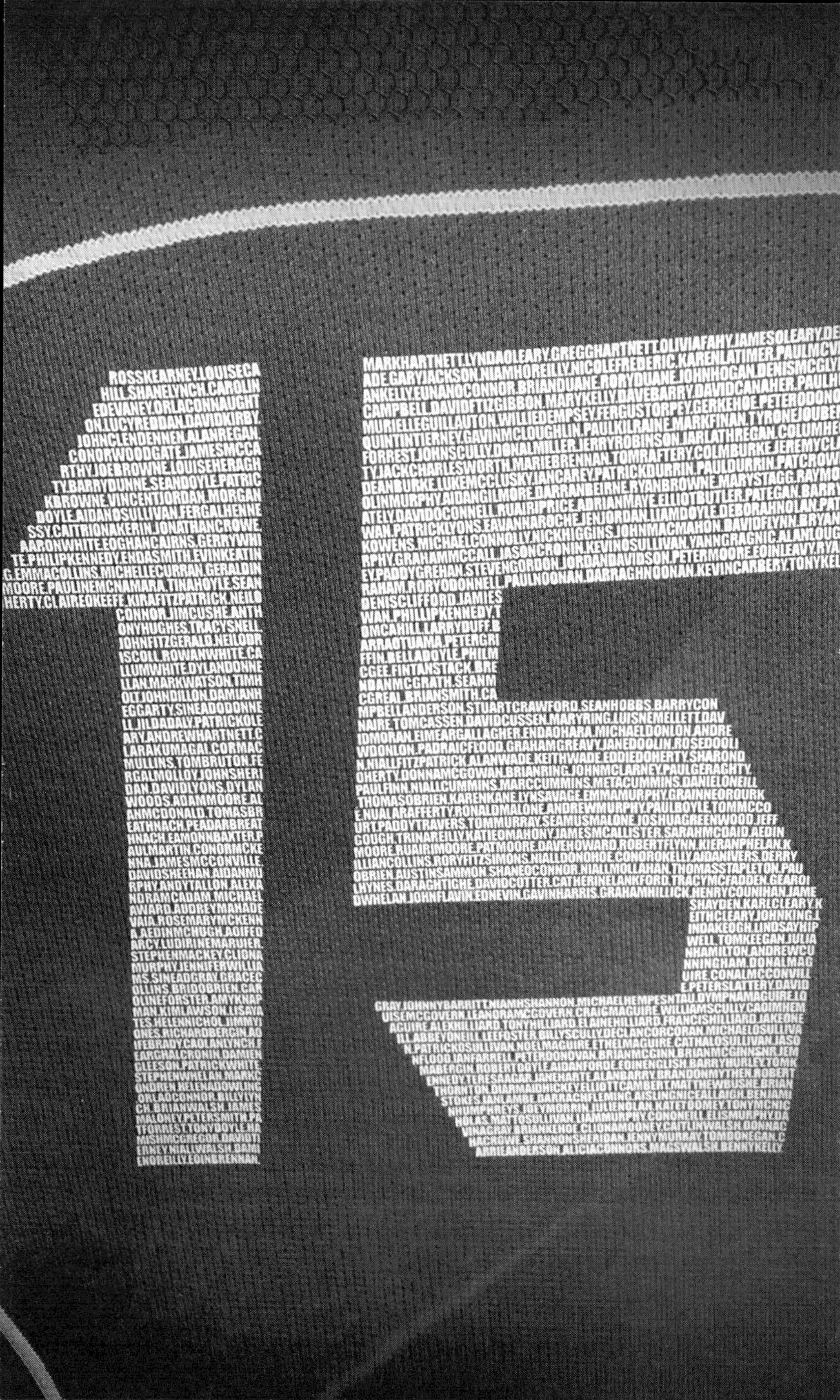

*For Ross, who has always been
with us, my family and Jess for their
constant love, support and strength.*

Reach **Sport**

www.reachsport.com

Written with David Walsh.

With thanks to David McHugh and Gill Hess Ltd.

Published in Great Britain and Ireland in 2020 by Reach Sport,
5 St Paul's Square, Liverpool, L3 9SJ.
www.reachsport.com
@Reach_Sport
Reach Sport is a part of Reach PLC.
One Canada Square, Canary Wharf, London, E15 5AP.

Hardback ISBN: 978-1-911613-65-7
eBook ISBN: 978-1-911613-66-4

Edited by Roy Gilfoyle.

Photographic acknowledgements:
Rob Kearney personal collection, PA Images, Sportsfile, Inpho.
Every effort has been made to trace copyright.
Any oversight will be rectified in future editions.

Printed and bound by CPI Group (UK) Ltd,
Croydon, CR0 4YY.

CONTENTS

1
___

THIS IS THE END

Saturday, October 19th, 2019. Tokyo Stadium, Tokyo

I t hurts at first. I am not happy to be called ashore. That's a reflex, though. No player ever wants to be hauled away from the action. As I head toward the bench, there is a separate part of me which is thinking differently. Thank Christ I am getting off this field.

We've lost this game. Sixty minutes gone. Nothing running right. I'm not doing anybody any favours by being out there. Get me off this field, thank you.

And yet another part of me is noting that Jordan Larmour has just come on. In twenty minutes, we will be out of this World Cup. Andy Farrell, our new coach, will start building towards the next one. This was potentially my last game for Ireland. Jordan Larmour is going the other way. He is the future.

If we are honest, this one was lost by half time. New Zealand were elemental in their power, ferociously grabbing territory from us, hitting us with big drives and stinging tries. Coming again with a combination of gut shots and haymakers. We'd said the right things to each other at the break but it was 22-0 by then and we knew that it was lost.

So it's over for me now and I'll have a little mental preparation time before we have to go out into the real world beyond the dressing room door. I know the shit that I, personally, am going to take and I know that I will take that shit personally. I know what will be heaped on us as a team. Everybody has an opinion and we are entitled to everybody's opinion. If this is the end, I won't miss that constant noise.

When the game is over, we hug each other and we troop back in to our changing room. I take off my boots and just sit there and think to myself. That's it. I am done, so done, with international rugby. I've had my fill. It's all hassle. Too much stress and hassle.

Ten minutes or so before we are due to leave the dressing room, Joe Schmidt comes in from whatever aftermath duties he has been dealing with.

He says a few words to us. He talks about how he is feeling and how proud of us all he is. He says how much he has enjoyed working with us, not just as a team but as people. It's the last time he will speak to us in a dressing room and I wonder if Joe is going to get a little emotional. I have never seen him be emotional.

Then Rory Best stands up. As our captain he thanks Joe for everything he has done and now Joe really does get a bit emotional and it doesn't feel right. Like seeing your dad cry. Players just stand up and shuffle towards him one by one. We need just to embrace him. I feel a huge affection towards him now, just seeing the flesh and blood side of a human being who lots of people have mistaken for a computer system hardwired for rugby. I wait my turn. Joey Carbery and Jordan Larmour are in front of me. Joe is saying something to them along the lines of, you guys, you guys are the future, you are the ones who are going to take Irish rugby to the next step. His benediction.

And then it's me. Old mutton. Very much not the future. But Joe looks at me and just says, ten years Kearns, we've been through so much.

All the seasons, all the training sessions, all the games since our paths intersected. A man from Kawakawa, New Zealand and a young lad from Cooley, County Louth. It's ending in a dressing room in Japan. I tear up now too. I was a little weepy a while ago out there on the grass when the last whistle blew. Now the tears come again.

After big games, the PR people take cattle prods from their briefcases and poke reluctant players in their ones and twos out into the media mixed zone to supply instant quotes to journalists. It's part of the job but you are reluctant to go out after a win because the dressing room is a happy place. You are more reluctant after a loss. Out there will be even worse than in here.

Keith Earls arrived back in from the mixed zone a little while ago just as I was preparing to go out and face the music. He was more bemused than annoyed.

"Do you know what they wanted to know? Would I be considering my position? Would I be retiring? Minutes after the game? They were asking, is that it for you?"

I do an about-turn. Keith is about eighteen months younger than I am. I've been reading published drafts of my own obituary in some papers for years now. I don't need this stuff now. Not today.

Back during the 2016-17 period, there was so much time when I really didn't enjoy playing for Ireland. We weren't winning and I was copping quite a bit of personal crap. Nobody had ever said that it had to be fun but that time was no fun.

I wasn't playing my best. I knew that. My body was breaking down on me. I had become obsessed with the caps. I was just accumulating more headwear. Running up the numbers. The numbers were the only thing people could never take away from me. Say whatever you want, write whatever you want, tweet whatever you want, but every cap I got represented one more time that I had got picked. One more time when I had got picked by somebody whose opinion really meant something. So I kept on going and Joe Schmidt kept picking me. While he had faith in me, I kept racking up those numbers.

But the criticism kept coming. I'm happy to take criticism and learn from criticism if it is informed and reasonable but some of the tone and content was personal. It got to me.

There are some guys whose bylines trigger bad reactions in the brain before you even read what is underneath. Gavin Cummiskey in the *Irish Times* gave me an awful going over in those years. I would have seen a lot of the stuff he wrote. I don't know why it got to me, he's not a major writer or a big voice but I felt that it was personal, that it was vendetta stuff.

He wanted me out of the fifteen jersey. He wanted me replaced by anybody that wasn't Rob Kearney.

Simon Zebo.

Jordan Larmour.

Jared Payne.

Anybody.

Around 2016 and 2017, this was really getting to me. I wasn't enjoying my game and the feeling was made worse by the texts and links that came my way.

– Cummiskey having a right slice off you today!

– Did you steal Cummiskey's last Rolo?

I remember having a chat with Enda McNulty, the IRFU's mental skills coach, about how I was feeling generally. I mentioned the media coverage.

"There is just this one fella who is just breaking me at the moment."

"Yeah," Enda said, "Gavin Cummiskey."

So even Enda had noticed. He suggested a solution.

"What I want you to do for the next six months at the end of every gym session, at the end of every training session, at the end of every piece of work you do and any time you practise, I want you to do one extra rep. Call it the Gavin Cummiskey rep. So, after gym, one more bench press. If you are running, just one more lap or one more sprint and so on."

So I did. Through gritted teeth, with clenched fists, on jaded legs. I did all my damn Cummiskeys.

I did lots of other things differently too and then, in 2018, everything changed. We started winning again. It was a bonus year, a late career dividend. I enjoyed my rugby and if Gavin Cummiskey, as it seemed to me, avoided me when things were going well, I didn't go seeking him or his byline out.

In 2018, I was back in love with the game. Once more there was joy in playing for Ireland. I was playing well. We won another Grand Slam. We beat the All Blacks again. We had our triumphant tour of Australia. I was just ticking off so many things that I had never done before and some that I had wanted to do again. I packed about as many good times into a single year as it is possible for a player to do. That year, with its avalanche of medals and memories, had to come to an end, of course. Now, here at the World Cup, we've been reminded that whatever we did last year couldn't inoculate us against disaster. Japan have beaten us in a famous victory for our hosts and the All Blacks have just handed us our asses on a plate.

Now I am stuffing gear into my kitbag and thinking that I may never be putting my boots on again in an international dressing room. If that's the case, I'm happy enough. I've had enough of days like these and also I've had more of the good times than I ever dreamed of having. No more games. No more mixed zones. I'll take that.

Sunday, October 20th, 2019. Tokyo

We are staying on here in Japan until Tuesday. Some of the group would like to be heading home sooner than that but I'm in no hurry. The last thing I want is to go home. I can't face going back to Dublin. I don't want to be there for the post-mortems and the inevitable backlash. I am embarrassed and I just don't want to see Irish people for a while. I don't want to have to talk to people about the game. I just want to be somewhere far away.

Last night we had a quiet evening back in the hotel. Not a wake but not a party either.

I had some drinks and a bite to eat. My mum is over here with my older brother Richard and two very good family friends, John and Mags McNally. Dad was here too but he is captain of his golf club Royal County Down this year and he had made the commitment that, for twelve months, his captaincy would take priority over any rugby he wanted to attend. So he had to go home during that week as they were hosting the R&A. The two events just happened to fall on the same week and he was gutted.

We have a team meeting at eleven o'clock this morning. Housekeeping notes mainly. Joe takes the meeting and once again he thanks us as players, he thanks all his backroom staff and he warns us that if we are going out on the beer today, we are not to mess around. The Japanese police take these things seriously and if anybody gets arrested they will be left behind. The team will be going home without the miscreants.

Joe makes a few more points and then he just floats away into the background. Straightaway Andy Farrell steps up and speaks to us. He will be getting a plan together for everybody over the next few weeks, details about which games we should play and how much holiday to take etc.

It's a full changing of the guard right there and then. Joe just moved to the background literally and metaphorically. Andy is the new main man. The king is dead, long live the king. It was the clearest imaginable moment of transition.

Here we are in a room in a hotel at Disneyland, Tokyo. The World Cup has ended and everything has changed.

Andy looks totally comfortable.

When the meeting wraps up, we grab whatever we need from our rooms and then pile onto a team bus. We're heading into Tokyo to roam about the city and, frankly, to go on the beer for the whole day. This World Cup hasn't ended well but it has been a long haul and we've been together so long that there is a little cabin fever in the ranks.

As a team we eat together, for the last time most likely, in a Tokyo restaurant. We linger till four or five in the afternoon then I wander out to meet my brother Richard and his friend

Paul O'Donnell. We wander the Golden Gai strip in Shinjuku, which isn't a very original idea. We bump into most of the team and half of Ireland as we roam. So much for avoiding Irish people for a while.

After months of pressure cooker preparation, it is good to feel the tension wash out of the body. I have the most fun that I have had in quite a while. It's less than twenty four hours after the game and the place is hopping with Irish fans and, in fairness, they are all in pretty good form. There are no recriminations. Nobody has a harsh word to say. The evening is just hours of meeting people who want to say thanks for everything that the team has done over the years. We appreciate it.

We have an unbelievable night. We fall into company with my brother Dave's housemate Nick Mullen and with Rhys Ruddock and that is pretty much it for us. We are set. We have drinks, laughs and trade songs in a little pub and suddenly it is two in the morning and we're all feeling good.

The tide of disappointment has gone out for now. I haven't a worry in the world apart from the nagging feeling that I'm going to wake up tomorrow with a headache and with an intrusive flashing neon sign in my head. YOU ARE NOW ENTERING THE REST OF YOUR LIFE.

But that's tomorrow's worry.

Then, of all the gin joints in all the towns in all the world, Gavin Cummiskey walks into mine. Well, the one that I am drinking in.

I'm healthy enough drinks-wise. Sober(ish) in a happy way. Richard is beside me. He knows exactly who has just walked in. He just nudges me an alert and I look over. Before Richard can say the words "just ignore him", I have let out a roar.

"Cummiskey get the fuck out of here."

Gavin Cummiskey turns around and walks out.

I'm not sure what I have just done. Or what I would have done if Cummiskey had, as he was entitled to do, just ignored me and sat down. Thankfully nobody takes exception.

There are other journalists in the joint. I haven't taken the decision to bar all media. In fact, we have been enjoying some great craic. Derek Foley is here, Ger Gilroy from Newstalk. There's a photo taken of me putting on a boxing glove and pretending to be punching Gilroy in the face. Just because he was media!

I think Gavin Cummiskey had his colleague Keith Duggan with him, a man who I've never met. God knows what Keith Duggan thought of me. Probably that Kearney is some ignorant fucker alright. More good PR in the battle for hearts and minds.

It's a great night but, from that moment on, I can't get the incident and my reaction out of my head.

Monday, October 21st, 2019. Team Hotel, Tokyo

The team is like one of those organs which can lose key cells only to grow new ones and regenerate and keep working. Joe is gone. Rory is gone. The World Cup is gone. But we have a team meeting this morning at eleven o'clock.

This gathering is essentially a chance to give some gifts to the liaison officer and the security people. Bestie got a gift and Joe got a gift too. Just a small way of thanking people for their efforts. Ger Carmody and Sinead Bennett, who between them plan and map out all our logistical operations, organised that. All the liaison staff and security would have got signed Irish jerseys. A nice touch for them. Joe and Bestie got a signed

Irish jersey as well. I'm not sure what they will do with them. And that was officially the end of it then. World Cup over.

The first thing I did this morning when I came to, was to send a text message. I don't have a number for Gavin Cummiskey so I wrote to his colleague Gerry Thornley. I said that I knew Gavin had said some unkind things about me in the past but that the way I had spoken to him was no way to talk to anybody. I asked Gerry to please apologise on my behalf.

Gerry's reply was very nice. He said it was understandable given there were a few drinks on board and allowing for the weekend that was in it.

I thought a lot about what happened. It didn't reflect how I felt in better moments. Gavin Cummiskey is doing his job whether he likes me or not. What he writes might genuinely be how he feels and good luck to him.

He still shouldn't be told to fuck off out of a bar.

It's just that, with the media, I've found it harder as the years go to just ignore it. I've had so much of it pent up in my system over a long period of time and when I saw him come into the bar I didn't even think about it. It was just a reaction. I was half joking and half not joking. Gavin Cummiskey didn't wait to see which it was.

Not a great end to what was a disappointing World Cup anyway.

Tomorrow I will fly direct from Tokyo to Dubai. Jess, my partner, is flying there from Dublin. Rory Best and his family are going. Tadhg Furlong, Conor Murray and their better halves are all coming. A mutual friend, Daniel Strain, will meet us over there.

It will be nice to be in Dubai with people who are feeling the same things. If I want to bitch about the game or what we might have done better than I can. If not, fine. I need this get away. I need a buffer. Home is reality and social media and journalists and pundits. Dubai won't be any of that.

October, Reality, Dublin

I came back from Dubai at seven in the evening on the last Monday of October and I went into Leinster training the next morning. Officially we had the week off but I've just had a break and I wanted to get going again. I had done absolutely nothing in Dubai and I am at that age now where, if I go longer than a week without work, I start to go backwards physically. So the best thing was to be back into the gym, back out onto a field, back into the system.

I wasn't being totally goody-goody about getting back to work. Jordan Larmour was still off for the week and I reckoned I'd get a little jump on him.

I was on the back foot coming out of the World Cup but my competitive instinct has kicked in again. After a week away, I noticed a huge change in my attitude toward my career since the All Blacks defeat. Back then I didn't care if I ever played rugby again. Now, a little over a week later, I care so much that I want to get a head start.

Physically, I feel fine. Mentally, though, it's tough going back in because it means starting off all over again. Bottom of the hill, looking up.

I put so much into the last four months with the aim of achieving one big target. That's over and done with now. They've taken the target away and given out the prizes to the winners. I am coming back into a new season already. I have to recalibrate but people around the club just want to talk to me about the All Blacks game. Stuart Lancaster and Leo Cullen in particular.

The club is a place of professionals. Nobody sugar coats things. Nobody says, other than that, how was the play Mrs Lincoln? It's why did you not do this on that move and why did you do that? That's their job. Asking hard questions of players is what makes Stuart and Leo the coaches they are.

They want us to absorb the learnings from the New Zealand game. The process will make better players of us. They have review sessions with each one of us to explain how Leinster play differently and what we are trying to do when we play this way. If this was us in this situation, they say, we'd try to get the ball to the edge here and take this space.

They are looking at our individual performances too. That is tough. I went through the game with Stuart and, for comparison purposes, he was also picking up images of the English back three from their game the week before against Australia. He was showing how the English back three worked from one edge of the field right across to the other edge. This is what he needs me to do.

The takeaway for me is that I am quietly pleased that Stuart is taking this time with me. It suggests that I am not written off yet. I should have a chance of some good playing minutes this season, maybe some big games.

How I finish is important to me. I don't like using the word legacy, it's more than a little bit pompous, but I do want to leave a good lasting impression behind. I don't want to be that pro who didn't commit to the last year because he was bitter and just stopped setting a good example. I don't want to be the guy letting down his team-mates with his lack of effort.

This is my fifteenth year, definitely my last in Ireland and, in short, I don't want to be part of something for so long and to have contributed so many things only just to drift further and further away. I don't want somebody to look around the Leinster dressing room one day and think, wow, is Rob Kearney actually still here? So sad.

This year, there will be myself and two much younger guys, Jordan Larmour and Hugo Keenan, each looking for time in the number fifteen jersey. I weigh up the pros and cons.

Pros: Experience. Reading of the game. A solidity which some might describe as boring. Just came back from a World Cup as first choice international full back.

Cons: Age. I'm not a project. Explosiveness is diminishing. That solidity which too many might describe as boring. My virtues aren't those that the club is looking for anymore. I'm not sexy anymore.

There is one more factor mitigating against me. Environment. Young players are so confident these days. Not entitled, just confident. The culture in Leinster now is so progressive and it leans toward developing and fast-tracking the younger guys. There is the philosophy that younger guys should be at the back of the bus in the seats where once the established players sat in their cliques, trading in-jokes and old war stories. Leo is particularly keen on this policy.

The young players are central now, not peripheral. The team is their team. That is a very clear policy led by the coaches, especially Leo.

Occasionally I think that the older lads are being pushed to the side a little bit and that is hard to stomach. On the other hand, it is working pretty well. We have forty or fifty guys all of whom have played a lot of games for Leinster, they expect to play every week and they play well when they play.

And then we have some guys like me who the club seems unsure about what to do with.

You can't argue against success though.

I've been here since the days when we got changed out of car boots. I have dedicated my whole career to this club and when I see the younger guys getting all the plaudits and being built up, I know that it's fine. The best way to kill complacency is competition. I can contribute this season by being part of that competition.

And I realise that I had the rub of the green when I was younger. I got those calls, I got so many of those momentum moments when I was starting out. If you asked me, I couldn't tell you how the older players faded away when we were young and coming through. Or how they felt about it. We were so hungry we never noticed anybody leave the table.

It's been a great career and I realise that I am fortunate to still be here for this period of change. I try to embrace it a little bit more. Still, if I was offered another contract at Leinster right now, I don't think I'd take it. It's not what I want. This year will be tricky enough as it is. Deep down, I'm just too competitive to enjoy not playing a huge amount of the time. I don't like watching from the bench or the sidelines and that is something I will probably be doing a lot of. This year is just a calculated withdrawal from the only career I have ever had.

I'm not sure what comes next. I will use the time to find out.

Most of the Leinster guys who had been to the World Cup came back to work quickly. We trained on the Wednesday and then we were put through an incredibly hard session on the Thursday. Stuart wanted to show us something. This is how we train and how we play and it's tougher than the training you do with Ireland.

The week in Dubai did my body some favours. I felt ok.

After some games, I can feel completely beaten up but physically I felt perfect after the New Zealand game. I had very few carries, not one carry in the first half and not a huge amount of work to do. We just didn't have the ball very often. Physically I could have played again the next weekend. Mentally? No.

At the end of the first week back, Leinster played the Dragons at home. Those of us who had been at the World Cup weren't required to go to the game but my brother Dave was playing, so I went along and watched a cruise control win with Mum and Dad. We were back in again on the Monday. We were to play Connacht the next weekend and I knew I would start on the bench.

In Galway, I came on with twenty minutes to go. I didn't have a huge amount to do. I touched the ball once and knocked it on. That got the biggest roar of the night in the Sportsground but it didn't make me smile at all.

I wasn't in the mood. It pissed me off to be back to the old hostile atmosphere of baiting and jeering. We gave a decent Leinster performance though and had picked up a bonus point before half time. The takeaway for me? I was happy to be back on the field. It helped me banish some memories of Japan.

Hugo Keenan started at full back in Galway. He's one of the young guys who hadn't played a huge amount before this season but already he looks comfortable. Hugo is young and comes from a sevens background which always stands to fifteens players. I've said to Hugo, as I have said to Jordan, that if he thinks that I can help with anything I'm always here. It's up to them.

Meanwhile, I understand the process. The club is developing

other full backs. That is good management and what I would expect.

Oddly, I actually enjoyed going to Galway. In the hotel beforehand and during the pre-game prep I felt so different to how I was just two weeks beforehand in Tokyo. I was relaxed. I was almost surprised to notice it about myself. The game was a chance to forget about New Zealand. The final whistle in Galway would mean that my last game of rugby was against Connacht. Not the All Blacks. I was back up on the horse.

With Leinster, all games matter but some games matter more than others. Those games are Heineken Cup games. The first of these was against Benetton Treviso at home. I could second guess the selection without thinking about it. I wasn't going to play in that one. The precedent says that Jordan now plays in the big games at home in the RDS. Those games suit his natural progression into the full back jersey.

A week later, we would be away to Lyon. That would be when my real value could be assessed. The team had a good win against Treviso, Jordan played well and on Monday morning I went to work expecting to be named in the team for the Lyon game.

The first person I met was Stuart Lancaster. He didn't quite avoid me but he would have if he could. He seemed uneasy and that made me uneasy. This is going to be bad, I thought.

Around eleven, Leo beckoned me.

"Can I have a word?"

Ok, here we go. If Leo has good news his face doesn't know about it but he says, you'll be back in at fifteen this week.

"Thanks," I say. Thanking him for putting me back in the team feels a little bizarre. He's not doing it to be kind.

I was uncommonly chuffed to be selected, though. Playing

in Lyon meant two things. The club still saw some value in me when it came to playing the big games in Europe. And they are going to give me a fair crack of the whip this year. My thoughts ran on. I decided that if I played well in Lyon maybe I'd get back in for the next big away day in the Heineken Cup.

It went pretty well in France. I had some big interventions in the game. Mostly defensive stuff. It was pissing rain and we were up against a big physical French side. They were keen. They were leaders in the league at that moment and the best team in France.

Afterwards, I went through our schedule again in my head. Hugo would start next week's Pro 14 game against Glasgow. Then we had back-to-back Heineken Cup matches against Northampton Saints. Away first. Home second.

Travelling to Lyon, I knew that I would need to be sensational to start in the home game against Northampton but if I played well enough I would definitely play in the away game.

I came off that Lyon field and weighed things up. Ok. Good game, I did some good things. I will play in the away game in Northampton.

I was happy and I allowed myself a few minutes of optimism. If I play well against Northampton will I have got myself back into the Six Nations window? Will Andy Farrell be watching? Will he see the sense of Leinster playing me in the tough away games and think about bringing my experience to the away games against England and France in the new year? Let Jordan take the home fixtures?

Why not?

I am trying really hard not to be completely overtaken by stress over selections. Last year, I would barely sleep on Saturday and

Sunday just waiting for the team announcement on Monday. I want to get to a place where selection isn't affecting my life outside of rugby. After all these years, it shouldn't be gnawing at my wellbeing.

I should be used to it by now. In 2017, I knew that Stuart, in particular, was pushing the idea of playing Joey Carbery at full back. Joey was young and he was playing sexy rugby. Stuart liked the idea of having a playmaker at fifteen. Quite often I wasn't getting picked. I was thirty one, thirty two and my club position was in jeopardy.

Fortunately, Joe Schmidt kept picking me for Ireland. Many in his position would have said, if you aren't playing at club level you can't play full back for Ireland but he stuck with me. Whatever Joe wanted in a full back he seemed to find in me.

Going into 2018, things didn't look good. Joey had played a lot in 2017 when I was injured and I knew that Leinster would have all-in committed with Joey had he stayed. No doubt about it, Stuart wanted that. Joey, though, saw himself as an out-half, not as a full back. He picked up a few niggles before he moved to Munster in May of that year. Jordan was on the scene but still not experienced enough yet for fifteen so I played all the big games and played well.

You just have to be a professional about it. Whether it's going well or going badly, it's never personal. I knew that Leinster had to pick me as 2018 ran on but, as it happened for me, 2018 was like a stretch of lovely summer weather that comes along after Hallowe'en. It was all the more enjoyable for being so surprising. I took some medals and a lot of joy out of the year.

My feeling this time, though, is that a similar reprieve is unlikely as we head toward 2020. If I don't play full back for any of the big European games this year, I will be wondering if management are privately thinking that Joe Schmidt made a big mistake picking me for the World Cup.

Stuart doesn't announce the team. Leo always does that. If you have a problem, you go to Leo. Stuart doesn't want anything to do with selection. He just wants to coach the team. He doesn't talk to players about selection but he has a say.

The week of the Northampton game, we were in the gym on Monday morning. The forwards were upstairs doing their video review. The backs were down in the gym. Leo came around, talking to people one by one. I eyed him as he made the rounds. I was gauging guys' reactions to get some idea of the lay of the land.

When he got to me he said straight off that the back three against Northampton would be James Lowe, Jordan Larmour and my brother Dave. Jordan had played on the wing against Lyon but against Northampton he would be full back. I had guessed they would keep him in the team regardless but assumed he would be on the wing. Leo said that they had brought Dave in because he is very good defensively and they needed him to mark the Fijian behemoth Taqele Naiyaravoro. Coaches can always give you a reason for selecting any particular player.

There is a touch of like it or lump it in these conversations with Leo. A lot of our chats have gone the same way. Leo will say, listen, we feel that Jordan offers us more in attack as a team. I will say to Leo that I think I offer more in defence than Jordan does. Leo will say, well, we value attack over defence. That's a pretty simple conversation and I can't argue that Leinster aren't that kind of team.

Sometimes I say nothing. I know that I will have bigger

battles to fight and it's best to keep the powder dry. In this instance I didn't say much. Leo asked me what I thought, which was unusual for him. I told him that I had expected to start the game. I thought I had done well enough in Lyon to merit that. I'd thought they would start Jordan at fifteen at home the next week. It's unusual for a player to give an honest assessment but Leo did ask! I hadn't expected to play the next week but I brought it up just to underline how much I had been expecting to play this week.

Things change so quickly that you can't stand still. I've been away from Leinster for almost six months. There are guys like Ronan Kelleher, Will Connors, Max Deegan, Caelan Doris and Hugo who have become real players while I was gone. It's an amazing crop.

As the season goes by and the stakes are ratcheted up, I know that every game will have its own subplot in terms of my own future. Seasons have always had that element but now, more than ever, it weighs on my mind.

If anything goes wrong when I'm on the pitch, the finger will be pointed at the older guy. And I hate that. As soon as you hit thirty years of age, it begins. They start writing you off. They whisper about getting a new model. It started even earlier with me, I suppose because I had started earlier. Somebody looked up one day when I was in my late twenties and asked, precisely how long has he been here? Forever.

For confidence, you look for the signs that you are not too far off where you were. The stats are coming at you relentlessly nowadays and you sift through them for encouragement. Then you ask your body how it is doing. The strength is the same but the explosiveness is seeping away. On the credit side, all the experience gives you a jumpstart when it comes to positioning. I realised long ago that all the moving parts of my body have to be maintained. Even at this age I am learning to run more efficiently, learning how to get more out of myself. I'm learning all these things that young lads are getting now on a daily basis from the time they hit the academy.

When I started off we would pull up in the car at Old Belvedere, get changed at the car boot and run out onto the grass and do a ninety-minute pitch session. Now we do an hour in the gym, just getting our bodies ready to go out onto the pitch. You are firing up all the muscles, hitting everything so you aren't taking chances on any small thing.

I tell the young lads to look after the body. It's your biggest asset, I say. These days, though, they have all that prep and then all the recovery strategies after the session and I'm sure they wonder what exactly I'm talking about. Why wouldn't a pro player take care of his body?

The two games against Northampton will stay with me as clearly as if I had played in them myself. Jordan Larmour made so many line breaks in both games that I gave up counting.

Late in the second game, I was warming up behind the posts in the Aviva and Jordan made a break up the touchline, jinking, slaloming, feinting. Leaving mayhem behind him before passing the ball inside to James Lowe. I just remember thinking very clearly, this is the moment. I looked around the Aviva. It was absolutely an epiphany. Absolutely. I was looking around. It's not the try at the end of the move that electrifies the place. It's all Jordan. He's sprinkled some magic there.

Well, that's it, I said to myself, the baton has been passed and it's fast disappearing off into the distance.

Jordan played so well in both games. People want sexy rugby and he gives it to them. For the last few years, the type of game I have played has not been sexy. It has been effective. It helped the team win but it is not box office, not what the punter wants.

I'm contracted to play till the end of the season but I see now how, with Leinster at least, it is going to unfold. A few weeks ago, I thought Jordan was the future. Now he is the present. He has arrived.

Two days after the home game against Northampton, I went north to County Down. Dad was hosting a captain's lunch at the Royal County Down golf club and we were all up there as a family. It was Sunday the fifteenth of December.

The golf club has a rule about not using mobile phones so when I noticed that I had a missed call, I made my excuses and went outside. The call lasted ninety seconds, two minutes maybe, and when I came back to the table nobody asked me about it and I said nothing. This captaincy in Royal County Down was Dad's World Cup. I was conscious not to take anything away from that by sharing my little bit of news.

We were driving home in the car later, myself, and my brothers Dave and Richard, when I mentioned it.

"I got the phone call just before lunch there. Andy Farrell. I'm done."

The training squad for an in-season camp was being named the following morning. Andy Farrell had said that Ireland were having a Christmas camp, stocktake stuff. Forty five players in. It's only a one-day camp. There will be some players from in the squad and some players who aren't in the squad.

Yes?

He paused for a few seconds.

Rob, you're not going to be in the squad.

I was a little rattled and not sure how to react. I didn't ask any questions. I literally just said cheers, I appreciate the call. I'll chat to you soon. Hung up. That simple.

For a moment, I had half a thought about it being unfair. I'm the most capped full back in the history of rugby union. Was I being a little precious in feeling that I deserved a face to face? What would that have achieved though? It's elite sport. There has to be a ruthless element to it and very little sentiment.

I just went back in to the table to the family and put on a brave face.

In the car, Dave doesn't really have to say anything for me to get some perspective. Dave has been playing very well this season. He knows he is probably going to be in the group named tomorrow. He had the disappointment of missing the World Cup, having being involved in camps beforehand. He's had some really bad injuries at really bad times. He knows how these things feel. One hundred times more than I do.

This was very definitely the first big setback for me and after the sunlit run that I've had, I'm just glad that it's his time for good things to happen.

Sean Cronin, Rhys Ruddock, Jordi Murphy and Jack Carty were also left out but I was the only one gone who had been in the starting fifteen at the World Cup. Forty five players is a pretty deep pool not to be included in. It was quite conclusive.

Over Christmas it affected me a little. It was there buzzing away in the back of my head. I was thinking, does Andy Farrell think that I'm the reason that we got knocked out of the World Cup? And my pride was bruised.

It wasn't so much the fact that I wasn't in the squad, it was more that I had been the headline casualty. The talking point for the following week was me. There was a bit of embarrassment to that.

We had worked so hard going to the World Cup and went off with such high hopes. I had imagined a scenario where we got to a final and, win or lose, we would have achieved something and I would have been the starting full back when 2020 came around. The Six Nations would be just three months later. The team that had done so well would get the chance to start. Surely? If I was good enough three months ago why would that change?

I saw Stuart Lancaster the day after Andy called and he asked me if I'd had 'the chat'. He knew. Stuart said that Andy needed to show change, that things would be different going forward. It was just an indication that the path was going to be different.

Then I got to thinking that this was all joined-up thinking by Leinster and Ireland. Leinster had been trying to tell me as much in the previous weeks. They were thinking the same way. Leinster and Ireland had made a clear decision to make Jordan the number one full back and to just roll with the punches from there.

The rest of the season, whatever it holds for the team, will for me be about keeping my standards up and just being a good team-mate. Also about being a good brother. Dave is getting his proper shot later than he deserved. I am happy for him.

It's a new world for me. When you are not in the team, you stop being relevant in subtle little ways. You don't have the usual level of interaction with the coaches. You're not quite invisible but you are now a blurry, indistinct figure in the background.

When the week starts and the team is named, nobody is

seeking you out. You keep working and observing the coaches, having the little side chats with the player who has your jersey. Did you see that Toulon did this at the weekend? Did you notice that? Yes!

Those chats aren't happening with me anymore.

But fifteen years is a good run. More than I ever expected. When I was young and as impatient as these guys are, I only wondered about how careers began. I never knew how they ended. The end, it seems, is like bankruptcy, it's coming gradually for a long time and then, very quickly, it's here.

It's all but done now and there is time at last to look back.

2
—

ROSS

— Robert, tell everybody what you want to be when you grow up?
— A rugby player.
— Aw! Good for you!

For as long as I can remember, I wanted to be a professional rugby player. At five, six, seven years of age, that was my dream. I wanted rugby to be my job. There was no plan B. Nobody had the heart to tell me that the game was still amateur.

The game went professional in August 1995. I was ten years old. I'll never forget that moment. I was in our kitchen and I was practising kicking drop goals up against the wall. It says something about the standing of rugby in our house that this was allowed. I remember Dad saying to me, rugby is gone professional today so some day, if you really want to, you can make it a job.

I was thinking, yes, definitely yes. What took so long?

My Mum, Siobhan, grew up in Dundalk. My Dad, David, was from the Cooley Peninsula not too far away. Mum and Dad were always in the same social circle. For a long time, their parents had been very friendly as couples so they hadn't strayed far from the nests when they found each other.

Mum and Dad's marriage is a strand of the consistency that runs down through the family tree. Mum's dad was a doctor. My grandfather on Dad's side was a farmer who ran the family farm in Cooley.

We all grew up in Cooley. If the main road from Dublin to Belfast is the beaten track, the Cooley Peninsula is the most beautiful of all the spots just off the beaten track. The peninsula is famous in mythology as the home of the coveted brown stud bull in the epic story, Tain Bó Cualigne, the cattle raid of Cooley. Apart from that we are a forgotten bywater.

Dad's great grandad had the family farm originally and it passed down the generations to my dad. There's a couple of hundred acres which is decent to biggish for an Irish farm but not exactly a ranch. Dad was born on the farm and he grew up there.

When my grandad ran the farm it was a full-time job. The farm was a huge operation back then. At peak times, Grandad employed as many as seventy people. Having endured harsh times either side of the Second World War, the Sixties and Seventies were good for farming. There were a lot of the traditional crops to be sown and gathered. Farming was a big business back then and there was a fair bit of money in it.

Since then, the whole way of farming has changed massively. There is one fellow on the farm now, he's sub-contracted and he comes in and does a little bit here and there.

Dad was the only boy in the family, the third child with an older sister and a younger sister. Adhering to tradition, he was always going to be the one to take on the farm.

He took an agricultural qualification when he was young but the farm itself would be where most of his learning would have been done. He came back to the farm in his early twenties and he is still there to this day. Over the years, at times, it's been a seven-days-a-week job for him and he has always been able to make the farm work, regardless of the vicissitudes of the economy or the broad changes in agribusiness.

Dad has spent his whole life out on the land but there was never any sort of pressure put on us when we were growing up to work on the farm. We were never nagged to get out to work. We could get involved after school if we wanted to. If not, that was fine too.

Now I am incredibly appreciative that I was able to play sports all day, every day. As a kid it was something that I enjoyed but I found it a little bit strange too. There were other farms around us at home and I would often be off playing sport while the kids from the other farms would be missing because it was a busy time for anybody on a farm. The other kids would be working while I was kicking a football.

I have some farming credentials, though. I did once get a good dose of ringworm on my leg. I appeared in a medical journal as a result and I still have the scars of the ringworm. Usually you have to be out working with animals to catch ringworm so I don't know how I managed to contract it.

Looking back, I'll concede that we were a little spoiled probably.

Dad owned a store in Bush, which was five minutes from our house. The business supplemented the income from the family farm. The shop was called Bush Stores and Dad sold general farm products, from cement to fertiliser and anything else that a farm might need.

My older brothers, Richard and Ross, would sometimes go down to the store with Dad. He'd let them tag along for company while he was working and to give Mum a break. She had enough to do running after me.

When Richard was nine and Ross was six they reached a small milestone in their development. They were given permission after some training to cross the road from the store all by themselves. You know what a big deal that is when you are small.

Once they had become qualified to cross the road, they would pester Dad to be given little jobs which would involve them crossing the road like grown-ups. One day, Dad gave them two letters to post. There was an old green post box almost directly opposite Bush Stores on the main road.

Richard and Ross went across the road with the letters and posted them. On their way back they saw another letter lying on the ground. Somebody had dropped their envelope on the way to the post box.

This was perfect. Richard and Ross went back into the store with the letter to ask Dad what they should do with it. They knew full well that Dad would say, sure, go and post it. It meant another trip across the road for them. Off you go, Dad said.

They went back out of Bush stores and turned the corner. Ross, all excited, ran ahead of Richard a little bit.

Richard heard the screech of the brakes, the instant smell of burnt rubber. Even now, decades later, that sound and that smell remind him of the day our brother Ross was killed by a truck.

It is a day of which I have no memory whatsoever. I was two and a half years old. It is Richard who tells me this story now years later when I need to know for this book. We have mentioned the day often but never talked in detail about it.

I cannot imagine the pain that Mum and Dad and Richard suffered but somehow the loss of Ross never hung over our lives like a dark cloud. Ross has permeated our lives as a benign and watchful presence.

They were young enough to try for more children and Dave was born the following June with Sara my sister coming the next December. A gift from Ross was how Mum described the arrival of a daughter after four boys. Any time something went wrong or someone in the family got upset it was always, don't worry, Ross is looking over you.

I have a lovely photo of myself and Ross, just the two of us. Ross asked for the photo to be taken just a few days before his death. Who knows why? I was just a toddler trailing after Richard and Ross, my two boisterous older brothers. I wasn't an afterthought but I wasn't central to their rough and tumble relationship. They'd knock lumps off each other, Dad says. What brothers close in age don't do that? Anyway, Ross decided that he wanted a picture taken with me and I am glad that he did.

In those days, you sent your films away by post to be developed. The photos were delivered to our house on the day of Ross's funeral.

I went to the local primary school, Monksland National School. Carlingford was our nearest village. It was five minutes away. Dundalk or 'town' was twenty minutes away. Monksland was a tiny operation. There were maybe ten people in my class and just one teacher for three classes in the school. It's a rural school. We had two infant classes then, one class from first on up to sixth.

Being honest about it, I didn't really enjoy primary school. In a small, tight-knit place it is sometimes uncomfortable to be regarded as different and I would always have been viewed as different when I was at primary school. I was from the big farming family. My brother Richard, who had passed through some years before, had gone off to Clongowes Wood and it was generally recognised that I was from a privileged background. I suppose we were regarded as an unusual enough family in the area and kids reacted in the way that kids usually do.

I think the bullying stemmed from the who-do-you-think-you-are view that we in Ireland sometimes exhibit towards people who aren't the same as us. If you are different, maybe you think that you are better? I didn't know who I thought I was but I didn't think that I was any better than anybody else. I was quickly marked out as being different though and once that happened, I noticed that I wasn't liked or included very much.

The bullying was just schoolyard stuff. I wouldn't like to overstate it. I played huge amounts of sport with the same people. At that time in my life, the changing rooms before games or the fields that we went training or playing on were the only places I could go and know that I would always be happy there. I was always the equal on the field.

Out on the grass with a ball between us, everything was always fine. As soon as the game was over we went back into the rut of it. I was the kid whose folks were said to be different. There was nothing much that I could do about it. Just suck it up.

Perception is a very powerful force in small places where

every difference is magnified. It probably did look to the other kids as if we were a little privileged but to me there is no reason why any kid should ever be perceived differently. We are what we are.

The bullies were a couple of years older. From the start I was always playing sports at age grades ahead of me, which never really helps too much either. I didn't belong on their teams and I was away from my own age grade a lot so I didn't fit in smoothly into either set-up.

I never mentioned it at home. You never do. I didn't want to involve my parents. You just live with the secret weight of it. You know you have done nothing wrong but you don't know what to do about it to stop it. So it goes on. It was mostly psychological and a bit of physical stuff around the eleven, twelve age. Then it just petered out when I was maybe fourteen or fifteen.

It's just the gap between who you are and who they think you are. 'They' are the people who don't know you.

I was a bit different. As well as being good at sport, I was a bit well-spoken. My big brother had gone away to some distant boarding school. These weren't decisions that I had taken but that's how kids are. It happens across every schoolyard in the country and it's worse nowadays because it is all online. If you are a bully, you hide behind your screen and your false name and you pour out the most vile and horrible things that you can think of. My school days were mild stuff by comparison. I can't imagine the lonely pain of any kid today reading that stuff. I can't count the amount of tragedies I've heard of or read about arising from cyber bullying. We need to be better people online and offline.

Anyway, the upshot was that at home I had one friend from

primary school days, a guy called Anthony White who lived five minutes up the road. Funny enough, Richard was very friendly with Anthony's older brother Darren and Dave was friendly with Anthony's younger brother. Anthony would be the only person from home that I am still friendly with.

As such I was counting down the days, literally counting them for years, before I went away to Clongowes Wood College. Which is unusual I know. Going away from home isn't generally a thing an eleven-year-old yearns for. Especially if his home life is as happy as mine was.

Maybe I let the bit of bullying get under my skin too much because overall I really enjoyed my childhood. Even school lessons weren't all bad. In primary, I was decent academically without being a great scholar. The teacher, Michael O'Dineen, was a big Gaelic football fan and being good at Gaelic helped me. I just really didn't enjoy Monksland and Clongowes always seemed to promise great things.

Richard remembers all the traffic stopping and the police coming from everywhere. Dad ran out from the shop and his face showed that instantly he knew the worst. Dad crumpled with grief. A Garda put Richard into the back of a police car and my brother sat there listening to the walkie talkies over the police radio. Mum arrived. She was hysterical too. It all kicked off again.

Richard says that he came home hours later and I was running around the kitchen in a nappy. Just running around and happy as a lark. Richard remembers that, at that moment in time, he would have given anything in the world to trade places with me. I was oblivious to the whole tragedy of our lives, insulated by my age. In the decades since, Richard would always have stored the memories of Ross in a quiet corner of his mind. We would never have spoken about those things. Talking with him now, this is the longest conversation we have had about Ross.

Richard was nine when Ross died on August 16th, 1988. It was a different time and people understood less about the process of grief. Neither Richard or I were brought to the funeral. It was seen as a bit taboo to put kids through all that back in those days. Children today would be fully involved in the grieving process. The world understands closure now. I was too young to be affected by Ross's death but for Richard it was different.

One day he had a brother who was three years younger. They were very close and they lived in each other's pockets. In a single moment, his brother was gone and Richard was left with the memories of the grieving grown-ups. Overnight, the next closest person in his life was a two-and-a-half-year-old toddler in nappies. Me.

As such, Richard and I never had any sort of relationship up until when I went to college in Dublin. Richard had gone off to boarding school at twelve. Then he went to Trinity College and in the summers he'd disappear to the States working on J-1 visas and doing some travelling afterwards. The gap between us was so big that we never had any chance to connect and grow closer.

He was the eldest in our family and one of the eldest of all the cousins. Whenever he was home, to him I was still a little boy running around with the tribe of little cousins.

He has told me one story that illustrates things.

He had been away to America on a J-1. On the day he came back late in the summer I was playing an under-14 Gaelic match, a final for Cooley Kickhams. He came to watch the game.

I was unbelievably excited that he was there. He would never have got to see me play sport but Richard was everything that I aspired to be. The compass and the road map. He had been where I wanted to go and he was who I wanted to become. This was the first time he ever got to see me play sport. I desperately wanted him to see me being good at something. We won the game and, as soon as it finished, I ran straight to Richard to ask him the one thing that I needed to know.

What did you think? What did you think?

He says he will never forget that moment. Me running towards him at fourteen years of age, desperate for approval. And he was thinking, I don't really know this guy at all.

Maybe that was just as well!

Mum feels that Ross's death impacted on me more than people might have thought, even at the age of two. Richard had a little bit more understanding of the whole grief process that he was sharing with Mum and Dad. My only way of expressing myself was to look for attention. As I grew, I became an awful attention seeker.

By way of explaining this (to myself at least), I suppose that I didn't understand what Mum, Dad and Richard were living through. And I didn't understand the sudden arrival of my younger siblings, Dave and then Sara. As I saw it, I went from being the youngest who everybody doted on to filling the gap between two demanding babies and a terrible grief. And judging by the stories I don't seem to have liked it very much.

I can pick one or two from the family collection. I was late for training once. Gaelic football training. Mum was on the old cord telephone. And I was nagging. Come on, we have to go, come on. Mum had been pruning branches in the conservatory or something. I went out into the conservatory and retrieved her scissors. I came into the kitchen, cut the cord on the phone and said, right, now we're going.

Apparently this was normal for me.

Another time they went away for a break on a weekend and I was left at home. We had an au pair or a minder. I can't recall the arrangement but I rang one of Dad's friends who is now passed away, Kevin Hanratty. He lived twenty minutes away. I called him and said, listen, I have rugby training in Dundalk in an hour. I need to be there. Will you come and collect me and bring me to training?

Kevin was so caught off guard that he agreed. He was even more rattled when he arrived to collect me. I came to the door and looked at him and asked, where the hell have you been? What's kept you lazy boots?

Dad's parents both died quite young so I have no recollection of my paternal grandparents. Don, my grandad, also went to Clongowes and pretty much came straight into the farm after school. He was a very good golfer off two and a keen rugby man too. He met my gran, Jean McCaldin, in Donegal and got married very young. Jean was born in Monaghan and came from a lovely family but unfortunately died very young and her death hit my grandad very hard.

We all grew up being close to my grandparents on Mum's side, Daniel and Phil. They lived in Blackrock in Dundalk, fifteen minutes away. Every Sunday night we would go to their house for dinner.

One Sunday when Gran, who was elderly enough at the time, was bent over in a press looking for pots and pans I just walked up behind her and kicked her up the arse for no reason.

I was six or seven years old. A couple of days later, forgiven of course, I asked her if she could tell me what heaven was like.

Maybe Gran was concerned that I was thinking about Ross and felt this was a dangerous and taboo area. She wasn't entering into the discussion.

She told me that we really didn't need to talk about that sort of stuff.

Why not Gran?

I don't know. I just don't want to talk about it.

Hmmm, I said. Well, Gran, you better find out because you are going there soon!

Mum's career was as a stay at home mum. Raising children is enough work for anybody, as she has told us on many occasions. Having a farm as the family business brings plenty of pressures on top of that.

The older I get, the more clearly it strikes me that our dad has always had a very soft side to him. Perhaps because of what had happened with Ross, he always seemed to have wanted us to live our lives to the fullest.

We were all obsessed with sports and we loved just being out there doing things and from Dad it was all encouragement. Mum would have been the voice saying, yes, enjoy it all and you can keep enjoying it if you look after your studies. They were a good team. Not exactly good cop, bad cop but each knowing their role.

I have never gone too far into the finances of the family farm but I do remember when I was growing up that Dad made sacrifices to get us all through our secondary education. He'd loved Clongowes and he wanted us to have the same experience. He worked hard to send us there.

Before Clongowes and rugby, however, Gaelic football was what I played mostly. If rugby was the family faith, Gaelic football was my number one game for a long time. It was what I played the most of because there was so much of it to play.

I only had access to rugby once a week, maybe once every two weeks on Saturday mornings in Dundalk with the minis. It was the club that Dad had been involved with in his twenties. He played for Dundalk and he played for the Leinster juniors. He was a centre. A good player but, at seventeen, he had a growth on a bone in his knee and as a result missed out on most of his last year at school.

Richard had played a lot of Gaelic with Cooley and he has the biggest collection of GAA medals in the family. In Clongowes he played lots of rugby too. He was a centre for the school in fifth year and a flanker on the Senior Cup team in sixth year. They got to the Leinster Schools Senior Cup final. For me, at eleven or twelve years of age, that was a huge thing. I remember going to watch Richard play in the Senior Cup and that being the highlight of my year. They beat Blackrock in the semi-final and a young guy called Brian O'Driscoll missed three dropped goals for Blackrock. I rejoiced but Clongowes went on to lose to Terenure in the final.

I knew that rugby was my future but those days of playing Gaelic were happy ones. Even when I did finally escape off to boarding school I had such a love of Gaelic that I was coming back home to play for the Cooley Kickhams whenever I could. All the guys who I had problems with in primary school were playing with the Cooley Kickhams too but the antagonism had faded in our mid-teens.

For starters, I had begun to grow bigger than them and it all became a little easier for me. I was a decent player and that changes the view of you. I loved playing and as I grew into the game the bullying thing outgrew itself.

Cooley Kickhams was two minutes from Carlingford, a rural club but big enough to be competitive. Sadly they haven't reached the same heights in the last decade or so. My last game with the club was the county final of 2004 which we lost by a point. It had been a long time, 1990, since we had won one before and Cooley haven't won one since. I've had amazing support from the people of Cooley throughout my career and, in particular, a homecoming when we won the Grand Slam in 2009. I'm very proud to be an honorary member of the GAA club and one of my Test jerseys hangs in the club to this day.

I was eighteen then. I was in the Leinster Academy but I wouldn't sign my Leinster Academy contract until I had played my last game of Gaelic. They had told me that as soon as I signed the forms, I would have played my last game of Gaelic football. So I just kept them waiting.

The final was in late summer in Pairc Clan na Gael. We played St Patrick's, the local rivals from Lordship which is halfway between Carlingford and Dundalk. That's a huge rivalry. They are the one club you did not want to lose to.

Pete McGrath, the legendary Down football manager from up the road in Rostrevor, did a lot of work with our team that year but we lost badly enough on the day. Only a point in the margin but we finished strongly having been well behind.

I'd played a game two or three weeks before and strained my quad. It was my first ever muscle injury. I played the county final fully injured. When I look back, there was no way I should have played. I still get pain sometimes if I kick a ball without warming up. But it was the county final. The first 'all peninsula final' the county had seen. A World Cup final for us.

I was always midfield, even at that age, but because I was injured I went to half forward in that final. Really, I couldn't move. I scored a point in the second half but that county final is the one game that I would love to go back and play again being fully fit.

I was a good fielder. I liked those battles in the air. I played Louth minor for three years on the bounce starting at fifteen. We got to a Leinster semi-final in 2003. We beat Longford, Kilkenny, Carlow, Wicklow and Offaly but lost to Dublin in a replay in the semi. Dublin went on to win the Leinster final. Mark Vaughan of Blackrock College and Kilmacud Crokes was on that Dublin team. He had the famous bleached hair and an equally unusual style and he was the big star that day. I remember that he kicked the equalising point four minutes into injury time in the first game.

I was injured for the replay but we got hosed.

So that was life back then. Constantly going. Definitely doing too much. Not enough hours in a day for me. I have had a lot of struggles with my body through the years and I wonder how much better it would be had I done less in those days. I would go from Gaelic into the Dundalk FC School of Excellence for soccer. I played tennis, did some golfing, went swimming. Always something.

For a while too I played soccer for Bellurgan FC from Lordship, which was ten minutes away. I played for the years nine through twelve and got picked for the Dundalk School of Excellence. We played in some of the Milk tournaments around Ireland and the UK. I wasn't skilful but I was quick. I played up front. They'd kick the ball over and I would win the race and bang! The meat and spuds stuff that works at that level.

I was never going to be at the races in the long term and I probably knew that even then. I had good potential in Gaelic football, though. I liked the physicality. I was athletic. I developed early so I was big and strong. I had a decent left foot without being the most accurate of kickers. But I had the basics of good fielding skills and athleticism. I played rugby all through the winter for those years and then came home and played Gaelic all through the summer.

If it wasn't for the rugby, I would back myself to have been able to play senior county Gaelic for a number of years. For Louth anyway. Nine of our 2003 minor team went on to play senior football for Louth. I wouldn't suggest that I could have played ten years at the top with, say, Dublin, but I would have enjoyed testing myself against them.

I was involved in an Aussie Rules trial at under-17. I was the only player from the county who went for that. Typically I had just played a rugby match that afternoon and the trial was being held that evening in Longford. I was getting older, seventeen years of age, and the prize was to get picked for a summer tour to Australia. I thought I could get away with playing rugby that afternoon but even at that age it's not the same as when you were thirteen or fourteen. The Aussie Rules boys went off to Australia in the summer without me but ironically I ended up in Australia that summer anyway with the Irish schoolboy rugby team.

If I had the choice that would have been one hundred per cent my pick anyway. That was the summer of 2004. Gaelic football was finishing for me. If I was ever to play in Croke Park it would have to be as a rugby player and back in 2004, that seemed a very unlikely thing to happen.

Rugby was a sporadic business for me until I got to

Clongowes. Down at the minis in Dundalk I had taken to the game quickly enough. I was playing it less but it was the game that I loved most. It was the one sport in our household that was always put up on the pedestal. It mattered. We were a rugby family.

Dad would have been going to Lansdowne Road regularly and he took me to internationals from quite early on. I remember, as a small boy, being up in the West Stand with him and drinking in the colour and the tumult all around us.

Later, more often than not, we were down on the touchline seats. Richard would get us tickets for there through school or Dad would get them. I know that when I was five or six, I pointed out to the pitch and declared that I would be out there some day. Which was an awful cocky announcement from a little boy. Even a boy who demanded a lot of attention.

Ross has always remained a part of our family but it is only in recent years that everybody can talk about him on a very adult level. I know that I can't sit here and write that his death had any effect on my life. A guilty part of me is so grateful that I don't have vivid memories of that day and the months that came after it. Another part of me, though, would love to be able to share the experience of Richard and Mum and Dad as well.

I have done some research over the years. After a tragedy like the loss of a child, marriages just end and relationships shatter. People lose themselves in their own grief. The numbers are frightening.

Sometimes I look at Mum and Dad when they are with each other and I think of all the trauma and the grief they have been through together.

ROSS

To bury a child is the one situation that every parent dreads. How did Mum and Dad stay together through that time and raise us all to be pretty good, fairly decent people? I don't know the answer to that but I just think it is the most amazing thing that I have known and that they are the most incredible people I will ever meet.

3

STARTING OVER

My first impression of Clongowes Wood College was, yes, this is for me. It wasn't the austere buildings or the mile-long driveway that led up to them, it wasn't the history peopled with so many major figures of Irish life and it wasn't the attractions of a classical Jesuit education. It was the sense of knowing that this was where I wanted to be and knowing that the things I was good at would serve me well in Clongowes.

Being a good Gaelic footballer had just about got me through primary school in Monksland, a place where, otherwise, I stuck out like a sore thumb. If I could be a good rugby player in Clongowes I knew that I would fit in fine. There was nothing I wanted more than to be a good rugby player and to fit in.

After primary school, Richard, myself and Dave were all sent to Clongowes. Kearney boys arrived at intervals over a number of years. Clongowes is a place of privilege. We knew that and we also knew that our dad had worked very hard to get us there. He had been sent to Clongowes himself and he had loved it. Dad was determined that his sons would have the same opportunity.

We arrived down to the broad green campus in Clane and each of us in our turn played rugby for the school. Dad took great pleasure in coming to see us play on a regular basis. Mum made sure that we got our noses into the books as often as was needed. Clongowes was already familiar to me when I arrived there. I had been down visiting Richard often and, more importantly, I had watched him play rugby for the school.

Schools cup rugby is the be all and end all of your world at that age. There is nothing bigger when you are a schoolboy. Especially in a place like Clongowes. Richard had played two years on the Senior Cup team and he was very good. Watching Richard, I had just got so captivated by that universe of schools cup rugby. There was no better day in the year for me than getting out of Cooley and going down to Donnybrook to watch my big brother play Senior Cup.

On my earlier visits to Donnybrook, I sat with Mum and Dad, always wearing one of Richard's jerseys. All the pupils wore the school jersey to matches and I longed to blend in with them. I knew all the songs and the chants. In one of Richard's Senior Cup years, they reached the final. At the semi-final against Blackrock, I got a little bit brave and went and stood in the midst of all the Clongowes pupils. I wanted to get involved in any way I could so I sidled my way in and nobody really noticed me.

Or so I thought.

That evening after the game I remember Father Bruce Bradley, who was the principal of Clongowes, beckoning me over. He was a lovely gentleman – as he still is – but when he said, I saw what you did today, I was bricking it. Was he going to pre-emptively expel me before I even got to Clongowes?

– Did I see you in with all the other pupils today?

– Yes Father, you did.

– Did you have fun?

I had no idea what the right answer was.

Clongowes had won. It was a semi-final v Blackrock. That lad Brian O'Driscoll had missed three drop goals. I had trespassed but yes, I'd had as much fun as a boy could imagine having.

He smiled at me and said, the only thing I ask of you is that for the final, you cheer louder.

I was thrilled. I had been licensed to go in there and cheer.

So when I got to Clongowes I had the clearest vision of what I wanted to do. Play rugby.

For me, there wasn't the sense of shock that some people speak of when they recall being suddenly dropped into a cloistered boarding school atmosphere, at the age of twelve. Some of the guys who arrived with me were stricken. They felt abandoned or intimidated. For me, this was what I had been waiting for.

I was just raring to go. I hadn't made many proper friends in primary school. In Clongowes you lived with your school mates all year round. The friends that you made were proper friends, people that you would have in your life forever. It was on a different level in terms of the friendships created. I badly wanted that part of it too. Having a big brother who had played on the Senior Cup team was a little bit of a headstart from day one. I was Richard Kearney's brother and I wanted to do what he had done. Going down to Clane felt as if my life was really starting.

I hadn't given much thought to the main aspect of a Jesuit education. The actual education bit. Books, study, exams, forming the man etc. As you progress through Clongowes from first year to sixth, each grade takes the traditional names of the divisions in Jesuit schools. From first year in Elements, through Rudiments, Grammar, Syntax, Poetry and finally sixth year or Rhetoric. These are the stages of learning a classical language. The primary aim of a Jesuit education is to create the *vir eloquens* (eloquent man) who is able to think and to speak for himself.

Being good at rugby would be useful but there was no mention in classroom of how to become a *vir eloquens* along the lines of Serge Blanco so, inevitably, the academic side brought me a little more stress than the rugby did.

Dad drove down to see us play rugby games. We had a sense that, like ourselves, he felt that if the rugby was going well, everything else would fall into place. Luckily for me, the school had figured all this out a long, long time ago. The structure of life was such that sport didn't impact on the academic side much. We had a daily routine in Clongowes. We were up at half seven and studying from half eight to quarter past nine. Then class all day from half nine till half three. Sport was next from four to half five. Then study again from six to eight.

And then sport again or some sort of activity in the evenings from eight to nine and then, from third year onwards, study again from nine to ten in the evening. The days were so structured and so jam-packed with (mostly) academic stuff that you had no choice.

There was no escape. When it was study time we went into a huge study hall. We each had our own desk and all our books were kept there. If you weren't sitting at your desk it was noticed straight away and questions were asked. We were watched from on high. A prefect sat at the back of the room on a tall chair watching over all of us so we didn't dare venture even a whispered word. There was always homework to be done and things to be learned. To not do it was just more hassle than actually doing it.

The tuck shop would open at 8pm. You'd gather up the pocket money and go treat yourself to a bag of crisps or a coke. Everybody loitered around the central area of the school when the serious part of the long day was over.

You were expected to play rugby in first and second year whether you liked it or not. It was compulsory, which was tough on the guys who hated it. It's a little strange maybe to make a sport compulsory when some people have no interest in it but everybody knew before they went that Clongowes Wood was a rugby school. Rugby, for some of us anyway, defined the pecking order and shaped the school's culture.

It was competitive. And to those of us for whom it really mattered it was very, very competitive. From the start, even at under-13, you had your A, B, C and a D team. Lads who weren't very good or who just plain didn't like rugby knocked around on the D team and tried to have a bit of fun with it. The rest of us dreamed of playing at a higher level or of being the best at the highest level.

There were other activities. The evening sport took place indoors. Table tennis, tennis, some snooker tables. There was a swimming pool and, in fifth and sixth year, there were gyms for us on site and we could go and lift a few weights. Football was played in the summer time. Cricket has made a little bit of a comeback in recent times but a rugby school Clongowes Wood was and probably always will be.

We stayed in dormitories. In the middle of the dorm there was an alcove, a common area with couches and chairs. For me, from first year onwards, Wednesday morning meant running to the notice board in the alcove. A piece of paper would be pinned up every Wednesday morning with all the teams on it. So many Wednesdays I woke up and jumped out of bed to go and have a look on that board for my name.

I played out-half when I was thirteen. A little bit as a flanker for a couple of years as well. Just in the back row. Dad saw me play as a number seven and confirmed what I already knew. I was all over the shop. I moved to full back in third year and knew that was where I wanted to play rugby. I played on the wing in the Senior Cup in fourth year. I was happy to be on the team, a big feather in the cap for a fourth year but I pined for the number fifteen jersey. I was a full back thereafter. I played three Senior Cups with Clongowes, the last two at full back.

Dad always took a good interest in our rugby progress. He would have come on a lot of Wednesdays and Saturdays from Louth down to Kildare to watch matches. Mostly he came on his own to games. Mum would always come for Leinster Senior Cup games.

Apart from the summers, which were my own, I only came home for some big games, championship matches for Cooley. In Clongowes you got home once a month from a Thursday afternoon to a Sunday night. You were allowed to go out on a Sunday afternoon for five or six hours. We'd go to lunch or to Liffey Valley shopping centre to see a movie or we'd go to friends' houses.

My younger brother Dave arrived in Clongowes three years after me. He missed home more than I did I think but he was the youngest and he had enjoyed primary school more than I had. He was in third year when I was in sixth year. He played on the senior team in fourth year as well but I had left the school at that stage. As Dad was at most of our matches, Mum and Dad usually only came down one in every three Sundays in a month and we'd be home for the weekend on the fourth Sunday.

In that way, the rhythms of the school became the rhythm of our family life.

As important to me as the rugby (or an essential part of the rugby) was making friends in Clongowes.

The school had four main dormitories for first years to live in. You started Clongowes life in one of those dorms rooming with three other people. I suppose the idea was to break you in socially. You could change around later. There were some single rooms and some eight-man rooms. You changed every three or four months.

On the first day of first year I walked into my four-man room and there was a guy already in there. He was wearing a South African rugby jersey, one of the old Nike ones with the Red Lion lager badge and the swoosh on the collar. They'd worn that jersey against the Lions in 1997. I was obsessed with rugby and with the Lions. This Springboks jersey was being worn by a small, shy ginger lad and I had common ground with him straight away.

This boy was Pierce Casey. We were probably twelve years old. He was my first pal in Clongowes and he's been one of my closest friends ever since. In sixth year when we played in a Leinster Senior Cup final, I was full back and Pierce was out-half.

I would have been pretty shy. I wasn't in any way confident at that time. Whatever confidence I possessed had been stifled by the previous few years in primary school. I was a little wary but excited to make some pals. That was one of the main reasons I had looked forward to Clongowes.

Pierce was born in England but had grown up in Glenageary. After college he lived in England for four years but now he lives two hundred metres away from me here in Dublin.

The two of us being shy probably made it easier. When you land into boarding school you aren't talking too much to people, you're just trying to sound everybody out and not give too much away yourself. It was common enough to wear any rugby jersey back then but South Africa and New Zealand were the cool ones. Pierce was a player too and I suppose we clung to each other for company and confidence early on.

I was in that little four-man cubicle for the first four months and then I moved to an eight-man about three or four months in. There I met another one of my best pals, Aonghus Smyth from Mullingar. Aonghus was older than us, over a year older, which is a huge margin at that age. He was the oldest guy in our year and back then he was bigger and stronger and more athletic than any of us. We became very close early on. He was a good rugby player but at thirteen or fourteen, his sheer size made him bigger and faster than everybody else.

Aonghus didn't get to play Schools Cup rugby with us in sixth year. He'd been a good centre in 2003 but the next year his age advantage undid him and he was too old for the team. He was involved though. He served as the waterboy in sixth year and he carried my kicking tee for me. Jeeves to my Wooster. The two of us became inseparable through school. One of us would never go anywhere without the other.

One of my fondest memories is perhaps one of Aonghus's most painful. Clongowes' grounds skirt what used to be The Pale and at one part it is thought that the ancient boundary was made of the Gollymochy River, which is a tributary of the Liffey.

Old folklore in the school had it that nobody has ever been able to jump the width of the Gollymochy. Aonghus being the quickest, the fastest, the most athletic of our year, announced one day that he might be the man to create history and leap the Gollymochy. Off we went.

We were telling him not to do it but secretly hoping he'd try. We'd have bet him a few quid. To cut a long story short, the long jump fell short and Aonghus shattered his ankle in fifteen different places and broke three toes. It took three surgeries to reconstruct his foot and ankle. He did get back to sport later but it was a horrific injury.

He actually made the newspaper though. Not for being the first man to leap the Gollymochy but for having to sit the first paper of his Junior Cert in Tallaght Hospital after one of his operations.

Before that he had stayed in the school infirmary for two weeks after his first surgery. He was permitted to pick a companion to come and stay with him as company while he was confined to the infirmary. I got the call-up.

The infirmary was in a wing off from the main area of the school and the two of us were delighted to be there. We got good work done in the infirmary. We didn't have to go to classes and our meals were brought into us like room service. One man's cloud was his friend's silver lining.

We are still close. I was best man at his wedding in August 2019.

When I won my first cap for Ireland, Aonghus had flown out to Argentina to see the game. My dad, Richard and Aonghus made that memorable trip together. When the tour finished, myself, Aonghus, Trevor Hogan, Malcolm O'Kelly and Tommy Bowe went on a ten-day holiday together to Brazil.

It was friendships like those with Pierce and Aonghus that I had looked forward to as much as rugby when I had dreamed about secondary school.

As time went by, I caught up with Aonghus physically. I had a major growth spurt in the summer of third year when I was fifteen. I came back to school from far distant Cooley in September and everybody was just looking at me. What happened to you?

How I saw the sudden change in my own stature was through the lens of rugby. In fact, when I think back on Clongowes, I generally measured my time there through rugby. I measure the years in terms of the games I played, the progress I made, the coaches I learned from. The other stuff, which the Jesuits would have hoped might be to the fore, seeped in slowly too.

Clongowes was my first introduction to a rugby life where I could play the game every day. It was a whole new deal for me to be playing day in, day out and I loved it. Secondary school was when a proper rugby life really began for me.

Under-13 was the first year level and everyone (as far as I could see, anyway) wanted to be on the A team. With that there definitely came a certain social status. Kids are so impressionable and sport means so much that rugby shaped the social order for us. Being good at rugby made me feel socially at ease for the first time.

As you got older you saw that effect most clearly with the Senior Cup team. If you were playing Senior Cup you were elevated to an undreamed of level of coolness within your year – even if, like me, you had been desperately uncool back in primary school.

So, at thirteen years of age, in our little world, being on the A team mattered so much that it gave you self-confidence and a real advantage in making your way through the school. Suddenly, just because I could play rugby, I felt that I was socially acceptable. I began aspiring even to a sort of popularity. Having spent my years in Monksland feeling isolated and bullied it felt like an incredible upswing in my fortunes.

Looking back now it is an unfair headstart for anybody to have at that age. There must have been boys who felt sidelined or excluded by the emphasis on rugby. Rugby mattered a lot even when it shouldn't have mattered. Yet it was massive for me at the time and anything rugby gave me I gratefully grabbed with both hands.

Clongowes meant starting from scratch again. Rugby was the means to reinvent myself. It was my chance to be part of something rather than sometimes feeling left out of things. For me Clongowes was even better than I'd thought it would be. One hundred per cent better. And rugby was the medium that made it better.

They say everybody at boarding school gets homesick at some stage and early on some lads were struck pretty badly. It's a huge life change for a boy. I had gone down to Kildare at twelve years of age though and I didn't feel the first pang of homesickness till I was fourteen. I was so happy with my new life that it took a few years before I even missed home. Even now I can remember being homesick for that one weekend but I can't remember why. That's how small a thing it was.

My first rugby coach in Clongowes was Stephen Grey. He was our year prefect as well. The prefect is a regular teacher but the prefects live on site with you. They look after the whole year for seven days a week. They teach a couple of classes but mostly they are looking out for you from 4pm till bedtime.

I got on well with Stephen but no coach at school really had a big impact on me until my senior coach. When I was in third year, Adam Lewis became my year prefect and then he was the Senior Cup coach in fourth, fifth and sixth years when I played on the team. Adam had a huge impact on me as a player and as a person.

First of all, Adam was a very good coach. He is an Australian with the broad interest in sport that seems to come with the passport down there. If Adam had wished, he could certainly have gone far up the professional ranks of coaching. He was so far ahead of all the other people involved. The ethos of professional sport wouldn't have appealed to the man, however. He had chosen to devote his professional life to teaching within the Jesuit system.

He was driven idealistically to make a difference in the life of every pupil he taught or coached. He held to the Jesuit aspiration that every boy could make a positive difference in the world. Most of all, he wanted us to behave. Jesuit education is very specific. 'Be a man for others' is one of the core philosophies. Not being self-centred, putting others' needs before yours. When you are away from home, if you don't get that upbringing from your parents it is very important that the school substitutes, *in loco parentis.*

Being a man for others just means putting others first. Adam genuinely believed in that. Even when we were fifteen years of age he was huge on instilling team values and humility into us. All those things which are so important now, those things which coaches try to instil as a tool to make their teams better, Adam was the first person who taught them to me. He taught them to us not just to make a team better but to make better people of us.

He loved rugby league and he had a weakness for the Sydney Roosters. He also loved the Brumbies, the rugby union team from Canberra, the city he'd grown up in. He brought us a lot of useful knowledge second hand from the Brumbies. His brother-in-law was Joe Roff, the great Aussie winger. I remember seeing Joe in Clongowes once and was blown away by the sheer size of him and wondered would I ever be big enough for professional rugby. It was nice to share a couple of beers with Joe after the 2013 Lions tour.

Adam was terrific at applying what lessons he picked up and transferring the knowledge to us. In fourth year in Clongowes, we were running Brumbies back plays. He was getting the play sheets from Joe Roff, all of the things that they were doing and running us through them. He was unbelievable at making players out of us and raising us as good people too.

Back at the turn of the century it was one Eddie Jones who turned the Brumbies into a great team. That was his breakthrough. In Clongowes, unbeknown to him, we were happily using a lot of his plays. That wraparound move that · Ireland and Leinster are so notorious for now? We were doing it at fifteen and sixteen years of age in Clongowes and we had taken it from the Brumbies via Adam.

He would talk a lot to the group about rugby and about life. I would have been very close to him. I was on the team and good at the game but at school he would never let me get ahead of myself. When I left Clongowes, there were a few instances in the following years where I did precisely that and I regretted it but the other part of Adam's influence was that he had prepared me for a life of pro-rugby straight after school. Coming straight out of boarding school and being thrown into an elite professional sport could have been a calamity but I survived.

Often the lessons from Adam would only seep in when you thought about them later. Sometimes his interventions were more direct. Like all young players, I thrived on praise and praise from Adam was a more valuable currency than praise from most other people. Typically, if I played a good game at the weekend, I would ask Adam how well I had done. It was me fishing for a little praise. Adam would never, ever give me too much. You were ok, he'd say, but can you do it again next week?

I had three years on the Senior Cup team but the year you play with the lads you came into the school with means the most. The first two years playing above my grade I learned a lot but those years felt like a bonus. When I was in sixth year, the whole Senior Cup business seemed much more important. It was the last chance and it was how our year and ourselves would be remembered.

I remember one week that season, we had a big game against Blackrock. It was a league game but it was taking place during the cup, so it was a huge match for us. Early that week the team hadn't been picked and there was this massive anticipation about who would be playing. In terms of understanding where we all stood as individuals, and collectively, this was the big game.

I wandered into Adam's office the night before the team was to be pinned up on the board. Adam wasn't around but, burning with curiosity, I ruffled around among some pieces of paper on his desk trying to find the teamsheet. In my heart I'm sure I knew that I would be playing but I always worried. That's why I had gone in there looking for Adam. When he wasn't there, I took the chance to end my doubts. I found what I was looking for. Number Fifteen, Rob Kearney. Brilliant. Delighted.

I hadn't played the week before. I'd been sent out with the second team but I suspected that Adam was giving me a kick up the backside just in case I was getting too cocky. He was right to be concerned. I was getting mentions in newspapers by then and it was my third year playing in the Cup. There were times when I was definitely getting ahead of myself.

Adam came back into the office at that moment and I turned to greet him, very pleased with myself.

"I see I'm starting," I said.

His face darkened. I knew that I had messed up. He was so pissed off. I'd crossed a line. Right there in front of me he picked up the teamsheet and crossed my name out. He wrote another lad's name in at full back.

Get out of here, he said.

I was embarrassed but I tried to front it out.

I argued with him. I was only trying to have a bit of craic.

Just get out.

Are you joking me? I asked him. Which wasn't a wise approach.

He said, no. What I had done was so disrespectful. Going through other people's stuff was not right.

I left. It was a big game, a match that my dad would have been coming to watch. I thought Adam would relent. He didn't. I didn't play.

What a lesson that was. I didn't get the lesson at first. I was embarrassed and resentful but the next day, some perspective arrived. It wasn't just looking through his desk that was bad but I had been such an idiot in my attitude. Why did I have to showboat and tell him that I had seen the piece of paper?

I knew he wanted to win that game against Blackrock but he stuck to his principles. I like to think that maybe if it was the Senior Cup he would have left me in the team but I wouldn't bet on it.

I can't recall now if we won or lost that game against Blackrock. My own little drama is all that I recall. The game was in Clongowes I know and I didn't even get on as a sub. I was just left to stew. I would have told my mates what had happened. I suppose I wanted them all to know I was actually meant to be in the team but I got pulled out of it, that I had screwed up. It was a face-saving manoeuvre really. In haste, I'd acted stupidly. Adam Lewis let me repent at leisure.

That year we reached the Schools Cup final although we had probably the least talented team of the three Senior Cup sides that I played on.

When I was in fourth year, I was a winger. We had lost to Johnny Sexton's St. Mary's. When I was in fifth year I was full back and we had a very good team and, from what I recall, we were favourites that year. We lost again to Johnny Sexton's St. Mary's. Same old story. Six-three, and Johnny kicked the winning goal.

When I was in sixth year, though, we were coached so well and we had a really good sense of togetherness. There was just a really good team spirit amongst that group and years later we are still friends.

We had a tough draw. St. Michael's. Terenure. Newbridge.

And then Blackrock. As they are most years, Blackrock were the big favourites. The first two games were very tough. Michael's was the best game, including Gaelic, that I had ever played up until that time. We had played them in a friendly during the season in St. Michael's and we had got pumped. I have one memory from that debacle. We were chasing the game with ten minutes to go. I took a quick line-out in the back field and I threw it to my winger, Fergus McFadden. The pass got intercepted and they took the ball and ran straight in under the posts. Easiest try ever given away.

The majority of the St. Michael's sixth years had been standing in a group on the sideline and they suddenly fell apart, reeling and cackling with laughter. Every single one of them broke into hysterical hooting. I mean these guys collectively broke their shit, just laughing at me.

On the way to the first round game weeks later, that laughter was still echoing in my head. There were no tries scored in that game but I was goal kicker that year. I kicked four from four. On my last kick when I knew the game had gone in our favour I went up toward where all the Michael's people were gathered and I cupped a hand to each ear. Not hearing any laughter now am I? I'm not sure that I want to ponder what Adam Lewis thought of that exhibition of arrogance but it was the first and last time I've ever done anything like that.

The following week we went to Donnybrook to watch the school playing in the Junior Cup (Dave would have been playing that day) and a journalist from the *Evening Herald*, (I think it was Des Berry) spotted me. I was walking back up the steps to the stand when he approached me with a question.

Have you been offered a pro contract yet?

I was like a teenager being asked if they'd been signed to a modelling agency. That was the moment when I was thinking that maybe it hasn't just been a dream. I could really play pro rugby. I was thinking, wow! A pro contract? An actual journalist just asked me had I got a pro contract? Is there anything that journalists don't know! The notion hadn't really been on my radar before that. I just wanted to be on the Irish schoolboys team and to get a sports scholarship to university. After that, I assumed that rugby life would just sort itself out in to a career of some sort.

At this stage, things did seem to be coming to me easier. My spurt of growth had been followed by a breakthrough with my game. I noticed the difference within myself. I got into the Leinster Schools team in sixth year. In fifth year I had been disappointed not to get in. I had thought that I was good enough but I hadn't been sent for the trials. The system was that your school coach sent you for trial and in Clongowes it was only sixth year players who got sent. In theory that kept our egos in check. My ego was the exception.

I knew that I should have stayed silent but I felt that I had to say something about not getting selected for the Leinster trial. It meant a lot to me so I told myself that I was justified in pushing the door a little. I knew better than to approach Adam so I asked Noel Murray, another coach in the school, why I hadn't been sent for a Leinster trial.

In Jesuit schools they move in mysterious ways. Noel told me that there was an upcoming charity match to be held in Donnybrook. The game would be between two Jesuit schools, Clongowes and Gonzaga and two Holy Ghost schools St. Michael's and Blackrock. Noel said that he'd send me along to play in this charity game. If I was good enough, Leinster would surely notice me and pick me up there. This seemed acceptable to me. A charity game sounded like a feasible platform to show the Leinster selectors what they had missed out on through my absence from their trials.

The match was played in front of four or five thousand people and I realised quite early on that sending me out to play had just been Noel's polite way of getting rid of me. I was ok but it was such a step up for me. This was much quicker and much more physical than what I was used to. There was another level to get to. Lesson learned.

From the outside, Clongowes would be seen as a hardcore rugby school. It is, I suppose, but there was a toughness in the Clongowes philosophy, a real emphasis on not letting the rugby guys get ahead of themselves. Senior Cup players were seen as heroes within the school and that was dangerous enough without the teachers adding to it. Noel Murray's style of handling me sat perfectly within the ethos of the school.

My time duly came and when I got sent in sixth year to Leinster Schools, my ability had taken a big leap forward. In fifth year I had been one of the better players but not near an Irish schoolboy team. In sixth year, though, I had such confidence in my game. I trained really hard. Adam was pushing me to work harder and to get better and better. He was always very big on running lines, running good lines. Thinking. Working hard. Rucking was a big thing of his. He was pretty well-rounded as a coach and ahead of his time. Most people back then thought that star backs had no business being anywhere near rucks.

The Leinster Schools trials were held around mid-season. We had a couple of provincial games after that. I played full back in all of them. That was maybe around Easter. The Irish schoolboys scene wouldn't start until the summer.

Meanwhile, in the Leinster Senior Cup, we had battled onwards and, without setting the competition ablaze, we had made the final. For the first time that year, I felt my self-confidence threatened by pressure and expectation. The Leinster Schools Senior Cup final was a big deal and there was a lot weighing on my shoulders.

Usually, on Senior Cup days, you go to class for the first two classes of the morning but the final itself is held on St. Patrick's Day which means a change of routine. We had mass at about half ten or eleven that morning. Then the whole school lined up outside on the drive for a massive guard of honour before we got on the bus. Four hundred kids lining the path to the bus. All in their purple and white shirts. There were six cheerleaders from sixth year all with big megaphones. They were responsible for starting all the different chants on the day.

I could feel some nervousness in myself but because I had played so much Gaelic over the summer and some big games with Cooley and the Louth minors I had sort of become used to the big day a lot more than all the other lads. And even though I felt the weight of the day, I was definitely the guy who wanted to play. Five years later, in the 2009 Grand Slam game in Cardiff, I would be a passenger and just hoping for a quiet game. If it is kicked to me, I told myself, I'll just catch it and kick it back. That was the limit of my ambition.

That day in school, though, I knew I was one of the better players on the pitch. I was trying to get my hands on the ball every second. We'd get a penalty and I'd take a quick tap and go with it myself. All these years later, I look back and it feels like I was an entirely different person that spring.

That afternoon we were backed by a big wind in the first half and we led at half time. In the second half we just got blown away by that wind and by a bigger Blackrock pack. It was heartbreaking to lose. Now if I look back on, say, the worst five defeats of my career, the Schools Senior Cup doesn't figure in the list but back then it was our whole world. As a kid, the only thing I had wanted to do was win a Senior Cup medal. It was in the immediate future. Touchable. I could see it. Now I'd had three cracks at it without success.

Still, there was a level of appreciation. I'd played in Lansdowne Road. I'd been asked if anybody had offered me a contract. Gary Ella, the Leinster head coach, had come to one of our games. Apparently to watch me. I was starting to get a bit of recognition. The *Irish Times* said I was the player of the competition. I was named as schoolboy rugby player of the week in the *Evening Herald*. This was just the greatest thing.

If my ego threatened to overflow, Adam Lewis worked hard to keep me grounded. If I talk about appreciation for all that season brought, the most profound gratitude would be reserved for what I learned from him.

Adam could have been a great rugby coach but he was always destined for great things whatever path he chose. He showed us that values did matter and, for Adam, it wasn't a show or a performance. He helped me at such a young age and he was young himself at the time, a man in his mid-twenties.

His coaching allowed Clongowes to punch above our weight. We had got to the final in sixth year without being especially good. Fergus McFadden was on the team with me but Blackrock were just on a different level. They had a good few decent players, including Luke Fitzgerald who was centre that day while still in fourth year.

Adam always put a bit of check on my natural exuberance. The *Irish Times*' report of the final described me as the player of the competition and I took reporters' opinions a lot more seriously back then. Adam had his work cut out to curb my cockiness. Coming to Clongowes, I had pinned so many hopes on starting all over and making friends that when it began to happen I probably lost the run of myself a little. I maybe had that touch of arrogance when I left school and went walking into the Leinster academy.

As for Adam himself, he has done well. He was principal of a Jesuit school over in New York and he has recently moved on to be the principal of a bigger Jesuit school in Boston. Not long after his appointment in Boston somebody sent me a quote. Adam was speaking to the pupils about sport. 'If kicking the ball on the weekend leads to a state title,' he said, 'I'll be the first to pat you on the back. But if it doesn't form you into a good man in the process, I actually don't care about the state title.'

That is definitely the man I knew.

4
—

CULTURE SHOCK

The really bright, academically-oriented guys at Clongowes were exceptional students. They were all expected to get six hundred points or very close in the Leaving Cert. They generally delivered.

I wasn't one of those guys. I was a four hundred and fifty points-range student, good without being exceptional. If I worked hard, it was because I had to. It didn't come easily to me. Also, I was put under pressure by Mum, aided and abetted by Clongowes.

I had discovered early on that being good at sport wasn't a free pass in Clongowes. If anything, it was the opposite. They came down a little bit harder on the sports guys. They did that for our own good and so that there would be no perception of leniency.

There was a time in Irish rugby when making a name for yourself in the Leinster Senior Cup did you some favours when the time came for you to get a decent job. This was true for me, only in so far as I was determined that rugby would actually be my job.

During my years in Clongowes, the notion of playing professionally and actually doing that in Ireland had become a realistic goal rather than a childhood dream. I just assumed that it would still take quite some time to find the right door into that world.

My burst of physical growth in my last years in Clongowes Wood and the benefit of playing a lot of games under a really good coach were standing to me. I had a good attitude and worked hard and I thought that, in time, I could play senior rugby for Leinster maybe. I was seventeen and if in my dreams I still got a little ahead of myself from time to time, it wasn't by too much. The gap between possibility and probability was closing for me.

The childhood assurances to my family about international glory could just wait. The idea that I would certainly play for Ireland was a relic of my childhood past. Lots of other kids, it turned out, had big dreams too, some of them identical to mine. All I could do was take things stage by stage and keep working hard.

I never would have spoken to Adam Lewis about becoming a professional. He would have clipped me across the ear for even suggesting it. Announcing that you felt you might be paid to play rugby would have sat poorly with a man whose constant emphasis was humility and usefulness. I listened to him always but didn't always absorb quite enough of the lessons about humility back then. I knew, though, that I had to keep working and improving. You earned things. They weren't handed to you just because you had dreamed about them.

When I was younger, nobody had ever dreamed of playing rugby for Leinster. There was very little provincial stuff back then. Leinster and the inter-pros was the sort of non-event in which I took no real interest. Only the international days sparked my imagination.

As soon as the game became professional I had begun thinking that I would love to do it. In one way or another. Just being a pro. Whatever way the game developed, I just wanted to be part of it.

I don't think that I assessed the odds of success too closely. I didn't map out any pathway. There wasn't one to map. From my schooldays, Fergus McFadden played Senior Cup for two years. He went on to be a pro as well. Despite Clongowes being a recognised rugby nursery, nobody else from the Senior Cup team I played on went on to a career in the game. I doubt if anybody apart from Fergus and myself gave the idea much consideration.

At first, beyond school, it was all about the Irish schoolboy team in terms of aspirations. Paddy O'Meara and Dan O'Connor were the captain and vice-captain of our schools team and they had both been in the Leinster Schools set-up too. Really good players.

I wasn't captain back then because I wouldn't have been a very good captain. In school, I was one of those players who was a little bit more worried about myself than the team. I was one of the best players on the team and I knew it. I was usually more concerned about getting myself right.

The game of rugby was evolving quickly. Leinster had won the inaugural Celtic League in the 2001-02 season and the game was looking at developing pathways for young players to become professionals. Being on the Irish Schoolboys was a good advertisement that suggested you were both interested and perhaps had whatever it took.

In sixth year, I had played in an Irish Schoolboys trial, Probables v Possibles, at Christmas in Terenure. I was on the Probables team which had reassured me. You feel in that sort of trial situation that it's yours to lose if you just take care of your own stall.

In the end, I had been picked for both Leinster Schools and Irish Schools. With Leinster, we had two or three games. We went on a trip over to Welford Road to play Leicester and won, I think. In the summer after my Leaving Certificate we toured Australia with the Irish Schoolboys.

At that stage, I had spoken to the Ireland Academy but nothing had been signed. I wanted to finish the Gaelic football season with Cooley first but I knew I would be joining the Ireland Academy not long after I returned home. They were looking for eighteen or nineteen-year-olds starting to come through the ranks. The idea was to recruit about ten to fifteen players from around the country. This was to be a paid contract, although the sum was fairly nominal. Five grand a year was the figure, I think, but that would have fully kept me going. I was low maintenance in that regard.

Beyond that, I was still slightly blurry about how my leap to being a full professional would come about. I hadn't chatted to my father about it at all. The only two things that I had given any serious thought to were the options of sports scholarships either at UCD or Trinity College. These had become apparent around the time of the Leinster Senior Cup campaign.

UCD was a straightforward sports scholarship. I was being

offered my fees and accommodation. There was some playing money too. At Trinity, every year they gave away one 'golden' scholarship to any sport. The offer was fees, accommodation, all your food and also some playing money. This was an unbelievable deal and Tony Smeeth, the great Trinity rugby man, had offered it to me.

I wanted to do Business, Economics and Social Studies (BESS) at Trinity. Richard, my brother, had been to Trinity and he'd done BESS. He'd loved it. I always liked the feeling of following in my older brother's footsteps and now I had the next stage all planned out. Trinity, rugby, food and board plus 5k from the Ireland Academy. My future was falling into place.

Critically, too, the Trinity deal had the royal seal of approval. I was quite excited about it all but Mum was over the moon. Mum thought that Trinity was the better degree and the better college. There was no fly in the ointment. Except myself.

Australia with the Irish Schoolboys was a great trip. I had barely been out of Ireland before that so this was an epic voyage of exploration for me. These trips down under only happened once every twelve years. We were lucky it fell on our year.

We left around early July time on a seven-week tour. Any future names? Johnny was on that tour. Duncan Williams was on it too, he's recently just retired from Munster. Sean Cronin and Devin Toner were there. Billy Holland. A few more if I think hard enough. Quite a few of us went on to have careers. We played seven games; six of them against club teams and one Test match against the Wallabies at the end. We lost the Test match – but not badly. We won all six of the games against the club sides.

On the trip I hung out with the Leinster lads I knew. Myself and Johnny would have been pretty friendly by then. We fell in with the Terenure out-half Conor Gildea and with Gavin O'Meara, the hooker from St. Mary's. There was a Leinster alliance I suppose. It was very much segregated. We knew each other from playing provincially. The national structure was prone to cliques even then.

Johnny, in those days, was a little different to the Johnny Sexton he would become. A bit more laid back. He was good already but he wasn't great yet. I don't think he started in the Test match. Even at the age of nineteen there were some games he didn't play in at under-20 level. Johnny would hit the big jump in his ability in his early twenties but in Australia that summer, not being in the team meant that he wasn't the leader of the group. That is a little hard to imagine these days.

The tour was a brilliant experience. A little bit of an insight for us all into the professional life. Especially for me. I had just finished six years in boarding school and this was my first taste of adulthood and freedom. It was unbelievable.

I wasn't a drinker. I was so obsessed with sport that it had barely even occurred to me to be interested in drinking. I didn't drink until I was eighteen or nineteen and even then only two or three times a year.

We would go out socially in Australia. There were two nights, I think, when we may have had some beers. I was not even close to being drunk. Most of the group was like that but especially me. I just had such a pure obsession with rugby that a little temperance was a natural by-product.

Another sobering factor was that I got my Leaving Cert results while I was down in Australia. My tendency to get ahead of myself had cost me. I had decided to do Honours Maths in the Leaving Cert. I knew that I was somewhere around the borderline with the maths and that probably I should have taken the pass maths paper. Even to this day I kick myself. A proper schoolboy howler.

I think twenty per cent of candidates failed Honours Maths that year. It was a freak year. I was one of that twenty per cent but my result was less of a freak than others. I had myself to blame. Now not only did I not have enough points for the Trinity scholarship that I had been offered but I couldn't go there anyway because I had failed maths. A pass in maths was compulsory. I broke down in tears when I was told. Mum was in tears at the other end of the phone telling me the bad news. Her Trinity dream was gone too! This just felt like it was the end of days.

By the time I got home from Australia, Mum and Dad had been busy exploring the background a bit more thoroughly than I could have. I thought that repeating the Leaving Cert might be my fate and the idea didn't hold much attraction, especially as I would have been too old to play a fourth year of Senior Cup rugby. Luckily I had stuck in the option of an arts degree in UCD as my last choice on the CAO application form for third level. I think the points requirement was three hundred and sixty or three hundred and seventy and, happily, you didn't need maths. When I got the offer I grabbed it like a drowning man grabbing a lifebelt. It might have been my last choice but I was bloody glad of it in the end.

I came home, finished my Gaelic football career and began with the Ireland Academy. I had been in the academy for two months when it got disbanded. The new provincial academies devolved from it. Suddenly I found myself in the new Leinster Academy. On the same terms. 5k a year.

So UCD, as it happened, just worked out perfectly for me. The Leinster Academy actually trained on the UCD campus.

I could finish training in the early morning and saunter off to lectures or exams. It was easy to combine rugby with the academic side of things.

I started off in first year doing economics, geography and social studies and, in second year, I opted for a pure economics degree. That was my way of getting a little bit of a step-up. If you did well in first year you had that option. Rugby looked promising but, as Mum might say, you never knew when it would end and when you would need 'something to fall back on'.

At UCD I think I was getting a thousand euro a month for playing rugby under the scholarship scheme so, from the age of eighteen or nineteen, I was doing ok. I didn't live the typical student life. Financially I was doing well as a student who didn't drink or go out.

I had been offered the option of student accommodation in UCD but I didn't take it up. We had old family friends Craig and Aveen Best from across the border in Rostrevor. Craig is Rory's uncle but the Kearneys knew the Bests long before I ever knew Rory. Craig and Aveen would be two of my parents' closest friends.

The Bests' daughter Gemma was in UCD as well and she had her own house five minutes from the campus, so I moved in with her. Gemma was a year older than me. It was a lovely house and not too far from the college gates. I paid rent. Or Dad did. Gemma had a car which she let me use to go back and forth to training. Leinster training was at six every morning. I'd train, drive back and then be off at college during the day. I trained with UCD under-20s on a Tuesday and Thursday. We played matches on Saturdays for the college under-20s team.

We had gym sessions with the academy too. The Leinster gym

at that time was in Old Belvedere, down in Ballsbridge. We'd train in a makeshift gym in a portakabin. The Leinster seniors did their workouts at a David Lloyd gym in Clonskeagh but they'd do their pitch sessions in Old Belvedere. We'd see them occasionally and wonder when, if ever, we'd be deemed good enough to join them. In that respect things moved surprisingly quickly for me. I was in the Leinster Academy for nine months when I got called into the seniors.

In April 2005, I captained the Ireland Under-19s at the Under-19 World Cup in Durban. We finished ninth of the twelve teams competing. We beat Georgia, Japan and Scotland but we got pumped by South Africa (who won the competition) and Australia (who finished third).

Then, at the end of that season in May, the Leinster Academy coach Colin McEntee called me in for Leinster's last game of the season. Declan Kidney was the head coach at this time. I was pleased but at the same time I knew that it wasn't such a big deal. It was more a case of being called up because the team needed a twenty fourth man. There's always a few of those 'body on the bench' spots in case somebody gets injured in the warm-up.

I made my debut in the next game which came around the start of the following season. Declan had moved back to Munster by then and my first game was Michael Cheika's first game in charge of Leinster. I was still in the academy.

"This is going to be brilliant for you!" Dad had said to me when he heard that Micheal Cheika and David Knox were replacing Declan Kidney. "Two young Aussies who don't care about what age their players are."

Dad got that one partially right.

My thinking was that Declan had only called me in a few

months ago as twenty fourth man but at least he knew who I was. This Cheika was going to come in and he would know sweet damn all about me. I'd be back to square one.

Michael Cheika, as it turned out, was a no-nonsense Australian. If you got past the gruff exterior there was just a gruff interior.

The 2005 Lions tour to New Zealand had taken place that summer from May to July and of the six Leinster guys who had been away, Brian O'Driscoll, Denis Hickie, Shane Horgan and Gordon D'Arcy were backs. Leinster were going to need a lot of spare backs so I did some training sessions with the senior team that summer. It went pretty well. I was going into second year at UCD and happy with my lot in life.

I played the Leinster warm-up games that summer. I scored a hat-trick in my first game, a warm-up match against Parma at Nass rugby club. That would have been August 2005. I'd started as I didn't mean to go on. I never scored a hat-trick again.

I remember that the Lions guys were only recently back in the country and Brian O'Driscoll came over to me at the end of the game with his shoulder in a sling. He said something nice about my performance. I had been playing on the wing and I think Eoghan Hickey might have been full back that day.

Girvan Dempsey wasn't back from holidays. Ireland had been on a two-Test summer tour to Japan in June and they had taken half a dozen Leinster players along (which meant Girvan Dempsey, Dave Quinlan and Kieran Lewis were also missing from our backs.) I was in the right place at the right time that summer.

Cheika was an odd character, though. For example, when

Joe Schmidt came to Leinster as his successor he began by having a thirty-minute one-on-one with every single player. Cheika didn't have that sort of instinct or interest. He wanted to change things straight away. He quickly got rid of a lot of what he saw as the deadwood in the Leinster team. He was brutal about culling the fringes of the squad. Nobody hung around anymore just being happy to be there.

Cheika wanted a really hard-edged group of players so he tried to break people in that first pre-season. He wanted rid of that soft-centred perception of Leinster. For me, that pre-season was my first proper one as a senior player and I thought that this was what was normal. Fifteen years later, I still look back on that pre-season as the toughest one we have ever done. The physical fitness element was a particular shock. Cheika's pre-seasons were on a different planet compared to other coaches' pre-seasons. The intensity and the sheer amount of fitness work we had to do was off the scale.

Leinster had been easy enough pickings when it came to the big European games. Now we did four fitness sessions a week. Sometimes, on a Saturday, we would go up Killiney Hill doing these crazy sprints up the big hill. For sections, Cheika would be running up the hill alongside you, roaring in your ear like a demented drill sergeant. Again, I thought that this was normal.

I learned too that he didn't give out credit easily and certainly not to the younger guys. There was definitely an element of younger lads having to work harder for his blessing. You had to be tough, hard-nosed, physically confrontational. I went to a leafy boarding school where the object was to turn us into men for others. Cheika and I weren't a great fit.

It was a blessing for me, though, that so many senior players were away and I was the only young person coming through. There was nobody else on the horizon. Jamie Heaslip was two years older than me. In my age group I was all there was. Another coach might have viewed me as the cream of the crop. To Cheika I was just the crop. Is this all there is?

On the playing field I'd had that dream start against Parma. Then we played Northampton the following week in Donnybrook. That was a bit of a step up. Bruce Reihana was the opposite full back but I started on the wing. Got through it. Did ok. No more. The following week was round one of the Celtic League against Ospreys away in their new Liberty Stadium. My first competitive game for Leinster.

We received a kick-off. A line-out on our own twenty two. Felipe Contepomi was playing ten. The first ball and he throws it out to me. I opt for a high clearance but I get charged down by Andrew Bishop, their centre. They score a try underneath the posts. This has been my first touch in an elite rugby competition. My career is over with my first touch. Thank God, I think, that I'm in UCD and will have 'something to fall back on'.

I felt sick. Felipe had thrown it to me behind the number 12, who ran short. I had opted for a big left foot. Charged down! The worst possible start. After that, I did ok. We lost the game by two but I scored a try at the end which made up for it a bit.

I got hit once in that game by Sonny Parker, a Welsh international centre. That was one of the few times in my career where I felt as if I had been properly hit and smashed. That was the moment where I realised that the physicality at this level was different to anything I had ever experienced.

At this stage I hadn't had too much interaction with Cheika. He took losses so badly. Almost frothing at the mouth stuff.

He's not a small talk guy at the best of times and certainly not with nineteen-year-old rookies. But not knowing what to do, I went over to him afterwards at the airport and I apologised. I didn't know if this was the done thing at senior level but I just said that I was very sorry about that charge down. He said, listen it's fine mate. I'm pissed with Felipe for throwing you the ball first ball of the game. That was fine and fair and I was glad I had made the effort. From there on, though, we had a very fractious relationship.

We were home for the next two games. I scored a try in each of the first four games of the league. How easy is this, I thought to myself. I was a full back in my head but young players do an apprenticeship on the wing even if they are going to be full backs anyway. It's a normal route, so I was on the wing. I got tries but the game was different then.

Cheika wasn't as pleased about it all as I was. There was something in me or my game that he took exception to. My attitude. An aspect of my play. I never really got to the bottom of it.

Personally I was surprised at how quickly it was happening for me. I knew there'd been a lot of players away on the Lions tour but I was surprised that after the initial shock, training wasn't that much of a step up from what I was used to. I'd thought the gap from international under-19 level would actually be an awful lot bigger. I'd played a lot with the under-20s in UCD but I didn't play any senior rugby there. I played for Leinster before I played for them.

I got called into a national camp when I was still nineteen. Very early, in hindsight. It was for the autumn 2005 game against New Zealand in Lansdowne Road. Anthony Horgan, maybe it was his last game, was on the wing. I was there or thereabouts I reckoned. I had played a few games for Leinster – five or six games – and I had scored tries in my first five games and now I had been drafted into the national squad. I was experiencing lift-off.

Eddie O'Sullivan was the national coach. When he was naming his team for New Zealand that weekend I knew in my heart that I wasn't going to be in the starting fifteen but, before the meetings to announce the team, he called me aside. Listen, can I have a word.

I didn't know what to think. He'd never spoken to me before and now he was just about to name the team to play New Zealand. This could only mean one thing. I'm thinking, surely not though.

He said, listen, I have just had a call from your UCD coach. Oh yeah? And he wants you to play in the Colours game this weekend. This tiny little bit of me was disappointed. Eddie O'Sullivan is not about to give me a shock debut against New Zealand, he's just telling me to go and to play in the Colours for UCD. That's how I came to play my one and only Colours game. We won but at the time it was a little bit of an anti-climax for me. Trinity weren't the All Blacks. Years later, though, it is nice to have had a Colours win.

I finished my degree over a period of four or five years. If that sounds like a young guy taking the scenic route through college I was a full-time professional and part-time student and Michael Cheika wasn't too keen on the academics. Given the pressure, I probably would have left UCD altogether if Mum wasn't a greater power than even Michael Cheika.

I suffered a bad knee injury in the 2011-12 season and ended up using the downtime doing a Masters degree in Dublin Business School. I was out for an entire season. The MBA was a two-year part-time course. I had half of it done when I got injured and the year off suited me perfectly in terms of getting it finished and keeping myself occupied. In terms of keeping my head together and investing a few brain cells in my life after rugby, it was the best thing I ever did.

David Knox had arrived with Cheika as backs and attack coach. Knoxie (there is no other phrase) was a little bit mental. After the Ospreys game, where I had been blocked down so disastrously, I remember one of the Ospreys coaches had come into our changing room and he was chatting with Knoxie. Nobody was paying attention until suddenly it turned into a shouting match arising out of something that had happened during the game. I had never seen anything like it.

Knoxie wasn't too shy to shout during games either. He got into a fair few arguments with other coaches and supporters down the years but this one was different. Something we'd never seen before. The other coach exited. I was glancing up, wondering what was about to happen next but Knoxie seemed to think nothing of it. That was a trend that continued a fair bit, Knoxie in arguments with people.

Otherwise he was pretty laissez-faire as a coach. He generally just wanted us to play good, sexy rugby as you would expect of an Aussie backs coach. It was just that occasionally he flew off the handle. One time in Donnybrook, we were playing Connacht and we had a back line at the time that was a galaxy full of big stars. Connacht's back line wasn't nearly so starry but at half time they were beating us. Knoxie lost it.

"You guys are a fucking disgrace. You are meant to be the million dollar back line and you are getting outplayed by this crowd?"

Some sheepish looks from the million dollar back line. The

jokes came later. Did he mean Australian dollars? Did he mean green and crumpled looking? Folded easily?

Mainly, though, it was Cheika's team. He ran it and in the process he always seemed to enjoy giving me a very hard time. He cherished the hierarchy within a team. He had his senior boys and he made them his mates. Brian O'Driscoll. Shane Horgan. Denis Hickie. They were the inner circle. Reggie Corrigan was there my first year too and Malcolm O'Kelly. Cheika sort of co-opted those guys and drew them in to him. The rest could sink or swim. Except me. I felt like I was being dunked under the water most of the time.

Gordon D'Arcy, I would have to say, was different. I played loads with Gordon. He was always a very independent guy and always had his own view on things. Gordon had been in Clongowes before me and, like myself, he seemed to draw his closest friends from his time in school.

At a time when I needed a small bit of mentoring, Gordon was somebody who was very good to me coming out of school. I would have met with him a few times just for advice and a bit of guidance. He was sponsored by Adidas at the time. I recall that he gave me two pairs of Adidas boots when I was in sixth year. I thought that was the most amazing thing ever. This was the year that he was the big star. He was Six Nations Player of the Year at the time.

Gordon's generosity and my naïvety was nearly my undoing in the Leinster senior dressing room. At one stage early on, Gordon kindly got me a pair of Adidas Predator boots complete with my name embroidered on the front. Himself and Brian O'Driscoll had boots with their own name on them. That was all that I noticed.

I thought I was pretty cool wearing my boots with my name

on them too. I never copped that nobody else in the Leinster dressing room had their own name on their boots. Just myself, still wet behind the ears and the two major international superstars. That ruffled a fair few feathers but at the time I was completely oblivious. This, I thought, is just what we hotshots do. I was so very green. Boarding school doesn't prepare you for the dog-eat-dog cliques and turf wars of a professional dressing room. If somebody had quietly said something to me about the boots thing for instance, I would have said, thanks Gordon and then just discreetly put them in the first bin I could find. I would have been mortified.

Some of the problems I had early on with Leinster were partly my own fault. I was progressing fast from a good ending to a schoolboy career. I hadn't had any major setbacks. It went to my head a little bit. The lads who had returned from Lions and Irish tours mainly did their own extended pre-season for a while. We'd only be seeing them when it came to Heineken Cup week or the week before. Then we'd quietly make way for them to return.

Denis Hickie got injured though in the week of the first European cup game. I wasn't due to be starting. I was marked down to be on the bench but I moved in when Denis was injured. I was thrilled with myself. It was our first ever game in the RDS. The first time for Leinster to have ever played there. I was in the team. We lost to Bath.

You react to defeats on two levels. How was it for the team? How did I play? The loss was bad for the team but I went ok. I was on the wing. Girvan Dempsey was full back. Shane Horgan was on the other wing. Brian was out injured with the shoulder problem. Gordon D'Arcy was in the centre. Felipe was ten and Guy Easterby was nine, I think. I felt part of it all out there on the pitch. It ended there when the final whistle blew.

The clique atmosphere was evident as soon as the Lions guys came back into the set-up full-time. There was no big, open-armed welcome when the senior lads came back in. If anything, it was probably the opposite. Just a coolness. There were no acknowledgements amongst us all in the morning at the start of the day. No chat. No, how are you going today? No banter. No interaction whatsoever.

We were training at UCD and at the David Lloyd gym. Leinster have their own section in David Lloyd in Riverview and back then we still did the odd bit of training down at Old Belvedere also, changing at the boot of the car when we arrived. Some small part of what I sensed to be a cold war may have been down to me. I was no doubt giving off a vibe that I thought I was the new good thing. If there was a bit of cockiness about me, though, that was how I thought I was expected to act around those guys.

In hindsight, they probably wanted to see a quiet, humble, unassuming young lad who would work hard, doff the cap and thank anybody who took the trouble to acknowledge his existence. I thought they wanted to see somebody coming in ready for a challenge, somebody looking to play in this team, demanding a spot. I thought they wanted cocksure swagger. I got that pretty wrong. And I wasn't behaving in the way Adam Lewis would have wanted me to behave. I accept that now.

On the other hand, I was a young guy coming into an established environment and today I would expect people to keep an eye out to make sure that I integrated well. There was an inside and an outside to it.

I was maybe the only young player in the country at that

time making any waves. As such, I'd be doing press interviews and photo shoots. I got some endorsement deals and ambassadorial stuff early on. I thought this was normal, just part of the package when you broke into professional rugby.

Cheika was old school though. He had grown up in a working class home with Lebanese migrant parents. I was from a posh boarding school and getting a lot of attention. The trappings which I thought were a normal part of the process were infuriating to Cheika and annoyed some of the older lads too.

From the outside there was this view of me as being the rising star of the domestic game. Meanwhile, inside the Leinster dressing room, nobody would give me the time of day and Cheika was singling me out regularly.

It's true that Cheika gave any young lad a very hard time of it but for a while I was the only young lad. Jamie was there a little ahead of me but Jamie was a forward which offered him some protection. Cheika had played as a number eight and he took Jamie under his wing a little bit. After me there were no other young players, no emerging academy players. I was by far the youngest and most inexperienced in the group. When Cheika needed to give somebody the hairdryer treatment I was an easy target for him.

I didn't know how to react so I fronted up. I didn't understand back then that a head coach should treat all players equally and not have favourites. For me, all those guys in that dressing room were up on a pedestal and I wanted to impress them but Cheika put them on a pedestal too. They were his guys and he wanted to make it clear that I had a long way to go.

When Cheika went hard on me I always took it. I would never, ever bite back. I was young though and I didn't want to rattle the cage. I'd take it all and look forward to being back playing with UCD the following week. He tormented me for a few years in the Monday video reviews. It didn't matter if I was the best, the worst or somewhere in the middle, I was getting slaughtered in review. Week in and week out I would dread those Monday morning reviews.

I don't remember a particular theme because I don't think there was one. If I made a mistake, it was showcased in the video session ad nauseum. If any of the older lads made mistakes, Cheika didn't embarrass them by putting them on screen. I was always the one who got the brunt. I was playing rugby, getting paid and I still hugely loved what I was doing. I just really didn't like having Cheika as a coach for those years. He was there for five years through till 2010 and it was only at the very end that things improved between us.

Other worries arose during that time. My second season at Leinster was 2006-07 and I just fell off the cliff. If there is such a thing as second season syndrome I definitely got a bad case of it. It was so noticeable that I remember Brian O'Driscoll slagging me about suffering from the condition.

I just lost my nerve. Luke Fitzgerald had come in. My second season was his first. I wanted to be a full back but at that time we were both left wingers and he was the new hotshot on the scene now. Luke would occasionally get picked on the wing ahead of me. The two of us were fighting it out for left wing. Shane Horgan had the right wing nailed down. Girvan was full back. I still saw myself as doing my time on the wing as part of the apprenticeship to become full back, that's the usual route but a lot of the time I was just on the bench.

I played some games that autumn. The one I recall best was against the Border Reivers away at Netherdale. I had strained my hamstring at the start of that week. I genuinely had no idea back then what hamstrings were all about. I didn't know how long it took a hamstring to heal or what it might take to make it heal.

On the morning of the game in Scotland, I did a warm-up and took a fitness test outside the hotel on a patch of green grass. It didn't feel right. Being young I didn't know that when a professional isn't feeling quite right he is supposed to go to the coach and announce that he definitely cannot play. If the professional doesn't do that, it can all blow up in his face.

I tested with the physio and mentioned that I didn't feel quite right. We went in to see Cheika. I was starting to explain that I had my doubts about the hamstring and Cheika just said, mate, you're fine. I saw you out there. Nothing wrong with you. You can play. The physio said nothing. So I played and it duly blew up in my face. I was awful.

I couldn't run with the ball so I kept kicking it back. At best my movement was seventy per cent of what it should have been. The message came to me from the sidelines. Tell him to stop kicking the ball. If he kicks it again…

I couldn't run, though, so I just kept kicking. We lost the game and in the changing room afterwards Cheika gave me the biggest bollocking I have ever got from a coach. Ever. A landmark in bollockings. He was jumping up and down, beside himself with rage, frothing, ape-shit mental. He was in the middle of the room. The whole team were sitting rooted in their spots. And I was getting ninety per cent of the flamethrower heat.

I remember that Brian O'Driscoll was going off to London or Newcastle or somewhere for the weekend. He wasn't coming home with the team. He just walked off with his wheelie bag for the weekend while we were still stuck with the frothing volcano that was Cheika. I had never wanted to be Brian O'Driscoll as much as I did at that moment.

We went in on Monday morning and Cheika had his squad list up for the week. Thirty players, including a few who weren't normally in the squad. My name wasn't there. I was sent off back to the wilderness of UCD for a couple of weeks as punishment. The wilderness has never been so welcoming a refuge.

I didn't get back into the team for six or seven weeks. I was still dropped the following week and after that I missed out on European games. I just played for UCD.

I missed out on Ireland's autumn squad selections that year. I had been in the training squad for the 2005 autumn internationals and had played with Ireland A but I hadn't been capped. Now this autumn Jamie Heaslip, Luke Fitzgerald and Stephen Ferris got called in and won caps. I felt they were disappearing off into the distance, heading towards great careers. I was falling behind and I feared that I would soon be forgotten.

Luke was out there playing for Ireland against the Pacific Islands. He was the youngest player to have played for Ireland for twenty nine years. Stephen was making strides with Ulster and he got his first cap against the Pacific Islands too. Meanwhile I was out in UCD with a great future behind me. It was a tough schooling and a difficult few years.

In hindsight, I regret not just going to Cheika privately and asking him what it was about me that he wasn't happy with. It would have been great if somebody had advised me to do that. As it was, I was just scared shitless of the man.

On the other hand, maybe if somebody had given me the

advice to go and face down Cheika, it still wouldn't have happened. Joe Schmidt is a more approachable man than Cheika but I would also be scared to take on Joe. Even at the end of my career, I would never take Joe on. There were a couple of times when I came close to asking Joe for a private chat. I didn't though. With Joe I could always say, he's still picking me, I am prepared to take the shit. With Cheika, I wish sometimes that I had knocked on his door. But I didn't.

Our relationship improved later on but I don't think he ever really took to me.

Even after the Lions tour to South Africa in 2009, when I had done so well down there, he just didn't pick me. He had me on the bench for the first Heineken Cup game. I felt that he had it in for me and he went out of his way to give me a hard time. If you asked him he would probably say, nah, he needed a hard time. I would argue back that I would have been a better player for him if he had been fairer or more encouraging.

I asked about selections a few times but never got far. I knew he was leaving at the end of the 2010 season so I was just prepared to suck it up. When we won the Heineken Cup in 2009 I had played all the way to the semi-final. I got sick with the mumps the week after the Harlequins Bloodgate game and I was in Blackrock Clinic for a week. My Lions tour was in jeopardy for a little while and I think Cheika probably made the right call not to to play me in that final. I was disappointed but had no real problem with it. I had only played one game the week before that and the back three, Isa Nacewa, Luke and Shane Horgan had played well in the semi-final. When he kept the same back three for the first round of the Heineken Cup the following season, though, that did bother me.

Even now, years later, if I see Cheika after an international

Looking over us: Ross *(left)* and me. Ross asked for this picture to be taken a few days before his death

Early days: *(Above)* me as a baby with Richard and Ross. *(Above right)* wearing Richard's Clongowes Wood jersey to make me blend in with the older boys

My world: Enjoying the mini-rugby at Dundalk RFC

Guiding the way: With Mum and Dad after my first Leinster schools trial. My parents are the two most incredible people I will ever know

Learning our trade: With younger brother Dave in 2004 at a past versus present pupils match in Clongowes Wood

First love: Lining up for a Louth GAA team *(back row, third from right)*. I played football constantly when I was young and it gave me the perfect foundation for the rugby career that followed

Kicking on: In action for Ireland at schoolboy level

Mentor: With Adam Lewis

Stars of the future: A team shot from an Ireland Under-18 get-together. Johnny Sexton, Devin Toner, Seán Cronin, Billy Holland and Darren Cave would go on to play at international level

Proud day: With Dad and Richard in Argentina (*above*) after I had won my first full cap. (*Left*) Scoring a try for Leinster in the Heineken Cup against Bourgoin in 2005

Euro star: Another Heineken Cup try, this time against Wasps in 2008 as a young Johnny Sexton looks on

Controversy: Mike Brown dives in to try and make the tackle during our quarter-final Heineken Cup win over Harlequins at the Stoop in April 2009 – the infamous 'Bloodgate' game

Leading by example: Ronan O'Gara took brave decisions on the pitch

What's your name again? *(Left)* training with Eddie O'Sullivan

Party time: *(Above, left to right)* Tommy Bowe, Jamie Heaslip and Stephen Ferris. *(Middle)* celebrating with the fans and *(top)* with the team after clinching our first Grand Slam since 1948 after a dramatic win over Wales in Cardiff

Good teacher: With Girvan Dempsey in the dressing room after the 2009 Heineken Cup triumph. Girvan and Geordan Murphy were very good international full backs who remained untrampled upon!

How do you like that? On the run and attempting to evade Italy's Andrea Masi. In 2009 I was the victim of a reckless tackle by Masi –and there was no apology afterwards

Heartbreaker: The famous image of me in the dying seconds of the second Test in Pretoria as the game slips away from us. *(Top)* Scoring the first try of the game

I'll say hello, nice to see you again. But, if I'm being honest, I've never really forgotten those early days. On the Lions Tour in 2013 we played the Waratahs the week before the first Test. Cheika was their coach then. Tommy Bowe had hurt his thumb the week before the first Test, Leigh Halfpenny was full back and there was an opening in the back three. I was half hoping that it might be me getting the full back spot.

I was talking with Cheika when he came into the changing room after the game. I said that I imagined Leigh would be full back. Cheika said, no mate you'll defo be full back. Leigh will be on the wing. I thought, mark the day, that is the first acknowledgment I've ever had from you that I might be half decent.

In the end, though, it has to be conceded that Cheika's achievement was to completely change the culture of Leinster rugby. He had us working hard and playing tough. The Harlequins quarter-final game in April 2009 was the first important away win for Leinster against an English team. We turned a corner. The final score was 6-5 and we defended our way to that win. Every inch. It was the first time that we showed that there was a hard edge to us. He had changed how we viewed ourselves.

When I look back at my relationship with him I think that in part he was just playing to the gallery of the older lads. Brian, Shane and Denis in particular. He would sometimes have lunch or coffee with them after training. None of the older lads ever came to me to say, don't pay any attention to the shouting. Of the big three, Denis would have been the one that I would have thought looked out for me a little bit but Shane and Brian had very little time for me back then. From the age of nineteen, until I was about twenty one or twenty two, it was that way. It was 2009 when myself and Brian and Shane became friends. Shane was just on the way out by then. He was vanishing from the international scene.

Before that there was an element of Brian, Shane and Denis having their own little private triangle for those few years. They were the top guns and Cheika's three best friends. It amplified the idea that they were the princes of Leinster rugby at the time. Until Rocky Elsom came along, of course. Then all bets were off! Rocky leapfrogged the lads into special friend status straight away but the impact he had was such that nobody ever complained.

As I said, I was grateful to have had a decent relationship with Gordon, and Girvan Dempsey would also always have been consistently generous. I will always be very grateful and thankful to them. Their kindnesses make for some lingering memories of that time of growing up in a professional dressing room.

The Leinster culture has done a full U-turn since those days. Sometimes myself and the older guys in our thirties joke that these wet-behind-the-ears academy lads get more respect from the coaches now than we do.

It's so inclusive now. We have sixty players in that Leinster squad and we all work together in the gym. We all know each other's names. Everybody greets everybody else every morning, every person in the organisation. There is no hierarchy anymore. It's not like the old days and as one of the old guys I can only say that I'm glad. It's all more enjoyable and much healthier. Coaches, staff, team, squad, academy and sub-academy, it all feels like one unit.

5
—

NUMBER FIFTEEN

On the way home from Japan after the World Cup, I was sitting with Johnny Sexton in the boarding lounge at Narita Airport when a man approached us politely. He was diffident and he was wearing a peak cap.

We were just a little bit down still and not much in the mood for chit-chat but the man just wanted to say hard luck to the two of us. He wished us safe home and the best of luck with the rest of our season. We said thanks and he said goodbye and he walked off towards his boarding gate leaving Johnny and I to pick up our conversation.

Johnny flicked his head in the direction of the guy in the cap. Jesus, he said, he was some player.

Who was some player?

The guy we were just talking to.

Who was he?

Chris Latham, said Johnny.

Was that…?

I have never fanboyed after my heroes but I got up off my chair and went striding off to look for Chris Latham. I needed to tell him that he was my hero growing up and to ask if I could have a photograph with him. He'd boarded his plane though and I never got to thank the full back who I had always wanted to be.

It wouldn't be correct to say that being a full back is a family trade but Don Kearney, my grandad, was a full back. He won a Towns Cup medal playing with Dundalk in 1937. My dad played full back at school. Dad would have gone on to play for the Leinster schools team at full back but he got struck with severe arthritis in sixth year and he ended up sitting his Leaving Cert in a wheelchair. He recovered from that and he went on to play centre with Dundalk and to captain the Leinster club team. These days, he has had two knee replacements and he has one full back in the family.

When we were younger, Dad used to do all the fixture lists for Dundalk rugby club. Back then they were a big enough club but the glory days of the late '40s when the Towns Cup came to the town three years in a row were long gone. We would go into the town to Mill Road and watch Dundalk play every Sunday.

The full back for Dundalk at that time was a guy called Conor Poole. He'd played for the Irish schoolboys. I was just always drawn to watching games from behind the posts. I watched Conor Poole a lot.

One day I was back towards the end of the field on my own and a ball got kicked out into touch and ended up almost beside me. I was maybe ten or eleven and at that age when the match ball comes to you, it's an exciting moment as if suddenly you are part of the action. I went to pick the ball up to give it to Conor Poole. He shouted at me, don't touch it, don't touch it. Too late. I was brimming with enthusiasm and helpfulness. I had plucked the ball up and thrown it to him before he was even through telling me not to do it.

I suppose I thought he'd say, nice reaction sonny, good throwing style. I think what he actually said to me was, gobshite. That was the day that I learned that you can't take a quick tap to yourself if anybody else has touched the ball. It may also have been the first day when I made a mental note that full back was a little bit of a lone ranger position. And that was attractive to me.

At Dundalk we only played mini-rugby so, until I reached my teens, the staple of my sporting life was Gaelic football. The first fifteen-a-side rugby game I ever played was under-13s at Clongowes.

I had an idea for a little while that I'd like to be the number ten, the boss, the quarterback. I was a good goalkicker. I kicked right the way through school and through schoolboys, even up to under-20s level (I have 1/1 at international level).

I played a little at number ten, and a bit on the wing. I did second year in Clongowes at number seven. Dad remembers watching me and recognising that his son was an absolutely clueless number seven. All over the shop was how I looked and how I felt. It wasn't until third year when I was moved to full back on the Junior Cup team that I knew I was in the right position. The coach was Brian O'Keeffe. I knew immediately that, yes, full back was where I wanted to play.

So I was fourteen years old and, to use a modern phrase, I

self identified as a fifteen. Throughout my whole career I have sometimes been too vocal about wanting to play full back. It was just where I wanted to be. They'd put me at full back. I liked it. I wanted to stay there.

Being a fifteen just suited my skill set. I realised that from an early age. I could kick, I was a competent catcher, I was quick. I had the attributes that distinctively went into the full back category. I set about improving those bits of my game and adding whatever else was needed. I'm still doing that.

Gaelic football must have been a big part of my development. There have been so many parallels throughout my whole career between Gaelic football and rugby, the whole aerial kicking and catching aspect of it. The skills I picked up in Cooley Kickhams can only have hugely enhanced my ability to be able to play the position.

When you are younger, rugby is always a little bit chaotic and everybody goes towards the ball in herds. It wasn't until fourth year and Senior Cup where it all started to become a little more structured and, like athletes coming off a bend after a staggered start, we could see who was ahead.

I played two years Junior Cup. In second year, I was on the bench as a utility player covering the back row and the backs. The next year I was full back. We lost to Belvedere in the semi-final but I knew that I had nailed down the position I wanted to play in. I was more developed than everybody else on the team. When you are a little bigger and a little faster than everybody else then you just wait for the ball to be kicked to you. Counter-attacking and scoring tries was easy until people started to catch up with me physically.

Also, I loved kicking the ball. I was naturally left-footed but at home living on a farm we had a decent-sized garden and if

Dad was out there cutting the grass or whatever he had always made me kick off my right foot. I had become comfortable early on with using both feet.

Back then you could take the ball back into your own twenty two and kick it out from there unimpeded. I remember so many times that I would catch the ball between the ten and the twenty two and run back into the twenty two to gleefully launch spirals long into touch.

I started spiral kicking the ball in third year. A guy in our year called Dermot Kilroy taught me how to spiral the ball in front of the cricket pavilion in Clongowes. I have such a clear memory of that.

Tragically Dermot died about three years after we left school but I remember him giving me a very simple cue. The ball has four seams on it. You have the valve here. This seam line should come to your left shoulder and just kick it with the outside of your foot. That is how I learned the spiral kick. I've fluffed many spiral kicks, so many have gone wrong for me down through the years but the first one I ever tried, I absolutely nailed. There is something so beautiful about watching a perfectly spiralled kick. I was addicted. I loved it and I practised it so much. In the early days in school I was one of the only ones on the team who was able to execute a spiral. That reassured me about my value within the team.

I have pretty much always spiral kicked up until maybe the 2012-13 season. The spiral was always my default kick, unless I was kicking a penalty to touch when I would punt it end over end. Or, if I caught the ball in my twenty two without being able to mark it and I knew that finding the safety of touch was imperative, I would never have spiralled. All other circumstances? Spiral.

When I was fifteen I moved up to the Senior Cup squad. I was a fifteen-year-old playing with eighteen-year-olds. I knew that it was a big feather in my cap to be the only fourth year on the team. I was still cocky enough to think that I should be the full back for the Senior Cup though.

There was a sixth year, James O'Reilly, who played full back. He was a good player; big, strong and quick. I know in hindsight that I was being ridiculous wondering why I couldn't be full back when I was fourth year but the two of us swapped in and out of the fifteen spot early in the year and I began to get ideas.

The Senior Cup team had scheduled a tour to England over the Christmas holidays. This clashed with a family skiing holiday. We had never been skiing before and this was a trip the family had being looking forward to all year. The holiday to Austria landed on the exact same dates as the school tour to England. It was a tough decision but I didn't go on the school tour. I remember texting Aonghus a lot during the tour. I needed updates on my campaign to be the fifteen.

"How is James O'Reilly playing?"

"Really well. Great."

"Yeah. Thanks mate."

"You did ask."

I didn't get to play full back for the rest of the year but it was a good holiday. I came back from Austria with no idea if I would even be involved in the Senior Cup. Aonghus hadn't sugercoated his reports of how well James had been playing. In the end, when I was named on the wing, I was ecstatic.

By fifth year I was the established school full back and Adam Lewis was my prefect. Adam was also our coach and one evening he called me up to his office and brought me into the living room and said listen, I want to show you a video here.

It was a two-minute video of Christian Cullen, the All Black full back. Just Christian Cullen player-cammed. The game was going on up and down the field but the camera stayed on Cullen the entire time. His work rate was incredible. He just did not stop moving. His anticipation, his concentration. He was back and forth, back and forth, for two minutes straight.

Adam showed me this and said, if you want to be a world-class fifteen that is what you must aspire to do. It was pertinent enough because I had always thought of Christian Cullen with the ball in his hand, sidestepping, feinting and just skinning lads and scoring tries. In this two-minute segment he never touched the ball, not once. But he never stopped working.

In terms of full backs, I loved watching Cullen. He was incredible. He had great acceleration. His ability to sidestep was magical. I was never gifted with an incredible, elusive sidestep though. Deep down I always knew that I wasn't going to be a Christian Cullen-type player. Cullen was the player who I thought was without doubt the best full back in the world but the guy who I really looked up to and wanted to emulate was Latham.

Chris Latham was simply a very good footballer. He was a left-footer, he spiralled the ball a lot, he ran good angles. He was tough and he was strong. He was the guy that I wanted to be like and a guy I learned a lot from watching him. Back at the beginning, though, that video showcasing Cullen's workrate made a big impact on me. It gave me a foundation.

Now, I will always tell any young player that so much of a good full back's game is what he does off the ball. If you are in the right position, the opposition's options are always restricted. You have to be anticipating and always trying to stay one step ahead of the game.

For a while after I left school, I think I stopped consciously trying to learn about the game for a while. I was playing and training as a professional and a bit too confident that what tools I had were enough for the job. There was more to learn but I was concentrating on just maintaining my own box of tricks. For maybe the last ten years, though, I've got back to learning and now that the end is so close I know that when I play my last game, I will still have a lot to learn.

I've made it a habit since I was about twenty three or twenty four that when I watch a rugby match I never watch the game from the viewpoint of what is happening now. I don't pay attention to what is happening in the moment. I have conditioned myself to always watch a game by anticipating what the next moment is going to be.

Every time I watch a game, I talk out loud to myself. He'll go short side. The ten is standing a couple of metres deeper. He is going to kick. If there is a breakdown here, I'm muttering that the ten is now there and the backs are setting up the normal line and the normal punter will be looking for it at the breakdown. I am always trying to think, ok where is the ball going to go next?

I try to train my mind to anticipate.

I enjoy it. As I have grown older and more experienced, I sometimes try to double bluff teams. I'll show them a space when I am in the backfield and I know that a kick is coming. I'll invite them to put it there. I am always looking at the number nine's eyes and the number ten's eyes. That is the only thing I am looking at. Those two pairs of eyes. There is only one player in the world who kicks a ball without first quickly glancing at where he is going to kick it to. As soon as a number ten does that, I know the ball is coming there. If a nine is rooting at the bottom of a ruck and he has had one little glance at a corner, I know exactly where the ball is going.

That is why Daniel Carter was without doubt the toughest player to play against. He was the master of the no-look kick. It was very hard to get a tell off him. He would look at one spot and he would kick the ball somewhere else. That made him the hardest person to cover in the backfield. He caught me out several times with his kicking equivalent of the no-look pass. I'm reading his eyes and as soon as he's glanced at a spot, I am already on my way to that spot. Just instinct. I am gone. I have departed. And then he just kicks it elsewhere. Inscrutable.

So then I have to make a call on what to do the next time he takes a look. Do I override my instincts and training, cancel my hair-trigger response and just stay put? I know full well that if I stay rooted and bide my time he will just put the ball where I should have been arriving a second or two ago. People will tut tut and say, look at that, Kearney hardly moved.

On the other end of the scale there were guys who were easier to read. George Ford of Leicester Tigers and England is somebody who always tells his centres what's happening. He always points upwards before he launches the Garryowen. Now, you still have to try to catch the thing, but at least you have the helpful warning. Incoming. Incoming…

I have always told Johnny and Ross Byrne that disguising their kicking intentions will make them even better out-halves because it makes it harder to cover the backfield. I tell them how I'm always looking at their eyes, looking for the tell.

Myself and Johnny have had great fun down the years when we have been on separate teams in training sessions. We would have a few quid down on whether Johnny will get a ball to bounce on me or if he will find a corner. He will be practising his no-look kicking and we will be trying to bluff and double bluff each other.

When I was in sixth year sometime after the Schools Cup final, in April maybe, I had a meeting in the Berkeley Court Hotel with three members of the IRFU staff. Eddie Wigglesworth, Mark McDermott and Pat Whelan. Myself, Mum and Dad got to the hotel in plenty of time. This was to be my interview to get into the Irish academy. We arrived and made our way up to the conference room at the top of the Berkeley Court.

There was no Leinster Academy at the time. Just an Ireland Academy. I don't remember much from the conversation other than they told me that I would never play another game of Gaelic football once I had signed up. Eddie asked me what was I prepared to do to be the full back on the Irish rugby team. I was a boy from Cooley who was still in boarding school. I had never been asked such a direct question before. I gave Eddie a pretty bland and pious answer.

I'll train really hard. I will work on my weaknesses. I'll sleep well. I don't drink and I won't drink. Just standard interview stuff.

Eddie Wigglesworth looked me in the eye and put it to me in a more emphatic way.

Who are you going to trample all over to get that jersey?

Oh. I'm thinking, what do I say here? Who will I trample all over? Is there a good answer to a question like this?

Who is the Leinster full back? Eddie asked.

Girvan Dempsey, I said.

Are you going to trample all over Girvan Dempsey to get that jersey?

I say, that, yes, I'd certainly try to trample all over him.

Geordan Murphy? Eddie said. Are you going to trample all over Geordan Murphy to get that number fifteen jersey?

Yes again.

I was glad I hadn't spoken about hoping to play for the Lions some day. That would have been too much trampling.

When we left the room, I remember that Mum was a bit unnerved by the ruthlessness of the whole thing. Her schoolboy son was going to trample all over Girvan Dempsey and Geordan Murphy? That is the one very distinct memory that she still has of my Ireland Academy interview.

As it happened, Girvan and Geordan were coming towards the end of their careers as I was coming into mine. There was no trampling. I learned from each of them.

In those early days, when the Leinster senior dressing room was a place of cliques and caucuses, I was very aware that I didn't really fit in. I found it quite an alien place. Girvan was the in-situ Leinster full back and it was my good fortune that he was an absolute gentleman. Personality wise, he was much quieter than the other lads. Denis Hickie, Shane Horgan and Brian O'Driscoll were the three musketeers, the true hotshots of their day and the dominant figures in the room. Girvan was different. He was a man unto himself and quietly aware of the undercurrents within the team at that time.

Girvan was never part of any clique and he was incredibly good to me. He just took me under his wing for those first few years. We roomed together. He was thirty and I was nineteen. It's very unusual for a very senior player to room with the youngest player or one of the youngest. Especially when they both want the same jersey.

Girvan was a Terenure man and just a welcoming guy. He taught me a lot about the game and his kindness was very important for me. When the caste system of the dressing room was getting to me, when some of the older lads weren't giving me the time of day, not even a hello, Girvan was warm and helpful. The fact that the Irish full back, who was on his way to eighty two caps, was taking time out to talk to me and give me advice was inspiring.

The best gift I got from Girvan in terms of learning was his understanding of a positional sense in full back play. Girvan was incredibly good at that. Full back was the only position that I wanted to play long term and I knew that positioning was a huge part of the position. Girvan never treated me as a threat to his position. He just quietly mentored me.

Girvan was an astute student of the game and a good teacher too. He taught me about anticipation, being a step ahead of the game and knowing where the ball was going to be kicked before it got kicked. Watching Girvan and listening to him I absorbed so much.

We would never get too much into the nitty gritty of reading the game. You absorb that over time rather than learning it rote detail by detail but Girvan taught me to be conscious of absorbing it. He would look out for me and it was necessary that I had somebody to do that.

As I have said, I was a cocky young guy and I repaid Girvan in my cocky way. It was around that time that I began saying in interviews that I wanted to play full back for Ireland. Girvan was the full back and Geordan was there too. I was being disrespectful but Girvan would have joked from time to time that, yeah, I was coming to take his place. I benefitted so much from his good grace and patience.

A lot of people know that this thing or that thing is what a team needs but they don't do those things. They talk the talk but the walking of the walk only gets done occasionally. You have team players and then you have the ultimate team players. Girvan was the ultimate team player.

The Leinster number fifteen jersey would pass from Girvan to myself in due time and it is the mark of the man that it felt more like Girvan was quietly passing it on to me than that I was ripping it away him.

When I made my debut for Ireland in 2006 in Buenos Aires, I was on the wing and Geordan Murphy played full back. I wouldn't play a big game in the number fifteen jersey until the day Ireland played Wales in Croke Park in 2008. There was uncertainty all that week. Who was going to be full back, Girvan or Geordan? I had been named on the left wing and I was delighted just to be in the mix.

The day before the game, Eddie came to me and told me that I would be playing full back. Neither Geordan or Girvan were fully fit.

Circumstance had been kind to me but I loved the opportunity that had fallen into my lap. We lost 12-16 but I felt that I played very well. I hadn't spoken too much in the media about being full back before then but full back was where I wanted to play and that was my best game of the campaign. Geordan was full back when we went to Twickenham to play England some weeks later and I was on the left wing. There was a general period of uncertainty.

Eddie was gone and Declan Kidney came in. We played Canada (Thomond), New Zealand and Argentina (both Croke Park) in Deccie's first three games and again I was on the wing. We lost pretty convincingly to the All Blacks. Having played full back against Wales in the previous Six Nations and having been at fifteen against Australia and New Zealand on the summer tour, that year I was disappointed. I was a little more vocal now about being full back than I should have been.

I've always been too forthcoming and honest in media interviews. I wasn't savvy enough with the party line. When people would ask what was my favourite position, I really needed to say, oh, I am just happy to have a jersey. But I would always say, full back. I want to play there. You have to show respect to the guy in the position. I was naïve and that was coming over as arrogant.

For the first game of the November series, Keith Earls arrived as another good young player who could play full back. It was Deccie's first game in Thomond Park. I'm on the wing. Keith is full back. I'm thinking, well, is full back gone now? Another Munster man and he is very talented and he has all the attributes. Is he the new full back?

Then, in the week of the Canadian game, Declan came to me and said that he knew that I wanted to play full back but for the moment I should just do what is best for the team. Declan was a very good man manager and very intuitive about just what his players were thinking.

Girvan was still in the picture. So was Geordan. I was glad of Deccie's words but there is never a guarantee when you don't have the jersey.

I got the impression that I was one of those younger ones that as a coach he wanted to bring through but that he'd take his time. Once I knew that Declan knew where I wanted to be though, I became less vocal about it.

I was very open to Declan's ideas after that. That was my first proper interaction with him really. When we played New Zealand the following week and lost 3-22 in Croke Park, Girvan was full back and I was left wing. When we played

Argentina, and won in Croke Park (17-3), Geordan was full back and I was on left wing again. I had thought that after the summer tour I had done enough to be the full back for the foreseeable future but it didn't happen that November.

At Leinster, Girvan was still there but we were in transition and I was just beginning to establish myself as the full back. Girvan was on the bench more and more. By the time it came to the Grand Slam Six Nations of 2009 Deccie had decided to put his faith in me as his number fifteen.

I remember feeling after the win in Scotland that it had been probably my poorest game of the championship to date. I had no disasters but not too much went right either.

I wasn't sure if I would be in the team for the Grand Slam game in Cardiff. It was still early in my career and there were no guarantees. He could go for Geordan and his experience. There was a perception that Geordan hadn't got a fair crack of the whip under Eddie. Himself and Eddie had their differences and were quite public about that afterwards. Geordan was battling it out with a very good full back in Girvan, though, who was perceived to be more solid. You go for solidity first. I am a big believer that big games especially are most often decided by one person's mistake rather than one person's genius. If your full back doesn't make a mistake, you always have a chance. So eliminate mistakes.

Anyway, there were no guarantees about Cardiff. Geordan was a superb player and hadn't started a game yet. He had been on the bench for all the games. That night in Scotland I was a bit down. We were staying in the Balmoral at the bottom of Princes Street and after the dinner Declan came up to me for a chat, which was unusual, and I was a bit unsure as to why. Was he going to break some bad news softly?

It was just a players dinner on our own back in the hotel late that night. We'd had the post-match function. The players' partners were around too but I was only twenty-two and I was alone. Declan asked me if I recalled when Ulster had won the Heineken Cup in 1999? I said I didn't remember too much about it. He said for me to take a look at the Ulster full back that day. Every time Simon Mason had got the ball in Lansdowne against Colomiers he just kicked it back to them. Mason had scored six penalties. David Humphreys a drop goal. Declan told me that and he just walked off. A typical Declan Kidney ploy. The riddler.

For me, the takeaway was that I was starting against Wales and I would be kicking every ball that I got. In a crunch match we don't want the ball in our backfield. Declan was telling me in his own way that every time I got the ball I was to kick it back. That simple. One job.

That relaxed me instantly. I didn't have to wait till Tuesday morning racked with worry. I had the game plan. Declan was a very new coach into the system. If he told me to do something and I didn't do it, it would not go down well. He'd be damaged by it and I might not be forgiven. Come hell or high water I was going to kick against Wales.

Declan had taken the weight of decision-making off my shoulders. I was gunning for a Grand Slam rather than a personal performance. I was to kick all afternoon. And that was how I played it. Every time I got the ball I kicked it right back. If I wasn't going to be Man of the Match I had the perfect excuse. I was just obeying orders. Was Deccie right? It was a good day for running the ball but I think the basis of his message was sound. I may have taken it too far on the day. I don't know.

As luck would have it, there wasn't much else I could do apart from kick. I had suffered a bad back spasm the morning of the game. We were in the team room in the Hilton in central Cardiff and I was on the floor loosening myself out. I moved awkwardly and my back just went into spasm. Immediately I got the physio on the case but there is not much a physio can do. It's just one of those things that takes a couple of weeks before it comes back to normal.

I'd slipped a disc in my back a few years before so there was a lot more going on in my back than just a spasm. I was unnerved but I just wanted to get out onto the field and to start the game. Painkillers were not going to do too much. My back was sore and I was very restricted in my movements. I'd lost a lot of flexibility and found it hard to turn or pivot quickly.

The idea of not playing never arose but the back got worse after the first half. Significantly worse. At half time I was trying to get it stretched and loose but I struggled to even get up off the physio bed after being treated. When you stop moving, the back seizes up and that is what happened. I came off the field after fifty five minutes. It probably wasn't noticeable but I know that I wasn't trying as hard as I normally would to get involved in the play. I was just trying to look after my own shop and do the things that would get me by.

Geordan came on and he did well. He was the one who caught the Stephen Jones penalty at the end and kicked the ball out. The last kick of the game, the last kick of the Grand Slam. He thoroughly deserved the moment. His Ireland career didn't allow him to achieve as he would have felt he could have but that was a great moment. Girvan and Geordan exited on their own terms and untrampled-upon, I am glad to say. They were both very good Irish full backs.

I think that I always liked the attention that came with being a full back. The full back works in isolation most of the time. Every other player is part of a team within a team. Everybody else is co-dependent.

Full back is a bit of a high wire act. The ball is in the air and time seems to stand still for a moment while everybody waits for the full back to materialise. There's a break into the backfield. Where's the full back? You get the ball and all eyes are on you. There is no hiding, no fall back, no safety net.

That can all be thrilling but when you are playing badly, the full back position is the loneliest place in the world. There are times when you just want to dig a hole in the pitch and jump in and pull the soil down over yourself.

Over the years I have tried when I take to the field to maybe give off a little bit of a swagger. I'd actually try to convey a deliberate air of arrogance or cockiness. I would like to think that I am not an arrogant or cocky person but taking the field in this way is a conscious decision. I'm trying to demonstrate to my own team-mates and to the opposition that I am ready. Come on, give it to me. I am not vulnerable. Try me. If you show any vulnerability at full back, teams will prey on it. You always wear a face that says, bring it on. Good out-halves smell fear in a full back the way sharks pick up the scent of blood in the water.

Again, there is a flip side here. Full backs get very harshly judged sometimes. It comes with being the last line. On the front line, if a number five misses a tackle, his buddy – maybe two metres away from him – makes the tackle for him. It's all good. You very rarely notice forwards missing a tackle. When a line break happens, though, the opposition have generally sent one of the quicker players up and they might have twenty metres either side of you to attack. The odds are always very heavily stacked in the attacker's favour but in the post-mortems, the team always died because the full back should have made the tackle but didn't!

I was a very good tackler at school. I enjoy contact and I enjoy the physical component of rugby but my tackling technique has let me down on a number of occasions. My problem is just getting my feet close enough to the attacker. I sometimes leave my feet behind me and lunge a little bit. The best last line tacklers get their feet really close into the attacker so that when they do lunge they are right there. It is much more effective.

More so than my tackling, though, I suppose the biggest criticism that I would have heard down the years was that when I receive the ball from a kick that I seem to just run straight back. People often say (or write) that I don't try to sidestep anybody. I just run into the biggest person in front of me.

Exactly. One hundred per cent. That is basically what I do when I am presented with a twelve-man kick chase wall.

For me, one of the most important measures of how good a game I have played was how much better I tried to make my team-mates play. How much more confident I made them feel. That was always something which was very important to me.

Paul O'Connell said something to me in our early years which stuck. Paul said that when he saw me catch the ball and run, striking hard straight back at the opposition, it was the best thing that he could see. He'd see me running straight and he knew exactly where and when the breakdown was going to be. That was the point. By running straight I would never get caught in a side-on tackle. Getting caught side on means you are getting hit at your weakest point and you are going to get knocked backwards which means your forwards have no access into the ruck.

So that was something that I very much did for the benefit of the team. In saying that, it is not as if I was ever this outrageously good broken field runner trapped in a reliable full back's body. I can't jink and sidestep people and do the things that Jordan Larmour does.

The game has changed anyway. Only people with Jordan's gift can do that now. Over the years teams have become well trained in stopping breaks from received kicks. They'll practise all week where they have thirteen people filling the front line. There is literally nowhere to go. You have to put the head down and run straight as hard as you can and make sure that the ball comes back first and foremost. Your job is to make sure that you don't get turned over in the tackle so that, as Paul said, your forwards know exactly the point of the breakdown so you are going to get quicker ball.

There are so many times over the years where I have done precisely this. I've just caught the ball and literally just run as straight and hard as I could. We might score a try or a line break off the next phase of play. I'm still the guy who served bread and butter when everybody wanted cake but I sort of take a small bit of perverse satisfaction in that. I'm not actually trying to run sideways or do a goose-step or run up my own arse looking for something for myself. We get quick ball and off the next phase we make something out of it.

The converse is that sometimes I will know that I have not been at my best at full back but depending on the plays which we have gone with, I might have run a couple of line breaks. I'm invariably deemed to have had a great game once there's been a couple of flashy moments. The same misconceptions come with the charge that a winger waiting for me to feed him a pass could starve to death.

It's percentages and territory. When I catch the ball in the backfield and the winger is there, unless I am up against the touchline, I will rarely pass the ball back to the winger. If I throw the ball ten or fifteen metres, that means it is in the air for three seconds. That three seconds to a good kick chaser is ten to fifteen metres. They want me to throw it out there to the winger. That's what's driving them. That interception is a definite try and a kick in the gut to the team conceding it.

My single biggest objective is to try to win the halfway line. So, ninety nine times out of a hundred, if I am in my twenty two and I get the ball, I will kick it. No apologies. If I am between my twenty two and the ten metre line, I would kick to an area contestable by myself to chase. Anything outside of that I try to get back to the halfway line or into their half as quickly as possible.

Chasing my own kick was something that I was very good at. Again, probably the Gaelic football influence. It is funny – catching is not something that I ever practised a huge amount. It is just something that I have always been able to do. That is probably not the best advice to be giving to a young guy. I look at a lot of out-halves and you rarely see them practise passing the ball but they are perfect passers, maybe because they have done it so many times in games and there is no better place to practise the skill than in the arena itself.

I used to love the roar that arose from the crowd when I kicked on twenty two, twenty five metres or so and caught my own kick. That was a joy. It's a dying art, though. It was an exciting part of rugby but it is a relic of old times.

Maybe six weeks before the last World Cup, World Rugby's head of referees Alain Rolland came to speak to us in the team hotel in Blanchardstown. I had a quiet argument with him about it. I said, we're losing this skill because when the ball is kicked up in the air every single person, including the referee and the two touch judges, focus exclusively on the ball in the air. They lose sight of what is going on down on the ground. Alain agreed.

Opposition players are entitled to run back but they are not entitled to change lanes. That is the terminology. Yet there is so much lane-changing going on now that is blatantly obvious but it is not being refereed. The contestable box kick will go out of the game in the next couple of years. It already has declined. It is just too difficult now to regain possession after a box kick.

Teams are blocking en masse. Saracens build a wall of three or four players in front of the catcher. The catcher will stand and four Saracens forwards will run back. You can't tackle the catcher, let alone get onto the ball.

As we move forward, contestable kicking will be limited to crossfield Garryowens. If you kick to the other side of the field there is nobody there to block. The only people who can block are the thirteen and twelve and they will most likely be out of position. It is a pity to lose the skill. A player like Dan Biggar is exceptional at catching his own kicks. Rugby shouldn't let that spectacle fade away.

I have always expected to make the catch every time. Two years ago in the Aviva, though, Biggar took a high ball off me. I was so frustrated that when he placed the ball back on the ground I just kicked it out of his hand. Completely illegally. A penalty given against us. Three points lost due to pure frustration.

But Biggar is just superb at catching his own kick. He has great technique. Most players when they catch the ball they cradle directly in front of themselves. He seems to catch it higher. Whatever way he does it, he is out there cradling much higher. His hands meet the ball at altitude.

After fifteen years of being an elite level full back these constant changes in the game and the thinking surrounding it remain a challenge. Adam Lewis got me to get into the learning side of rugby but, as I have said, that very much stopped for me for a long time after I ceased to be under Adam's influence.

I wasn't a very good student of the game in my twenties. I was obsessed with rugby. I loved it. I lived it and breathed it but I wasn't a real student of the game. I could still do my job well without really understanding all the intricacies, without appreciating that rugby is a very complicated game.

It took until I was twenty eight, I would say, before I started understanding rugby better. To be fair, a lot of that is down to Stuart Lancaster. I'm not Stuart's type of full back and for me that has been a challenge and a learning experience.

Stuart's biggest strength is really educating a team on how he wants us to play rugby and why we should want to play rugby his way. Stuart's idea of a full back in the modern style of game is very different to how I play. As a result he has influenced me in how I have tried to change my game over the last few years.

Stuart, very simply, asks that the full back operates as a second out-half. Saracens are the team that he will show us as Exhibit A on a weekly basis. He'll tell us to watch how Goode and Farrell work in tandem. The ball doesn't always go through Farrell. Goode plays down short side as he steps in at first receiver and becomes a second threat for the team. That has been the weakest part of my game.

I know what the answer will be if I say to Stuart, look, this is not the kind of player that I am, I have different qualities. He will say, that's tough Rob. That's the kind of player that we need you to be.

There is no doubt that if you have a second playmaker in the back line it enhances your attacking ability ten-fold. I would always try to argue a little bit with Stuart in saying this doesn't necessarily have to be the number fifteen. Why not the number twelve or thirteen? He is usually of the view that, yes, he would like them to do it as well but he is dead set on the fifteen being the second playmaker.

And that's the odd thing. After so many years wearing a number fifteen on my back, I will finish while still on a learning curve. My career, it seems, may be destined to finish abruptly after the time of lockdown and virus and uncertainty. That was unforeseen but while I have been methodical about planning when and how I will leave the game, I am surprised by how much I am still learning as I leave.

I never thought I'd feel like extending the lease on number fifteen, and I won't be able to, but leaving is harder than I expected it to be.

6

IRELAND'S CALL

In hindsight, lots of things happened very quickly for me. In real time, though, it all felt quite slow.

There was a World Cup in September 2007 so Ireland had pencilled in a summer tour for late May/early June. Eddie O'Sullivan drew some fire for leaving his first fifteen behind. That was the start of the 'Untouchables' as they were called – but for me it had been a break. I'd made my debut against Argentina in Buenos Aires in the second Test against Argentina. We'd lost and I hadn't done very much of note in the game but nothing bad had happened either.

I didn't get any feedback afterwards. Eddie was a stoic sort of character in that way. He just didn't communicate in that manner with players. Even today I could count on one hand the amount of conversations that I have had with Eddie.

For a young player it was all a bit mystifying. Every coach provided different terrain to negotiate. I had a head coach at

Leinster who didn't appear to like me very much. Meanwhile with Ireland, Eddie didn't seem all that certain that I actually existed.

So it was encouraging to be involved in the extended squad of forty or so for the World Cup warm-up camp during that summer. I measured my progress by external factors like that. This has happened so I must be doing ok. That hasn't happened, should I be worried?

No coach was coming to me and saying you are doing well but you need to work a little on this or improve on that. I got picked for games or squads or I didn't get picked. Nobody explained anything. There was the day to day showing up and working hard but there was no big picture. There was no guiding hand on the shoulder. Was I at the point where I was supposed to be at along my career path? Who knew?

I didn't play in many of those summer warm-up games but I wasn't expecting to. I was along for the experience. I remember Ireland played against Italy in Ravenhill in August and there was a game in France against Bayonne that turned into a massive brawl. And they played against Scotland in Murrayfield on the day when Geordan Murphy broke his leg. At that stage, I thought I maybe had a slender chance of making the World Cup squad. Looking back, Gavin Duffy was in that squad as was Brian Carney, a former Clongowes boy, who had converted from a rugby league career in the spring and had played in the first Test in Argentina. He made the World Cup squad.

I didn't allow myself to get too hopeful but again in hindsight and looking at the big picture which I couldn't discern at the time, just two years later I was playing on the Lions team so perhaps I was closer to selection than I thought.

Jamie Heaslip remembers the exact moment that he got told he wasn't going to the World Cup. I don't really. I know we were on the pitch somewhere and Eddie just said, listen, you won't be required for any more training. I was happy enough. I would not have been ready to go to a World Cup and play games on that stage. In terms of mentality or ability, I was not ready. I came back to Leinster and played loads of games while the internationals were all away. I benefitted in that way and after the World Cup I got called into Eddie's squad for 2008.

So, by early 2008, I had been training with the Irish team on and off for about sixth months. We were approaching the Six Nations and we were training at St Gerard's College. Back then we used to stay at Killiney Castle Court Hotel and for training purposes, St Gerard's was just ten minutes away in Bray.

We were in a team huddle at the end of training and Eddie was talking to us, just making his few points. He was addressing me about something that I had done in training. He paused and stood there looking at me slightly baffled and then he began clicking his finger in my direction.

"What's your name again?"

Malcolm O'Kelly leaned down and whispered in his ear.

"That's Rob."

Eddie said, "Oh yeah Rob."

It was bizarre. The national coach trying to recall my name and having to ask for help. I looked around and all the heads were down, guys smirking at their boots. That was definitely another 'back in your box' moment! There's whatshisname. He thinks he's the next big thing!

I wasn't the only one. If Eddie was looking for Graham it was actually Jamie Heaslip he wanted. Jamie took real offence to this. He has a brother called Graham. That was Eddie's way. You could take broad encouragement from things which he might say in team meetings but he wouldn't come to you as an individual and speak one to one.

I played in the Six Nations under Eddie in 2008. I was on the bench the day we played Italy in Croke Park. Gordon D'Arcy broke his arm twenty or twenty five minutes in and I came in on the wing. Luke wasn't near the Irish team at that point. I think Andrew Trimble moved into centre. I played pretty well and I was happy. Afterwards I felt that I had a good chance of keeping the place.

France were next up. Next week will be my week, I told myself. We had won. I had played somewhere in the range of ok to well. I had fitted in and I didn't look out of place. The team for France was read out in Killiney Castle. On a Monday in training coaches would go with the team that finished at the weekend. Then they would name the team for the following weekend that night. The team officially gets released at announcement time on the Thursday but we always know from Monday or sometimes Tuesday who is playing.

I was named on the left wing and I was really pleased. It's Paris. Six Nations. One hundred per cent a big game. I am chuffed but I am also properly shitting it. Paris will show you what you're actually made of.

That afternoon in the Stade de France was my real baptism for Ireland and it was the first time in my life that I was hit by proper, real match nerves. I always got nervous before games but this was to another level, stomach-churning stuff.

The Stade, that day, was like nothing I had ever experienced. 76,500 but not our own people like I had experienced in Croke Park against Italy. Also Aurélien Rougerie was to be my opposite number. And what a number, 6ft 4 ins and 16 st 4 oz. I was marking a monster of a guy, the star of French rugby at that time. I forgave myself the nerves and the churning gut.

On the first play, Rougerie literally bounced me off up the left wing, running right over the top of me. Somehow I just held onto the bottom of his jersey and he didn't get away. I ended up playing well after that. France beat us 26-21. Typically, we had started making a comeback toward the end but they had a big enough lead banked having scored three first-half tries. I came home knowing that I had done ok. That was when I first started to have a sense of belonging at the highest level. We had lost but it was a big personal win for me.

Eddie was under some pressure at this time so, as usual, there was not a lot of feedback. I was waiting game by game to see if I would stay in the team.

When we played Scotland I was on the wing again. Geordan was full back and he had a good game in the absence of Girvan, who was out with a hip injury. We won well. I scored my first try for Ireland that day, going over in the corner after an incredible twenty five metre pass from Brian O'Driscoll. I think that score won a try of the year award in Ireland. I felt I had done enough to stay in the team for the Wales game at Croke Park.

The discussion all week before Wales was about who would be full back, Girvan or Geordan? Geordan had done well against Scotland but Girvan had been fifteen for the two previous games. All the chat was about the two of them and, meanwhile, I was named on the left wing. Happy enough.

And then, the day before the game, Eddie told me I would be playing full back. I loved that. A green jersey with the number fifteen on the back.

I had a big bust-up with Shane Horgan on the field that day. We had still not formed a good relationship at that stage. I remember him going absolutely mental at me about something. I had never been oblivious to the fact that he didn't think too highly of me but it was at that moment I realised that, Jesus, this guy really has a problem with me.

It was a work rate issue in the backfield. Shane had decided I was not working hard enough to cover a play. He unloaded. I hit back. That was the first time ever that I responded. Usually I just sucked stuff up. And then, ironically, it was Brian who intervened to calm us both down. Fuck it lads, get over it. Move on.

To be fair, Shane and Brian were never nasty to me back then. Just indifferent. It was a bit of a studied indifference. I wasn't deferential. I thought the appropriate response was to just act like I did belong. I'm sure they looked at me and asked each other, who does he think he is? If they wanted a new friend it wasn't going to be some nineteen-year-old snot. The snot didn't quite get that though.

We lost 12-16 to Wales but again I felt that I had done enough. In fact, I felt that I'd played very well in that game. I hadn't spoken too much in the media about being full back before then. Now I'd had a Six Nations game as number fifteen and it had been my best game of the campaign. I was a bit too relaxed about telling the media that I wanted to be the full back. Having got in there on a week when Geordan and Girvan were both injured, it was a bit disrespectful.

Geordan returned at full back and I was on the wing when we got pumped by England at Twickenham the following week but I scored another try in the corner. An odd thing that I recall from that weekend is that Dave had played a game the night before for the under-20s against England. He was on the left wing and scored exactly the same type of try as I did in the exact same minute. Both on the left wing, both of us taking a switch against the grain.

England had been our final game and Eddie was gone then after that. We had been 10-0 up at one stage but that was as good as it got. They just smashed us really and we lost 33-10. With England, when they get on top they keep going. They never take their foot off your neck.

Overall I had enjoyed a good campaign. I felt seriously involved in the group. I had put a calling card down for the full back position. I had announced myself as a potential starter for the Irish team.

Meanwhile, back at the ranch, the door at Leinster was opening slowly but is was definitely not wide open…

I'd been two years at Leinster but there was no feeling that I was established, not even close. There was a real element of, well, not under-appreciation as such but of me constantly having to question myself. This coach doesn't seem to think as much of me as he does of the other guys. Is it him or is it me?

I had played a lot of games that pre-season and then Denis Hickie abruptly retired at the end of the 2007 World Cup. He was meant to play that season as far as I remember and then he was gone and it was a surprise. When he packed it in, he left behind a little opening for me to get into the first team on an established basis. I had been getting game time and I had played some games in Europe but I wasn't a guaranteed starter. You aren't really established at Leinster until you are playing in Europe and I was on the bench more often than I was starting.

Girvan was full back and was seen as the better full back.

Shane Horgan was on one wing and there was no way he was ever being ousted. Gordon and Brian would be centres and Felipe was at ten. That left myself and Luke battling for the other wing.

You had to factor in the injuries, of course. The only time I had been getting into the European team was when other players were injured.

So what progress I made in the pecking order with Leinster was more down to performances for Ireland than for Leinster over the next year an a half. In those days, I was waiting for the Ireland games to come around because that was my time to showcase that I was a better player than Michael Cheika was giving me credit for being.

Declan Kidney had been announced as Eddie's successor but Deccie wouldn't be taking the position up until November.

In the meantime, we had the 2008 summer tour with Michael Bradley in charge as interim manager. I played full back in Australia and New Zealand and had two very good games. We lost both times but they were gallant losses of the sort we used to have back then. We could have won both matches. We'd brought a decent team down there. Again it was us losing but me being privately pleased. Bradley was good but we all knew it was just a two-game tenure and that Declan would be coming in. We just wanted good reports flowing back to Deccie.

At Leinster, as the new season starts in late summer of 2008, I'm now an Ireland player so I feel that Cheika is under pressure to pick me. I play all of the European games that season bar the semi-final and final with sickness. This is the year that I really get a little bit chirpy about wanting to play full back.

Having done well with Bradley while playing full back in two Tests, I was a little disappointed when Declan picked me on the wing for the autumn campaign. We played Canada (we won 55-0, I scored two tries) in the first game and Keith Earls was at full back. My thought was that I had just played full back against New Zealand and Australia and now they were picking somebody who has never been capped and giving him his debut at full back in Thomond Park? In my head I was getting a little shirty with Deccie. I didn't say anything to him though. Duly he came to me instead. I appreciated that he had acknowledged it.

When we played New Zealand the following week, Girvan was full back. The series finished up with Argentina and a win in Croke Park. Geordan Murphy was full back and I was on the left wing again.

By the end of 2008 I had arrived at an odd place in my career. I still wasn't completely happy with Leinster and continued to feel like a bit of an outsider. With Ireland, although I didn't even have ten caps to my name, I felt more comfortable and valued. Maybe not being seen as part of the Leinster hierarchy was a help in the Irish set-up.

Declan, having taken over the Irish team as planned for the autumn schedule in November, had decided to gather a large group of players together before Christmas for a couple of training sessions. It was to be a chance to introduce himself and explain what he was all about to those not already familiar with him.

We met up at Johnstown House in Enfield. Padraig Harrington came to speak to us for an hour or two one night but the get together is better remembered for what happened at a different group session amongst ourselves.

It was a strengths, weaknesses, opportunities and threats exercise. SWOT to use the business acronym. We were in a team room, forty of us, and we were split up into different groups and asked to all go off into our own separate rooms. Each of the groups had one leader and nine randomly chosen players with him. I was with Ronan O'Gara's group.

We went through the usual procedures with these things, guys chipping in with things but nobody really trying to reinvent the wheel.

When it got to the discussion about our weaknesses, I said that when I looked at the Munster lads they seemed different when they played for Munster than when they played for Ireland. I didn't say that they cared more for Munster or that they tried less for Ireland. When the story grew fine hairy legs a few months later and turned into a full blown myth, that inference became a key part of the telling.

I said that, for me on the outside, there was a real sense that Munster had great team unity and team spirit and they were obviously very proud to play for their team. Incredibly passionate.

I mentioned Thomond Park and the white hot atmosphere down there. It seemed as if it was the most incredible place to play rugby for your team. I looked at Lansdowne or Croke Park and we didn't have anything close to that. Munster played in that seething cauldron of passion. Everybody supported them and when the Munster lads played for Munster we were sat elsewhere watching the scenes. Big men crying their eyes out before the games, the crazed commitment to the red jersey, the unity of the crowd and the team. It was just the most passionate thing we had ever seen in rugby.

I said that when I looked at the Irish team I didn't see

anything that came close to that. Anywhere. I said that, for this Irish team to be successful, we need to have that. We needed to have what the Munster team have at that time. It was Harry met Sally stuff. We'll have whatever they're having.

It didn't seem like a big deal to raise the issue in that small room. At this time there was lots of talk about exactly this problem in media circles and in rugby circles. Everybody loved Munster at that time. That strange creature, the Lunster was roaming the land. Leinster people who were caught up in the Munster craze were driving around with Munster flags or stickers on their cars.

So I just tried to articulate that. I don't recall who else was in the group. Nobody else said anything. ROG just wrote it all down on his flip chart. Then somebody else said a few words about some other topic and then Declan was knocking on the door and herding us back into the main room.

There, all the leaders read out what they had written on their flip charts. Ronan read out what was on his. He rattled through the points. We need to be better under pressure. We're not fulfilling potential. We're less than the sum of our parts. We're underachieving. A lot of the standard stuff that you get from these exercises. Then he added that there was a feeling that maybe Munster players aren't producing the same level of performances for Ireland, a feeling that Munster players look like they are enjoying Munster more. There was a pause and a slight change in room temperature. I'm thinking, ok, just get on with it ROG.

He didn't mention who had contributed any particular point. He just read out the points as he had noted them. He was getting toward the end when Marcus Horan stood up. Marcus had been in another group.

"Sorry Deccie, I have to stop it here, but there is a big elephant in the room here. We can't move on until it is discussed."

ROG stopped talking. I'm thinking, oh fuck. I have just offered something in a small room and now there is this unbelievably awkward silence within the whole squad and apparently there is now an elephant in the room.

Now that Deccie was being brought into it I hoped that he might jump in and save the young soldier who had said these things in the private little sub-group. I hoped he'd take hold of the conversation and steer it to wherever he needed it to go. Please Deccie, don't have me defend this in front of the whole group. But Deccie just stayed quiet at the end of the room. He was loving this. This was precisely what he had wanted to happen. He just stared around the room with an expression that said, ok lads, let's just see where this takes us.

That's Declan Kidney's forte. He wanted this subject to be out and aired and he subtly created the space for it without leaving his fingerprints. The Munster and Leinster thing was being talked about in public and in the newspapers but nobody ever spoke about it in the camp. Deccie wanted this big moment. He knew, though, that it had to come from within us. He couldn't just hand down an edict.

Deccie couldn't know who within the team would raise the issue but I imagine he could have narrowed it down. Deccie couldn't really tee up one of the Munster lads to raise the issue. He'd been their leader for the previous three years and presumably there was the usual tension between club structure and the national team in that time. Leinster had done nothing on the pitch, just a Celtic League the season before that. So it didn't seem as if the established Leinster guys had the standing to bring the topic up. Lads from Connacht and Ulster felt that it just wasn't their business. So it was probably always going to fall to somebody who was a little disaffected with the Leinster set-up. That somebody was feeling the heat now.

The silence felt like an eternity as Deccie just stayed, sitting and waiting. I had walked myself right into it.

I took a decision. Ok, I have said it in the sub-group and if I don't stand up now I am going to look like a coward. Fuck it, I need to stand up and face the music. The music would be easier to face than the silence. So I got up and said the exact same things that I had said in the sub-group.

I said, it was not a direct criticism. I was not questioning the Munster players' desire or questioning their level of passion when they played for Ireland but when I looked at Thomond and when I watched Munster playing I saw a different group of players. There was a different vibe down there. I said that, quite frankly, I was just unbelievably envious of what they had in Thomond Park. I wanted to be a part of whatever that is. If we could get that going in Lansdowne or Croke Park, this Irish team could become really successful.

It wasn't exactly the Gettysburg Address but it was just as short, even shorter. Forty five seconds to a minute. Nothing more. Just confirming myself as the person who'd said the words and then repeating them. I sat down, waiting for somebody to give me some sort of support or acceptance. Even for somebody to just acknowledge it. There was nothing. Not a murmur. Again, Deccie stayed quiet. Jesus Christ, I was thinking, somebody please say something. Let's have a row about it. Or a group hug. Anything.

Then the rest of the points just got read out. I sat there hoping that the meeting would go on forever. I didn't want it to end because right then it felt like I had accused Munster of something heinous. What was coming next? I was really uncomfortable. Then the meeting was over and it was time for dinner.

I went straight to my room. I didn't speak to anybody. I reckoned that I was the pariah of the group.

I was sharing with Jamie but we were staying in these two-bed split-level villas in the grounds. I had a room on my own and I just retreated to it. I didn't leave the room again until breakfast the next morning. I had no idea how it was all being taken or what was being said. I was hoping that the others might appreciate the honesty and know that it wasn't a personal attack. On the other hand, maybe they'd take it as a criticism of who they were or where they came from. Maybe I had made things worse.

Each of the villas had a little path from the front door which led onto the main path. As I walked out on my own, who did I see on their way to breakfast but Donncha O'Callaghan and Marcus Horan. Two of Munster's finest walking up their path, a couple of larger than life icons. Uh, oh.

For a second, I decide to put the head down and walk towards breakfast just hoping that they won't have me for breakfast. They've seen me coming out my door, though, and they know too that I have spotted them. The three of us just stop because it is unavoidable. And incredibly awkward.

Donncha just says, fair balls to you kid. It took a lot to say what you said.

Marcus said, yeah, that needed to be said by somebody. Well done.

Nothing more. We moved along straight away but what an unbelievable relief it was hearing those words from the mouths of those two Munster men.

Donncha and Marcus were two of the senior guys. What they said carried weight. I relaxed after that. Nobody else said anything to me but nobody was ratty or distant with me. If anything, I came away feeling that I had earned a little bit of respect for saying what I had said.

My other memory of those couple of days is of Deccie sitting myself and Jamie Heaslip down in the video analysis area of the team room. Deccie was a great man for asking questions. He said to Jamie, who was Ireland's standout player at the Under-20 World Cup? Jamie was embarrassed but conceded that, yeah, maybe he was that player.

Deccie turned to me. Who captained the under-19 Ireland team at the World Cup? I did.

Ok, I need the two of you to start stepping up as leaders now in this team.

That was the night before the SWOT analysis incident. He had emboldened me a bit.

I concluded that it wasn't going to offend Deccie if I spoke and contributed within this team. He saw myself and Jamie as part of his plan.

It was my first time getting that positive prompting from a coach. With Cheika, it had never happened and never would. I had played maybe six games under Eddie and there was never any dialogue between the two of us. We just never really had a conversation.

It was so welcome for me as a player to have a coach who was feeding me a little bit of love. That was Declan's biggest strength. Man-management. Creating a player-driven environment. Being the invisible hand.

When Jamie and I ended the conversation with Deccie, we both came away feeling really valued.

The next night I raised something at a team meeting, something which had never been spoken about within the group. Of all of us in Enfield that night in 2008 Deccie was probably the least surprised to be told that there was an elephant in the room.

7
—

GRAND SLAM

Ireland v France

We regrouped in early 2009 to prepare for the Six Nations game against the French. We trained in Limerick, based in the Castletroy Park opposite the university. I hadn't seen any of the other players too much since Enfield and I was still a little rattled as that first week approached. I was convinced that everybody would have been thinking about all this over Christmas and maybe talking among themselves.

My brief chat with Marcus and Donncha had put me at ease a little bit and Brian O'Driscoll had phoned me the week before the Limerick camp to reassure me about things. I'm not sure if that was prompted by Declan or if Brian initiated it himself. He just said, listen, what was said was said. It needed to be said and it needs to be put behind us now. So put it behind you. Move on and go forward. Nothing had been leaked to the media which was a relief. In Enfield, before we broke up, Declan had said that what had happened within the four walls in those last couple of days was to stay between those four walls.

France was always going to be a tough opening. They had beaten us in Croke Park in 2007 in a bad game that we should have won. We had lost again in 2008 in the Stade de France.

Limerick turned out to be a tricky week for me. On the Friday during the last session we were on the field and I was running backwards when I accidentally tripped over Alan Gaffney. I wasn't expecting anybody to be behind me. The upshot was that I was told that I had a grade two ligament tear. This was eight days before the game. In the normal course of events, that's more than an eight-day injury.

My physio at the time was an American guy called Brian Greene and he was unbelievable. We went to Dublin that week. We were staying in Killiney Castle. Brian was treating me four or five times a day right up until we headed into town for the days before the match.

The Shelbourne Hotel, where we always stay during this part of our pre-match preparation, actually has a sad role in our family history.

My brother, Ross, died on August 16th, 1988. His anniversary is on the same day as that of my paternal grandmother Jean Kearney. She died in the Shelbourne Hotel at the reception for my Auntie Pamela's wedding to Aubrey Bourke, a very well-known rugby character and talented player in his day. She was forty-eight and she had a heart attack on the grand staircase. We go up and down those stairs all the time in the days before international games. I have made that climb and descent hundreds of times. Always once or twice during those days it will strike me that Dad lost his mum and his second son on the same date of the year and one of those tragedies happened right here.

After one of the internationals, Dad came up to the team room with me and as soon as we walked in he told me that this was the room into which the whole family had been ushered when they were told that his mother had died. He was eighteen. Not for the last time, what was meant to be one of the better days of Dad's life had become a tragic event. On this occasion, he and the rest of the family ended up grieving between the four walls that would become Ireland's team room.

Anyway, when we arrived at the Shelbourne on the Wednesday before we played France, I still hadn't passed my fitness test. So Brian stepped things up further. He began coming to the bedroom at two in the morning and five in the morning to treat me. He was making sure I was getting attention right through the night, which was above and beyond any call of duty.

There was a huge bleed in the ankle and the joint, a lot of fluid in there. Brian would come into the room to mobilise the joint and get the fluid moving so I didn't lose too much mobility during the night. When he'd leave I'd go back to sleep with the Game Ready machine switched on, compressing and freezing my foot at the same time.

The morning before the game I was slotted to do my fitness test at lunchtime. I was in the physio room and Paul O'Connell looked at the ankle and said, you are hardly thinking of playing with that are you? He was right to be concerned. It looked a mess.

I hadn't done a fitness test and I hadn't even run on the ankle since the previous Friday. I had done a little bicycle work but the main priority had just been getting the swelling down on the joint. The more movement there is in the joint the less painful it becomes. The manipulation sessions with Brian were sore but in the neighbourhood of uncomfortable rather than torture. The joint just wants to lock. The trick is to stop it.

In Croke Park, I got strapped for the fitness test. I took some painkillers before the test. Ten minutes after taking them I just got sick all over the tunnel in Croke Park when I was on the way out to the pitch. Whatever painkillers I'd taken were now gone, spewed up near the sacred turf.

I did the fitness test over the far side on my own while the guys were doing the captain's run. It is just myself, Brian Greene and the doctor, Gary O'Driscoll. With ankle trouble, running straight lines is easy. The changes of direction and the turns are tricky but the strapping makes things easier because you have some stability.

I did some straight lines, a few turns and some kicking. After you run you know that the ankle will swell again so you do the bare minimum to prove your fitness. The test went well. I felt pretty good and was able to do the things I wanted to. Not 100 per cent but enough to get by. Generally, if the player says, yeah I'm good to go, nobody is going to stand in his way unless it's a concussion issue.

Still, I won't miss the stress of that type of week. I've had a lot of them where I have been injured or had a niggle and on Saturday I'm standing for the anthem and wondering if I am really fit. Should I pull out? Even now?

There have been weeks where I actually have pulled out on the day before the game and that is the single biggest head-melting experience that I have had. Your brain has been trying to get into the game all week but the brain has also been listening to your body which just won't play ball. On the Friday, you call the whole thing off because your body wins the argument. And then your brain worries about it for the entire weekend.

More often, though, you don't pull out and the adrenaline just surges up within you. As the clock ticks toward game time, you start second guessing yourself. You're not fit! You will be found out! You'll make a show of yourself! You'll let everybody down today! You'll be taken off after five minutes and the boss will go mental!

Against France on the day, we played very well. Jamie scored a great try. Brian O'Driscoll and Gordon D'Arcy scored one each also. Gordon hadn't started. He'd been out for a long time. When he scored everybody jumped on him. There was a real sense of the team just being happy for him, it was just a joy that he was back and scoring a try in Croke Park. He'd had a bad run of it. He'd broken his arm a couple of times and had trouble getting it healed properly.

I played well. When you get into the game, if your first touch has a positive impact then everything is fine. Bring it on. The first few touches of a game are so important in terms of how that game goes for you overall.

The French kicked a lot of restarts right down the middle of the field that day. That gave me a bit of work to do. I made a good half break for Jamie's try off the first phase when I stepped back inside and got an offload to Tommy who made another half break. Jamie scored under the posts.

We had made a conscious decision that year to try to improve that element of our game. Mervyn Murphy was the analyst with the team but he took on much more of a coaching role that year. Whereas normally he would have been filming training sessions with his camera, now he was actually down on the field with the clipboard masterminding some of these plays.

When Joe Schmidt came in a few years later, Mervyn took more of a back seat again because that stuff is Joe's forte. But Mervyn is somebody who could, if he wanted to, be a very good coach. He was on video analysis with the national team for twenty years until he moved on last season.

He is back in the west now working with Connacht on a scheme to develop talent. The young guys he is working with probably don't know it but Mervyn had a huge impact that Grand Slam season.

We beat France and the good start we had energised the media. It always works that way if you win the first one. And it is always premature. Grand Slam talk shouldn't happen until after round three.

The next morning my ankle had swollen again. We did a pool recovery session in town at the back of the Westbury Hotel. I remember a few people who might not have seen the ankle during the week spotting it and there were gasps. The state of it! It was still blue and purple and I'd had a lot more bleeding in it but appearances aside, it was fine. I was recovering.

I trained on the Tuesday, got through it and from there it was business as usual.

I just kept it strapped for the remainder of the tournament.

I was pleased though.

In my mind, Enfield had put me under a little bit of pressure within our group.

I'd shown that I was able to talk the talk. Now I needed to walk the walk, purple ankle or otherwise.

GRAND SLAM

Italy v Ireland

A lovely warm day in Rome. My first time to the city. It was beautiful and it was all new and different for me. I had played away in the Six Nations the year before but the support in Rome is always huge because it is a great trip away. The bus used to take the team through a big square, the Piazza del Popolo, I think, on the way to the Stadio Flaminio where Italy used to play. There would always be ten to fifteen thousand Irish there. My own eternal memory of playing in Rome is of driving through that square and gazing out at the tide of people. It always gave me a lift.

In the Stadio Flaminio that day the sun was splitting the rocks and a few minutes into the action I got decapitated. A ball was thrown to me. It hung in the air for a fraction too long and my opposite number, Andrea Masi, came at me fast with a swinging arm. Suddenly my whole body was parallel with the floor. I sort of turned as I went down and I landed pretty much on all fours. I came straight back up which was good for my street cred with the lads, speaking as a 'Leinster ladyboy' that is.

Masi stood and shouted over me, "you like that motherfucker?"

The tackle looked much worse than it was but it was an incredibly reckless tackle nonetheless. Masi got sin-binned for what would be an absolute stone-cold red card today. An eight to twelve weeks red.

He didn't come over and speak to me at the end of the game. I saw him at the post-match function and he looked at me and walked away and didn't acknowledge me. It is one of the few times in my career that has happened. Normally you will go to a player afterwards and apologise. I couldn't understand his attitude. He could hardly have felt hard done by? It was a blatant offence. I bounced straight back up. I hadn't made a meal out of it and on the day he had got away lightly. He received a three-match ban later but that was hardly my fault. I've played against him a few times since but there has never been any dialogue.

I came off with ten minutes to go. Geordan came onto the field and while waiting for the game to end Karl Richardson, the PR man, came up to me and said, listen, as soon as the final whistle goes follow me and we will do the Man of the Match interview. I said, ok, good. Thanks Karl.

Just after that, Luke scored his second try. The full-time whistle blew and I went to Karl.

Karl said, oh sorry, they're actually giving it to Luke now!

We had done nothing socially after the French game as we had promised Declan that we would be sensible. We were getting a break after the Italy game so there was a big session in Rome. We had a great night out. In Rome, you could feel the team coming together. There was much more unity. Relationships were developing and bonds being made.

We were up and running in the campaign and we were becoming a proper team. And nothing bonds a proper team as much as a good night. That is an old school tradition that still holds true even in the clinical professional era. Just enjoying each other's company makes a team better. Guys drop their guard.

For the week after a good night out there is all the chat and the reliving and retelling of it and the laughter at the things that happened. Those are the memories. We don't ever really talk fondly of the inside break someone made. We talk about the nights out though.

As luck would have it, I found myself in the early hours coming back to the hotel in a taxi with Marcus Horan and Donncha O'Callaghan, just the three of us. We had a few drinks on board and I said to them, there is something special brewing this year boys.

Ireland v England

We were a good mix. O'Connell, O'Gara and O'Driscoll were our three leaders. They were icons and very influential on the team. Myself, Jamie Heaslip, Luke Fitzgerald, Tommy Bowe, Stephen Ferris were the new guys just brought in to this scene. Tomas O'Leary as well. Then you had the other layer, the established players. The likes of Marcus Horan, Jerry Flannery, Jonny Hayes, Donncha, David Wallace. The guys who had been around the block and knew where the ambushes might come from.

The Grand Slam team of 2018 was a better team in terms of the democratic spread of skills and responsibilities but the back row in 2009 was exceptional. Wallace, Ferris and Heaslip! That was a platform to build from. Jamie was a new age number eight. Unbreakable. He was a game changer for us. Countless line breaks in a game. Very good over the ball. He could do everything on a rugby field.

In 2018 we were blessed to have had so many more guys who were at that level with O'Connell, O'Driscoll and O'Gara. Nobody had to carry the burden the way that those guys did. They each had massive moments throughout that 2009 campaign which contributed to us winning. In 2018, so many people had massive moments. When I think of the English and Welsh games in 2009, it is those three guys that I think of. There were times when they were dragging us along. The three of them were the musketeers lifting everybody else. And as I've said, we also had a very special back row.

Martin Johnson was now coaching England. They had been surfing the crest of a wave until they'd crashed to Wales in their second game of the championship.

I had played the Six Nations in Twickenham the year before. I had scored a try but we had been hammered there. Danny Cipriani's game. He scored eighteen points and was brilliant on his first start. Eddie O'Sullivan's final game. It felt like an ending. It was a tough experience.

Now, a year on, with a new coach, we knew that England were a serious team. For me this was probably the biggest game of my career to date.

I don't remember too much about the game. As a nation Ireland had been plunged into the depths of a sudden recession. Declan's big thing was how we had the ability to make people in the country happy. That was a huge motivation for him. He was very genuine about that. He framed the national team in the context of the country's mood. The people who come are all paying money to be there and to see you guys. Pay it back. We believed him. People really care about sport. He was putting the burden on us a little bit but it was an added motivation. We felt we were in such a great position to be able to change people's day.

The first half of the game was a lot of kicking, just very scrappy stuff. We looked very tense. We had been hearing murmurs about how with our new coach and a couple of wins under our belt, people could now see us winning the championship, maybe the Grand Slam. We looked like a nervous team but we defended very well.

Brian got his try (and our only try) in the second half, a few minutes before the hour mark. They closed the gap late on. Phil Vickery got sin-binned before our try. Later Danny Care got sin-binned for tackling Marcus. It's always nice to see an opposition player getting yellow carded. You have a good advantage for ten minutes. In a dog-eat-dog situation, those incidents fed our belief.

I hadn't actually played too much with Brian at that point but that England game was the first time I can remember looking at him during a match that I was playing in and saying, wow, yeah, this guy is class.

We'd always known about his sidestep and his ability to make a line break and to take teams on. That's what we grew up watching and admiring in him. But in that game his defence was unbelievable. He was over here scavenging, over there poaching balls, he scored a great drop goal and he scored that try. He was in there doing work usually left to a forward. For him to step up and take that role upon himself was hugely impressive.

And Brian got a couple of big bangs that day. At one point, a few minutes before our try, he looked as though he was going to have to leave the field injured after a pretty brutal block from Delon Armitage. This came minutes after being steamrolled by Riki Flutie. We were all surprised when he had stood up and played on after that one.

For a while, Brian looked as if he wasn't quite there. I would have been a small bit conscious that day of how often and hard he was getting hit. There wasn't that level of concern about concussion back then as there is now. We hadn't developed the same duty of care to players. It was almost accepted as a little bit normal and heroic to finish. Ah, he'll be fine.

And he was. His try was so vital. A few minutes after Brian had been decked by Armitage, we were camped on the England line but unable to get across it. We were driving forward, feeding it back and driving again. Progressing inch by inch, if at all. If you watch the game again as we were constantly recycling the ball, Brian, the most marked man on the field, was almost tiptoeing across from the periphery on the right until he was standing just to the left of the ruck. It was stealth in plain sight.

When he took the shortest pass from Tomas O'Leary, he was more or less standing still but as the leather touched Brian's fingertips it was like a switch had released a current through him. He generated his acceleration in the space of one yard and his chest was almost parallel to the ground as he crossed the line. He had the ball on the grass before any English player had properly reacted. Using the amount of hits Brian took that day as a gauge, you can only imagine how many times the English players had forewarned each other about watching Brian O'Driscoll at all times.

The try was just the cherry on the icing on the cake after the meal. That day Brian played rugby on a different level to everybody else. Great performances like that mean a player walks off the field with even more of an aura about them than when they ran on. That was Brian O'Driscoll that day.

With a couple of minutes left, we put ourselves in slight danger. England were still minus Danny Care and maybe we allowed ourselves the luxury of noticing our own fatigue and looking forward to it being all over. Mike Tindall broke through the centre. We were jaded and didn't react quickly enough. He offloaded to Andy Goode, who made a little grubber kick which Delon Armitage scored a try from. It was the first try we had conceded in the campaign. It was also the last.

England was a big step. You never fully know where you stand until you play England. The pressure ratcheted up. We were now the only unbeaten team in the Six Nations. Before the England game we were described as having won our first two games. After the England game we were 'maintaining our Grand Slam challenge.'

Scotland v Ireland

The feel of our season had changed. The headlines fed the hype and the country slipped into great expectation mode. It might have been six decades since we had won our only Grand Slam but now, with two games left, delivery was almost being demanded. The conversations now had skipped ahead. People were talking and writing about the final game in Cardiff. 'The Grand Slam Game.'

Everybody was making big and dangerous assumptions and the Scots, who we were playing next, had to have noticed. Suddenly, for us as a team, the Scotland game became a banana skin while for the rest of the country, it was a springboard formality. We'd beaten Scotland the last eight times we had played them, hadn't we? All the Irish hard luck stories, all the championship chokes and the final furlong flops down the years were forgotten about. Optimism has a short memory.

I have never liked playing in Murrayfield. I hate how the track runs along half of the pitch. It leaves you very disconnected from the supporters. That always got to me out on the field. I just didn't like it. When you get this idea into your head early on that you don't like playing somewhere and you feel that you won't play well there it can become self-fulfilling. Murrayfield is one of those stadiums for me.

Declan ruffled a few feathers that week and changed a few faces in the team. Denis Leamy started. Peter Stringer started. Rory started. Jamie was on the bench having played very well in the games before that. It was just good management by Declan. Why not give players an opportunity to make them feel more involved, and to give them ownership. If they are on the bench for a full campaign when they felt they deserved a chance, it will get them down a bit. That's just the time that you don't need any negativity. On the other hand, having beaten England at home with a great and gutsy performance, the lads who started would have expected to hold onto their places.

The gamble for Deccie was that if he won he would have been hailed as having given a masterclass of player management. If we lost he'd face the firing squad for attempting to fix something which was never broken.

Conditions in Murrayfield were tough and windy. The forecast was for a flurry of high balls being hoisted into my workspace. Good.

For a while, it looked as if Deccie's gamble was going to break him. We fell behind 9-3 and we looked a little jittery. We brought it back to 9-6, Ronan O'Gara's second penalty brought him past Jonny Wilkinson's Six Nations scoring record. We conceded another penalty. Ronan scored another one. It was 12-9 at half time. It was dour and not a very attractive game and it looked like Scotland's win at that point.

With the wind up, Scotland were predictably sending the ball up a lot too. It's supposed to be unsettling but I really love those days when there is a ball dropping from the sky and I am racing to be under it.

Luckily, Scotland are always a hit and miss team. Some days they are great, sometimes not. Within that context, though, Edinburgh is always a tricky place to go to. You never have the game won after fifty minutes. Brian made another huge intervention and, right on cue after fifty one minutes, Jamie came off the bench and scored a try that was all Peter Stringer's making. Suddenly Deccie's bets were all paying off.

I had got to know Stringer a little. He wasn't one of the players I was very close with. He was quite shy, one of the quiet guys on the team, but he was incredibly professional. Peter took great care of himself physically. At scrum-half you don't take too much contact but Peter made his career last forever through sheer will and professionalism. He was Man of the Match that day in Murrayfield. Another day of great service from him.

Wales v Ireland

My memories of the Welsh game itself are poor. There was a week of insane excitement and hype which we tried to ignore. And then a rugby game which we had to win.

Running out in Cardiff was the first time that I had ever seen the two trophies side by side. The Six Nations and the Triple Crown. If we won, we would be taking both home. If Wales won, they would be taking away the Triple Crown and the Grand Slam 'trophy' would be going back into the cupboard.

In that context, the hype made perfect sense. This was a scriptwriter's dream thriller of an ending. Some would be going home happy and some would be going home hurting.

Another twist. It was my first time playing in the Millennium Stadium and I was blown away by the noise. It was a different level to anything I'd experienced in volume and intensity. The Stade de France is pretty loud but not as atmospheric. In the Millennium, the crowd are so on top of you it's possible to make clear eye contact with somebody in the crowd. In every other stadium you just see a blur of faces.

Paul O'Connell took some incredible line-out balls that day. Tommy Bowe had a storming game. Brian O'Driscoll burrowed over for his fourth try of the championship. A few minutes after Brian had brought us back into the game with that try, we scored again off a crossfield kick from Ronan O'Gara. This was one of Mervyn's plays which he had brought in that week, having scouted and studied the Welsh.

It was also probably my first experience of us introducing a play specifically because of something that the opposition did. With Joe, every play was chosen on that basis but the Wales game was the first time I had seen the idea of us playing on a specific weakness of the opposition.

Mervyn had spotted that the winger on Tommy Bowe's side tended to move a lot earlier than he should have. I think Shane Williams was playing very flat up in the line and left a lot of space behind him. Gavin Henson had moved to full back at that stage after Lee Byrne had gone off injured. Mervyn's thinking was that if the kick went in and Tommy had a headstart, he would win the footrace to the ball.

The kick came off a scrum. The open side was left, short side on his right but quite a central position. It was a perfect kick from Ronan O'Gara. He placed it diagonally just behind Shane Williams, right in the gap between Williams and his full back. Maybe a forty degree angle.

They were blitz defending and coming very hard off the line and they left us that little bit of space and it bounced perfectly.

The full back Henson was in that nightmare position of coming but knowing now that he wouldn't quite get there. Tommy sidestepped just as Henson launched himself hopefully into the air, not sure if he was grasping for the ball or the player. He got his right arm in the way but Tommy brushed past. Shane Williams had that bit of acceleration but Tommy had too much of a headstart. Once you are coming forward, stopping, turning and having to reaccelerate, that is a big ask. With Williams in pursuit, Tommy just ran diagonally right through the posts and scored.

Ronan had his moments of inconsistency off the tee in that championship but that day in Cardiff he made two huge plays. That cross kick was literally inch-perfect and famously, nervelessly, he kicked the drop goal. That's why I put him on the pedestal alongside O'Driscoll and O'Connell. The three of them dragged us to that Grand Slam. In 2018, we didn't have the feeling of looking towards somebody to make the big play. In 2009, there were times when the rest of us almost felt like, 'come on lads, do your thing and get us through this.'

At the end I was in a fair bit of pain and I went off with fourteen minutes to go. I was glad I wasn't on the field when Wales got the late drop goal with minutes to go. It was such a high pressure situation.

Some players revel in that situation. I wasn't one hundred per cent, I wasn't feeling great. I hadn't been burning the house down. Sometimes on a good day you come off and you feel, hey, I could have been the difference. I wasn't feeling that though. And it gave Geordan a chance to get on and I was happy for that. He had his deserved moment and he enjoyed triumphantly launching the final ball of the day into the crowd.

When the final whistle went there was such a release. My

parents and Richard had made it to the game and I remember going up to them in the stand afterwards and getting some photographs together.

This was the first significant thing that I had ever won in my career. I had a Celtic league with Leinster which felt great at the time but compared to what Munster players had on their mantelpieces it was small beer.

That night in Cardiff we went to a nightclub called Tiger Tiger just around the corner from the hotel until three or four in the morning. I left the nightclub with Jamie. It was late and we were half tiptoeing back into the hotel. We got to the team room and everybody else was in there. We kept going the night through.

Then home the next day. The big homecoming on Dawson Street on the Sunday. There were ten or fifteen thousand there and Tommy Bowe gave the Black Velvet Band a good going over. After the Mansion House we went back to the Killiney Castle hotel for a big function with family and friends. We then went to a pub down in Killiney, a small pub, and drank into the early hours.

Monday afternoon found us in Keogh's, off South Anne Street, squeezed into the snug. I have a memory of the Gotham pizzeria next door sending us in six or seven boxes of pizzas. A Monday afternoon in Dublin. A Grand Slam. Cold beer and pizzas. That was the first time that I felt this rugby life I had chosen was just the best thing ever. Whatever the bumps in the road, weekends like this one would always make it all worthwhile.

People tell you that if you fail a lot before you succeed you will enjoy the winning more. It's not quite the case all the time but I couldn't say 2009 meant more to me than it did to John

Hayes or Ronan O'Gara, who had played the Six Nations for ten years. I was very aware of the circumstances and the significance. We hadn't done it in sixty-one years. We were aware of how special it was.

I still have my jersey from the Grand Slam of 2009. That year, O2 were the team sponsors and they had run a competition whereby supporters of the team could put their names on the back of jerseys. Each player's number would be made up of people's names in small point size. O2 had got onto me the week of the game and said, is there anybody whose name you would like to put on the back of the jersey?

I hadn't told Mum or Dad about the promotion. After the game, we were downstairs in the Hilton in Cardiff. It was sheer carnage. People everywhere. I asked Mum, Dad and Richard to come up to my bedroom so we could have a few quiet moments together.

I threw Richard my jersey. He was like, ah, is that today's jersey? I told him to look at all the names on the back.

"See," I told him, "they're all supporters' names."

He was looking through them fascinated.

"That's really cool," he said.

I said, "Take a look at the first name."

He said, "It's Ross Kearney. Wow. Who's Ross Kearney?"

"It's our brother Ross. I put his name on it during the week."

Richard just left the room. Outside he got very emotional.

My dad says that, to this day, that was his proudest rugby moment. Not the fact of the Grand Slam but that particular moment in the room and learning that his son Ross Kearney's name was on the back of the jersey I had worn.

To be able to give him that moment was better than any medal.

8

CUP FEVER

With all that transpired afterwards, that night back in Enfield grew into something bigger than it really was. A lot was made out of it, much more than needed to be, but every great win has to have a myth behind it.

If it brought us together a little bit I'm glad but inside the team it just became a bit of a running joke. Going into the Six Nations after Christmas the slagging at training was invariably Enfield-related.

– What was that guys? Was that some Munster thing?

– Hah, typical Leinster ye'll understand rugby some day.

It turned into a joke but at least it was in the open and that was the healthy thing. Nobody referenced it in huddles, caucuses or team meetings. The ice was broken and that was what Deccie had wanted.

On a personal level, Enfield just meant that within the team I moved up a notch in some people's eyes. It was perceived that

I'd been the one with the balls to speak up. I wasn't suddenly a leader within the team, though. You don't become a leader after a two-minute speech to a group of players at a team meeting. Deccie had wanted to clear the issue so he could have a foundation to build on. He got that. But I'm sure he knew that what would really make the difference was something else. Hunger.

By that time, although I was comparatively quite young, I was just so desperate for a bit of success. I think most of the guys would say that. There was just a mad hunger for winning and that, more than anything, was what drove 2009. We had the makings of a great Irish team and we wanted to prove it.

In the aftermath, of course, the media always want to find a point that they can put the finger on and say, aha, this is where things changed.

It became part of the folklore that we turned a corner after I made a speech at Enfield. If we had ended up with the wooden spoon in 2009 would I have been the villain of Irish rugby? I reckon so. The story would have been about how one of the Leinster players criticised the Munster players about their priorities. I can imagine the words. *Leinster upstart ... crossed a line ... bitter anti-Munster rant ... hurtful ... can of worms ... unforgivable ...*

What's happened to this Irish team in the years since then is that we've had some success and Leinster and Munster players get on well.

The next year was the first time that I remember there being proper friendly relationships between players from various provinces. These days, Conor Murray often stays with me in Dublin. Pete O'Mahony stays with Johnny. That was unimaginable back then. I just can't imagine Anthony Foley or Brian O'Driscoll doing that back in the day. It would never have been thought of.

When things are going well, it seems as if you are always straight into the next thing. Reminiscence can wait. You move on very quickly. We had three or four days of fun after the Grand Slam, then it was back into Leinster on the Wednesday or Thursday of the next week, just trying to get moving again. Time to sweat all the badness out of the body.

Leinster had a game on the Saturday. Those of us who had been with Ireland sat that one out but we were all back on the field as a group the next Monday getting ready for what, for us as a team, was virtually another final. We had Harlequins away, the game that we would regard as a watershed but which most people remember as the Bloodgate game.

It was very challenging having been out of the Leinster environment for a couple of months to come back in without having played a game and then head straight into a European quarter-final. I was the regular starting number fifteen for Cheika now. I had started in all the games up till this point and had properly established myself as the first-choice full back. I wasn't sure if that was because Cheika's view of me had changed or because, in terms of optics, he had no choice but to play the Irish full back as the Leinster full back. By this stage, I didn't mind too much either way.

We knew that Harlequins would be a backs-to-the-wall day. Big time. For Leinster at that stage, big matches away from home were always a very tough challenge. The Stoop on a day like this would be a cauldron. It was precisely the sort of game that we had struggled to close out over the previous few years. We had the talent but the other ingredients weren't there. Now, we had the talent and we had the belief and we had an Australian. Harlequins were good back then without being great and we had established in our own minds that we were tougher now. Cheika's work and the arrival of one Rocky Elsom from Australia had given us the belief that we now had a harder edge to our game but we hadn't shown it yet.

If we were ever going to lay down a marker, this was the game to do it in. We needed to announce that we were now a different Leinster team. That would be Cheika's biggest achievement, getting that toughness into us.

On the day, of course, Bloodgate happened, but we had no idea what was going on. As players, we were completely oblivious to it. I know now that Nick Evans, the Harlequins fly half, went off early in the second half. Chris Malone came in but then he tore his hamstring and Tom Williams came in for him. Mike Brown was now left to take their kicks and he missed a penalty to give them the lead. Then Williams seemed to suffer a blood injury which allowed Nick Evans to come back onto the pitch.

We did think it was a little weird that Nick Evans came back on. We knew that he had been nursing an injury throughout the week. He'd been substituted off and now all of a sudden he was coming back on. In the heat of the moment, though, you are not thinking about whatever dramas are going on off the pitch.

We saw a little commotion on our own sideline with Ronan O'Donnell, our team manager, and the late Professor Arthur Tanner. Both of them suspected that there was some chicanery going down. They complained at the time but to no avail. Whatever we as players noticed, we forgot about it straight away. You can't get distracted by stuff on the sideline.

The game went on with Nick Evans back on the field. He had a late drop goal attempt to win the game for them but he missed. And that was that. For us as a team, that day at The Stoop was less about the Bloodgate scandal than it was about us having made a big statement. If Nick Evans had scored his drop goal attempt, the fallout would have been much greater in our minds but in the aftermath we had proved a point and we had a semi-final to look forward to.

The Leinster softies, the 'ladyboys', were no more.

I had a good game. Defensively solid behind what was a great defensive display. I had the type of game that I always thought got me a little bit more respect from Cheika. The flashy displays where you might score a try or two didn't impress him much.

There is always a little bit of tension between the provincial set-ups and the national team. It is very much us and them. Winning a Grand Slam with Ireland doesn't cut much mustard back with Leinster. The club still has its own priorities. So the Harlequins game was good for me in that sense. I was thinking that the tide was turning in my favour.

We had Munster in the semi-final. Whatever bit of warmth the Grand Slam experience had created between the representatives of the two clubs would be set aside for a while. It wasn't hard to imagine Munster training away and smiling at the notion that Leinster were now tough guys because they'd beaten Harlequins. Let's see how they do against the swarm of red jerseys.

After Harlequins, I went into training on the Monday morning. It should have been one of those mornings when you hit the day full of the joys of spring. It was a spring after all that had brought a Grand Slam with Ireland and a breakthrough win with Leinster. I felt poorly though. We were in the gym and my glands had swollen in my throat. I was chatting to Felipe Contepomi and he was evidently sizing me up as we spoke. He asked if I was ok. I told him no, actually, the glands were sore and I didn't feel ok at all.

It was lucky that it was Felipe that I had been chatting to. He has medical degrees up to his own glands. In his Argentinian accent he just said, you are ill Rob. You have the mumps. Get out of here. I really liked Felipe. He was a popular figure in the group. On the field sometimes he flashed that bit of Latin temperament but he was much liked in the club and with the fans. He was both a maverick and a warrior. He told me to go and see the doctor. I went to Professor Arthur Tanner who sent me straight home.

I went back to my apartment. I was living at the time down in Spencer Dock with my brother Richard. Mumps is a word that everybody has heard but in my case at least I hadn't thought about the virus much, ever. Was this even mumps? Was this serious? Mumps? It felt serious. Maybe it was something different? Check Google. More serious. Quite quickly I felt myself deteriorating. Some people just get the puffy cheeks and swollen glands under the ears. I got the whole selection box. Headaches. Fever. Fatigue. Muscle Ache. Loss of interest in food.

I didn't leave the apartment for three or four days. By then I had accepted that I wasn't going to be able to just tough this thing out on my own. Then there was one evening at around nine o'clock that I felt really, really sick. The thing just escalated. I was feeling something like a really bad flu with hot sweats, I was as weak as a kitten, my glands were swollen and sore, I was vomiting now and unable to eat anything. One hundred per cent the worst that I have ever felt.

I have never been one for calling doctors but I felt so wretched that I dialled Dr Jim McShane, the Leinster team doctor. It was late to be calling Jim but he knew me not to be a hypochondriac who kept several doctors' numbers on speed dial. He could tell that something was far from right with me. Jim arrived to see me an hour or so later.

Felipe, of course, had been right. It was mumps. There was a small outbreak in Dublin at that time, especially in UCD where I'd been a few times in the previous weeks. I don't know how I had picked it up but you can easily contract it off water bottles at training, surfaces or airborne droplets. We all know more about viruses now than I, for one, did back then. I was the only player in the Leinster panel who did catch it so I assume that UCD was what made the difference. Some of the other Leinster players got vaccinated the day after I was diagnosed.

In the midst of all the sweats and head-in-the-toilet moments, I found myself sitting at home in the apartment one day watching the announcement of the squad for the Lions tour to South Africa. It was live on *Sky*, the first time they'd presented the squad announcement as a TV event.

I knew the Munster game was already out of the question for me. The way I was feeling, perhaps a possible final for Leinster would also be impossible for me. Beyond that it would be touch and go. I was there on my own, feeling like death. The sickness hadn't even reached its lowest point but I felt so bad that my thinking was that even if I did make this Lions selection there was a good chance that I wouldn't be able to go to South Africa anyway.

Thankfully, the tension was brief. My name was the second to be called out. They started at number fifteen instead of at number one. Lee Byrne first. Me second. I'd had strong hopes about making the squad but at that moment I was too sick to even be pleased about it. I was so ill it hardly registered.

The next day, I checked into Blackrock Clinic. Richard drove me out there and I stayed for a week. Very ill. Still not eating. I lost seven or eight kilos in less than two weeks of the mumps. I didn't hear from Michael Cheika from the time I had left training that Monday morning after speaking with Felipe. I was at home for a week and in Blackrock Clinic for a week and not a word. Not that I was watching the phone but some contact would have been reassuring. Twelve days later, on the Friday evening, I got a call from him. I was still in Blackrock.

How are you doing? Yeah? When will you be back in?

The next day he did a press conference. He was asked about me and he said, yeah, I have had a few really good conversations with Rob. I wondered if I'd been having these really good conversations with him through fevers and hallucinations?

I also got a call from Dr Gary O'Driscoll later in that second week. Gary is Brian's cousin and at that time he had recently become the club doctor with Arsenal. Prior to that he had spent eight years with Ireland and he would be the Lions doctor for the tour to South Africa, his second Lions tour. He was ringing just to check up on me and to see what progress, if any, I was making. He had heard that I had the mumps. We had a good chat and he was very sound and reassuring about things. He told me that he was going to tell Ian McGeechan that I would be fine.

I believed him that I would be fine but when I left Blackrock on the Saturday I was far from fine. I didn't know what the immediate future held. I still couldn't eat much. For another week after getting out of hospital I still couldn't train. That was three weeks of training missed. I had lost a lot of muscle and a lot of fitness. Those are the two things that go first. The first time I tried to train, I threw up after just a few minutes. I went into the gym to do a low intensity circuit of body weight work. I lasted five minutes and my head was back in the toilet. Screw this for a game of soldiers.

This was the week of the semi-final. When you have your head in the toilet you get great clarity. Not only have I zero chance of playing, I am a long way off being fit for a final if we get that far. A lot of Leinster players will have that Munster game down as one of their top three occasions to have been involved in. A pivotal moment. For me it was the first time that I had missed out on a really big occasion.

Isa played fifteen that day. He played unbelievably well too. As he always did when the need was great. His level of performance never dipped much and on the biggest days he always turned up.

So I missed Croke Park. 82,208 people there and I was on the line doing water duties. I was well enough to have some use. I was just back doing light training. To be fair to Michael Cheika, he did make me feel involved. I was on the mic back up to the coach giving messages. It is funny how little things like that make a big difference. It meant a lot to me on the day.

It was also a little marker for me that the gap was closing between the two of us. That our relationship was getting a little bit stronger.

It was a difficult experience overall. My first time going through that. I look back on my whole career and there have been countless times when I have been on the line since then but this was the first and it was huge. It's a cliché in team sports to say that everybody who wasn't on the field was just as much a part of it as everybody who was on the field. It's a nice thing to say but it doesn't feel that way. An injury would have been easier to accept but being high-tackled by the mumps made missing out hard to live with.

That semi-final was the day that the pendulum swung in our favour. Leinster would start beating Munster regularly after that. The club had been beaten so badly by them back in 2006 that it was always going to take something momentous to banish those memories. Munster were the superpower of European rugby during my first years with Leinster and in 2006 they had pummelled us in Lansdowne Road which was filled with and brought to boiling point by Munster supporters.

Croke Park at least was very much fifty-fifty, in terms of the red and blue in the stands. That was a sign of the change as much as how the team put the game away. The monkey was gone from our backs but, as Cheika would be quick to remind everybody afterwards, we still hadn't won anything.

On a more micro-level, I was just happy that beating Munster gave me a chance to be involved in the final in some way. I convinced myself that evening that I stood a good chance of seeing action. I was delusional.

At the time of the Munster game, I hadn't trained or played and I was doing everything in my power to regain the weight I had lost. Between then and the final, I played one game away to the Dragons when we put out a very young Leinster team, almost an academy team. My brother Dave made his debut that day. We won and I played ok without being spectacular. I remember my fitness was lacking. I came off after sixty minutes or so. Yet I recall that when Cheika announced the team for the final and I was named on the bench, I was still disappointed.

My absence had let Shane Horgan in for the semi-final with Isa moving to full back and things stayed that way. Shane was near the end of his career. The Grand Slam year had been the year that he hadn't been involved nationally. He was one of the players that Declan had moved aside. He was playing well, though, and even if fit I couldn't argue too much after how the back three had played in the semi-final. I heard the team being called out and that was it. Suck it up and get on with it. Worry about the next thing.

The next thing was the Lions tour and there was the possibility that this absence was all going to have a knock-on effect for me. I hadn't played much rugby since the quarter-final and I'd played no rugby for weeks before that. The little optimistic part of my brain kept telling me to cheer up, that I was back fit and I was on the bench. There was a chance that I would be used in the final.

We had an induction day with the Lions on the Monday of the week of the final. The Lions were insisting that we go over to spend the whole day there. Cheika knocked that back immediately. No way. So we trained on Monday morning with Leinster and then the four of us were rushed to Dublin airport in a taxi which brought us right out onto the runway and onto a private plane with five seats on it. We flew into Farnborough, a private airport near Pennyhill Park in Bagshot. We were picked up by a Lions Land Rover right there on the runway. We felt like proper superstars. That was the first and last private plane trip of my life.

At Pennyhill, we met all the players and coaches, we each did a piece to camera, we had photos taken, collected gear, resized it, we did all the admin stuff that was needed. We each got a mountain of gear plus a case, two sports bags and back pack.

We just came home with an empty Lions bag to put our own personal clothes and bit of stuff in. The rest we could collect on the way to South Africa.

We were in Surrey for no more than five or six hours. I got to meet most of the people, many of whom I wouldn't have spoken to before. I had never spoken to Lee Byrne before. He was a quiet guy. When we were chatting, he asked me if I was playing at the weekend.

"No. I'm on the bench."

"Really? Why is that?"

"I've been sick for a couple of months."

I was thinking this conversation wasn't a great start in terms of laying down a marker with Lee. He hardly went home feeling his spot was threatened by Mr Mumps and his convalescence.

As it turned out, it was a tight final in Murrayfield. Leicester brought the experience but we brought the hunger and a couple of other elements.

Leinster supporters had arrived as a new phenomenon and again they showed up in their hordes. We felt that we had grown a very strong support base which historically we had never had.

And, of course, we had Rocky Elsom – Man of the Match as he was in most of the games he played for Leinster. He was incredible that whole season and seemed to get Man of the Match in most of the games. He was on the level of an O'Driscoll, an O'Connell or an O'Gara in terms of his impact in big games.

Rocky was a very quiet person who didn't interact too much with people. He was only with us for a year. Twenty one games. He lived alone. There was a little bit of a running joke about

Rocky being out on his own, floating around town, having the craic any weekend that we hadn't a game. He trained very rarely. Part injury, part reluctance. He would wear a hoodie in the gym. Little things that made you wonder, was this guy really bothered? Then, come Saturday afternoon, we'd see a different man. I have never known a player who could turn the switch on quite like he could. One of the worst trainers in the team. He didn't try to go hard even when he did turn up to train. On a Saturday afternoon, though, he was sublime.

After a couple of months when he'd been doing what he was doing everybody just said, ok, you keep backing it up on Saturday afternoon like that and we aren't going to complain if you never train. And who could complain? He became an instant cult hero. He was the first of the Leinster overseas cult heroes. I have never known a group of supporters to love one person so much, so quickly. The crowd worshipped him. Instantly. He delivered for them and the relationship fed both Rocky and the crowd. It was the perfect scenario.

That final also saw the birth of Johnny Sexton. That celebration. How comfortable he was in the final. What he was born for. He didn't look in any way intimidated. He has that belief about him. He had been knocking on the door there for a long time without getting too many chances. Felipe was always very clearly the number one and Cheika loved Felipe. Cheika always loved his inner sanctum material. Johnny, meanwhile, was a young guy working his trade. That day, in a game decided by three points, Johnny's drop goal from out wide just inside his own half was a perfect cobra strike.

We had started out together at the same age. We had a slight bond but I went into the pro ranks a little quicker. Johnny was playing under-20s and playing for Mary's and we didn't play a huge amount of games together in those years. He was working for a bank. He was always very confident, though, as if he knew deep down that he would get there. He needed the break. He got in the Ireland Under-20s squad after the coach had seen him play for Mary's.

I was very happy for him. He had trained very hard. You love seeing guys who take their chance when they get it. Even to try the drop goal and then pull off a perfect peach of a strike. It was a Johnny Sexton thing to do. I had hit a drop goal for Ireland in the Churchill Cup against the Maoris in San Francisco from the exact same spot. I had always teased him about that drop goal that I'd got. It was the first thing he said to me after the game. That was better!

I came on for Luke on the left wing late in the match. I didn't have a huge amount of involvement. My first play was a kick to the corner of a midfield scrum on the halfway line. It came to me and I kicked left footed down into the corner. Fairly business-like. That was my last play too, my only involvement of the game.

At least I had got onto the field. I was number twenty two. Girvan was number twenty three and Girvan didn't get on and I felt for him. He had contributed so much to Leinster for ten, fifteen years and he didn't get to be on the field when we got over the line. I thought at the time that it was very tough on him. He was long enough in the game to know that there is no sentiment in the coaches' box when you are making decisions in a tight final but I hope that he understood how much he had contributed to getting everybody to Murrayfield that day.

Myself, I felt a part of it to an extent but looking back at the finals of 2018 and 2012 when I started the games, I felt a lot more involved. Those medals mean more to me than the one that I was on the bench for. I know I had contributed earlier on but starting a final is what you want to do. It makes a difference to the quality of your memories.

The celebrations are better at club level where there are closer bonds. Even at international camp you (sometimes) gravitate towards the guys you know from provincial rugby. We came back to Dublin the night of the final, on a chartered flight. We spent no time in Edinburgh, just went straight to the airport. Players want to come home. We never stay overnight after a provincial game. The scenes in the airport were incredible. Thousands of supporters on their way home. It was straight back to Dublin, straight to Harcourt Street. Leaving Krystle nightclub at four in the morning.

I'm not sure if I slept but I know that Brian O'Driscoll picked me up in a taxi at 7am as we were going to South Africa that day. We were both in a delicate condition.

For Brian at that stage of his career there wasn't a lot of novelty left with all this stuff. I was just pleased that I was actually going to be getting on the plane after all the weeks of stressing. I didn't care what condition I was in. If the tiredness helped me keep a lid on my excitement, I was relieved. It could have got embarrassing.

For me, the Lions had always been the ultimate in rugby. I always remember Brian's try against Australia in 2001. I was fifteen years old at home in Cooley and I watched it live. Then I watched it on the VCR again. And again and again. Our machine didn't have playback, it was just rewind, play, enjoy. Repeat. I just watched that try forever. Now myself and Brian O'Driscoll were driving to the airport together to go on a Lions tour.

We flew to London and went straight to Pennyhill Park to

link up with the Lions guys who had been together for the week. We arrived not looking great but in that sort of old school culture which still lingered in the game we were fully expected to not look great. It was lauded a little bit by players and coaches. There had never been any expectations that we would arrive fresh and bright-eyed and with a pep in our step.

I hadn't really spoken to Ian McGeechan yet and I knew that I was very much on the back foot fitness-wise. I hadn't played eighty minutes for the guts of two months. I was tired and I was thinking that I might never get up to speed but I was just happy to be on the plane. I wouldn't be landing in South Africa with any huge ambitions of laying down any markers.

A few weeks into the tour, your mindset changes but that's how I took off. We only had two full backs so it was very much a fifty-fifty shoot-out. Lee Byrne was incredible that year. Between the two of us, I assumed that Lee was probably the number one full back in management's eyes.

Taking off that day were Jamie, Luke, Brian and myself from Leinster. Paul O'Connell, Ronan O'Gara from Munster and Tommy Bowe who was with Ospreys. Tomas O'Leary had got injured for Munster a couple of weeks before the tour and Jerry Flannery had got injured that week in Pennyhill Park in Surrey and had gone for surgery. Nobody on the plane was more pleased to be there than I was.

I grew up loving the Lions more than Leinster or Ireland. For me it just was the best about rugby. I remember entering a *Sunday Tribune* competition to win a Lions jersey. I was eleven or twelve years old. I wasn't in Clongowes yet but I was obsessed with rugby. The question the newspaper asked was 'who was the only person to have played, coached and managed the Lions team?' I had no clue but I wanted that Lions jersey very badly so I went and asked Dad. He said Syd Millar. Google had yet to become a thing so I believed my source, filled in the form and sent it off. A few weeks later, when I had all but forgotten about it, I got a call from somebody in the *Sunday Tribune.*

"You have won the jersey."

They could tell from my voice that I was pretty young.

"You have put medium down for the jersey. Are you sure that's what you still want?"

I backtracked and said, ok, well maybe a small one.

A Lions jersey with the Scottish Provident logo from the 1997 tour duly arrived. Growing up, I would never have got replica jerseys or anything like that. As a kid this was the greatest thing that I had ever won. I remember that so vividly. Pure joy. The small size was massive on me. I could have got lost inside it. I still have that jersey at home.

At that stage I had played more Gaelic football than I had rugby but rugby was the real love and passion and that 1997 tour had really fired my imagination. It had been key and winning in South Africa in 1997 got the Lions back on track. Now, twelve years later, we were setting off to do the same thing. On the tours since 1997, the Lions had won just one out of six Tests. We needed to set a level that the Lions would never dip below again. We needed to be really competitive.

I knew these things but leaving England below us I was just glad to be healthy and along for the ride.

9
—

LIONS AND BEYOND

I have never grown tired of touring.

Going away on a playing trip has always been the high point of any year. No matter how often I do it, the excitement of heading off with a kitbag and team-mates still makes a boy of me again. At the end of a season, to be travelling off to Australia or New Zealand or wherever has always had a little bit of a school's out feel to it. I've been on so many enjoyable tours and some successful ones but all these years later, the 2009 Lions tour to South Africa still stands out from all the others.

Nothing since then has matched the excitement, the newness or the fun. Ireland's 2018 tour to Australia was the most successful tour that I have been on. Going one-nil down in the first Test but coming back to win the series two-one was memorable and satisfying. But the 2009 Test series in South Africa is still the measure against which I judge all other expeditions.

In part, this was because those weeks with the Lions were the last stand of the old-school rugby tour. I am lucky. My career has been long enough that it has one foot back in those far off days. I fully embraced the era of high grade professionalism but I have a lot of sentiment for that time when the definition of a good tour was more holistic. In 2009 we weren't just there to play rugby. Playing meant a huge amount but I also built up so many great friendships from that tour.

In the years afterwards, you remember your Lions roommates more clearly and often more fondly because you were with them for a full week. You were thrown right in at the deep end and, for me, Wasps' Simon Shaw was as good a start as I could have wished for. A huge man. A really gentle type of guy. He was funny and very laid back. Just a very nice fella.

After Simon, other guys became friends too. Matthew Rees, Jamie Roberts, Ugo Monye are the names that stand out for me. Ugo and I got on very well on that tour as two young players each experiencing being Lions for the first time.

Ian McGeechan, our manager, was very much about the old school type of tour. Once you trained you could then do what you wanted. Train hard. Play hard. What you did in your own time was up to you.

So many new experiences. That tour was the first time I had been exposed to Mike Phillips or anybody like Mike Phillips. A character like that just seemed so un-Irish to me. Previously I'd have looked at him from a distance and thought, Jesus this guy is such a gobshite. In South Africa, I was struck by how likeable he actually was. Somebody can have a huge public persona like that but still be very good company and be a very funny and decent person.

Not only did Mike have a very funny schtick but you were always glad that he was your number nine. He was unbelievable. Everything you wanted in a scrum-half. Like Conor Murray, what a superb player he's been for Ireland. South Africa, being such an abrasive place to play rugby, was made for him. He played the best rugby of his career on that tour. He was a person we would gravitate around, the centre of the laughs and the craic in the team room. Mike would just have been one of those big characters that we were naturally drawn to.

Professionalism has washed away the old way of touring. Now, how you prepare for a summer tour is pretty much how you prepare for the November internationals or the Six Nations. It is literally like staying at home in Dublin and preparing for another Test match. The intensity is the same. You train. You play. You recover. You don't go out for midweek drinks or do anything off the wall. Maybe one drink after a game but nothing more.

Tours are so compact now and there is a greater onus on winning the games. Years ago, Ireland could go away on tour in the summer and results weren't the be-all and end-all of how the tour was judged. Now the scorelines matter a hell of a lot more.

A change of scenery is still as good as a rest, though. On tour you get to know the people you play with better than you do within the normal work days at home. You have a break from the daily responsibilities and demands that nag at you all through the rest of the year.

In South Africa in 2009 we trained hard. We went out for drinks during the week. We enjoyed our down time. We had a lot of fun. Ultimately we didn't win the series but we played well and our performances were important in keeping the Lions project alive. It was a great experience and another turning point in my career.

The Lions for me was always primarily about making good friendships and seeing if I could fit within an elite group, not just socially but on the field as well. It was the opportunity I had dreamed about since childhood but it still forced surprising adaptations on me.

With Ireland, for instance, I have had the same seat on the team bus for the last seven years. I sit at the very back in the rear left corner by the window. Your seat on the bus is a hierarchy thing. When you are young and just happy to be there, you sit in the first free seat that you can find. Usually near the front. As you grow older you gravitate towards the back where the big boys sit. For the last few years of his career, Brian and myself would have sat beside each other in the back row, chatting on the way to games.

At the start of my career, I used music as part of my pre-match preparation. It seems now that all players listen to music going to the game but in latter years I have actually moved away from it. I prefer to chat with somebody on the way to the ground. It works as a way to ease the nerves. I love being able to hear the sirens of the police escort and the noise of the crowd slapping the side of the bus. It fuels the energy.

And I like to be able to look out at all the movement and the colour around us. I feed off being able to watch people and make eye contact with them. I specifically try to lock eyes with supporters. I get a sense of their excitement and how much it means and I feed off their passion.

For away games, it is generally best to avoid locking eyes

with rival supporters. I don't do a good death stare so I try to take in a broader view of the whole scene. I like to look at the rivers of support converging as we join them approaching the ground. I like the feeling of us all being swept along to some roaring sea.

The Lions experience was different even in that small matter of the bus. Everybody has their own spot where they sit with their national teams so when you got on the Lions bus people wanted to sit in their own spot and there was a bit of awkwardness. Was it better to be polite and give way or hold out for the familiar spot that kept you in your comfort zone?

On both of the Lions tours that I went on, I missed the preparation week before take-off; the training, the socialising the going-away dinner. Leinster had finals on both occasions. That leaves you a bit behind socially. In 2009, though, I was young so when I got on the bus I just sat wherever was free. The bigger personalities staked their claims and made the noise and banter. Most guys sat on their own with their music. I was still just happy to be among them.

Lee Byrne and myself were the only full backs on the tour. I had no illusions. It was a short pecking order and Lee was ahead of me. I was the understudy and he was playing the best rugby of his career that year. He was up there as one of the best full backs in the world. I accepted that and wanted to have a good relationship with my opponent, especially as this was a Lions tour.

The two of us never really spoke to each other, however.

It wasn't as if we didn't get on but there was just zero dialogue between the two of us. Lee was a very popular guy on that tour but between the two of us there was nothing. I look at the friendly relationship I have these days with Jordan Larmour, for instance, and it was nothing like that. Not unfriendly but just no rapport.

Lee was a superb spiral kicker. Of course, I fancied myself with the spirals too. At the end of tough training sessions, the two of us would just spiral balls for an extra twenty or thirty minutes every time. We were trying to outdo each other without talking to each other. There was no teasing or banter. We were just silently launching these balls, each of us eyeing the other and trying to better him. It got to the point where my legs were sore from the amount of joyless kicking we were doing.

We won all six of our pre-Test games. I played the second game against the Golden Lions and played again in the fifth game against Western Province on a bad day at Newlands.

I got a nasty dead leg that day and limped off late on. That meant that I wasn't available for the last warm-up game which was against Southern Kings in Port Elizabeth. Lee Byrne wasn't playing either as he was being rested for the first Test at the weekend so Keith Earls was put in at full back. It was a tough day for Keith. He hadn't played much international rugby at that point and he was the youngest guy on the tour. I may have been young and fresh-faced but it must have been a crazy time in Keith's head. That tour was a massive learning experience for him and an experience that helped make him the player he is today.

Somewhere along the line, Rob Howley sat Lee and myself down and said that there was nothing between us, it was nip and tuck for selection for the first Test. We should both keep going for it. I think the three of us knew that Lee was nip, I was tuck and that nip would be in the team. I certainly did.

On the week of that first Test Lee was, as expected, named as full back. I remember being in a gym doing extras for my rehab. We were still in Cape Town and the gym had a view down over a lawn to the ocean. I was working hard and outside on the grass Lee was holding up the number fifteen jersey with a scrum of photographers taking pictures of him.

That is such a vivid moment. I didn't resent him but I don't think I have ever wanted something so badly as I wanted the shirt that Lee was holding up. I'd come on the tour just glad to be healthy and relieved to even be part of it all. There and then, though, I promised myself that by the end of the tour it was going to be me holding that jersey.

As it was, I was named as number twenty two on the bench which surprised me. Usually a winger or a centre on the bench will serve as the reserve full back. As a specialist full back, there was only one player on the field that I could be used as a replacement for.

In South Africa the journey into the grounds on Test match days was unnerving. Absolutely nothing like driving through leafy Ballsbridge towards Lansdowne Road on a Saturday afternoon or passing through the big piazza of happy people when we play in Rome. Here, there was incredible hostility. I was pretty nervous as we passed through the crowd the first day in Durban. South Africans were banging on the bus, shouting abuse, giving us the middle finger, throwing things at us, and making it an unbelievably uncomfortable experience. I was shocked by it and how visceral it felt.

We walked out on to the pitch before the warm-up, just wearing our tracksuits and runners. It was a different story. We took a deep breath. There were so many Lions supporters filing in, their cheery presence diluted the hostility. It was reassuring.

The team made a slow start that day and when Lee Byrne got injured in the thirty eighth minute, we were twelve points down and a bit dazed. Sitting on the bench knowing what was next, I just remember sort of bricking it a little bit. At no time in my life when I had dreamed about playing Test rugby for the Lions had I dreamed of coming on two minutes before half time when we were twelve points down.

ROG was sitting on the bench beside me. His reaction was typically businesslike. Take your gear off. You are fucking ready for this. You are made for being out there.

That was huge to me.

The first action that I remember was taking a high ball over Bryan Habana after the two of us went for a ball from a box kick off the nine. Bryan had a great career but he didn't grow up fetching high balls for Cooley Kickhams. I grew into the game after that catch and I got some really good touches. It was the best that I had played since round two or three of the Six Nations that year.

We almost resurrected ourselves that day. We were gone after forty five minutes, we trailed 26-7, but we dug ourselves out and had a chance to win that first Test. We dragged ourselves back into contention. Two tries, one from Tom Croft (who had one in the first half also) and one from Mike Phillips brought us to within touching distance.

And three times we should have had another try. Ugo got bundled into touch once and had the ball smashed from his hand at the last second another time. Phillips was just over but a desperate last-second invention from Bakkies Botha forced a knock-on. Heartbreaking stuff.

The second half was almost entirely Lions pressure and we forced the game to a knife edge of a conclusion but we had given them too much of an easy start. An incredible game to play in.

Afterwards, I thought to myself, this is as tough as it gets. The ultimate level. There was that taste of a disappointing defeat mixed again with some personal pride. I was delighted that I was a Test Lion and that achievement could never be taken away. There is a big difference between being a Test Lion and being a tourist. I had something now that could never be subtracted.

I also had no idea what was coming the following week.

I wasn't too sure as to Lee's position. He was back training on Monday wearing a thumb guard and apparently back in contention. To me that was surprising. With a thumb injury, you usually wouldn't be available the next week.

I recall Shaun Edwards saying, if you stay down on the ground and don't get back into the defensive line you had better have a broken leg. Those words will always stand out for me as epitomising the spirit of the Lions in South Africa.

Lee had played well but I knew that I had played better. There had been a huge amount of aerial bombardment. My bread and butter. I had finished really strongly. I knew that there was a chance of starting the following week. The week before I had been surprised to be named on the bench, now I would have been surprised not to start.

When I got named as full back for the second Test, nothing was said between Lee and myself. There wasn't a good luck, a handshake or anything. Lee had been available for selection. The game was never mentioned between us. We would have made small talk in training but there was no camaraderie. I don't remember if there was another injury complication but Lee didn't end up playing again on the tour.

Dad and Richard had got their timing right when they booked. They arrived in South Africa for the second Test. Dad has a very good friend, Chris McCann, who grew up in Rostrevor and moved to South Africa maybe twenty years ago. Mum knew that Dad would be fully occupied and was happy enough to stay at home. My sister Sara was sitting her Leaving Cert and Mum was always Head of Academic Affairs in the Kearney household.

It was good to see Dad and Richard but I remember being very nervous before the game. The Lions had been a dream since childhood but here I was and the dream, having been achieved, meant the result mattered more. If we lost this game the series was lost. To go two-nil down in a three-match series is awful at any time but back then, the Lions concept was coming under pressure.

People were asking if the Lions were worth the trouble, wondering if this wasn't an anachronism that needed to be phased out. Since the 1997 victory in South Africa, the Lions hadn't gone well and there was a feeling that maybe people had seen enough. There was that pressure and the fact that I knew from the first Test that these games were a step up from anything that a player would have experienced.

Willie John McBride, the emeritus leader of the Lions project, had given us our jerseys before that first Test and spoken of what it meant to represent the Lions in a Test match. It was hairs on the back of your neck stuff. I remember shaking his hand, collecting my jersey and just the sheer size of those hands was something that stuck with me. Those hands and that jersey could make you feel very mortal. That was just the first Test. Now the pressure had ratcheted up again. I'm not religious but I prayed to all the gods and to Ross, my lost brother, that on this of all days when I needed to find my best rugby it would come to me.

It was a stunning day. I remember walking the field beforehand and the sun being very bright and glaring. I was wondering how it would be for catching high balls. The sea of red in the stadium was incredible and comforting again after the usual hostile welcome to the ground.

I don't remember many specifics about the minutes before that game in Pretoria. On days like that you try to stick to the routine that has taken you this far. You want to take things in, but not be overwhelmed. It's a delicate balance.

For games in Dublin, I will try to pick out my parents in the crowd during the national anthems. I know where they will be. For away games, I try to find a young kid and mentally I bring myself back to when I was a boy watching internationals. It doesn't matter who the kid is supporting. The kid is there for the occasion which is so much bigger than he is, the huge noisy arena, the bubbling excitement. Focusing on that kid brings all those feelings back to me. When I remember being that wide-eyed kid, I never take any of what is happening around me for granted. Every chance to play in games like this is a privilege.

My memory of the game itself was how blessed I felt as it unfolded. How everything I touched just seemed to turn to gold for me. It was a heartbreaking day again, a killing loss for us, but on a purely personal level it was almost perfect.

Everyone says it doesn't matter how you've played when the team loses. That's just not true. There is consolation in having found your best self when you needed it. I was in a state of flow all afternoon. The performance came out of nowhere. Considering the preparation that I'd had since the mumps, I had no right to hope for anything better than surviving that match with my confidence intact.

For all the science of preparation, there is an element of luck to these things. You do the same things before games. Some days, everything clicks. Some days, nothing does. For one reason or another, that afternoon was pure. Everything seemed easier than it should have been. It was one of those days when you just didn't make mistakes. It doesn't even occur to you that you can make a mistake. The process of making decisions was barely a process for me. Just an instinct, like breathing. Things were coming off for me every time. I was kicking the spirals. I was making the catches. I was getting the right bounces. I was taking the high balls. I was hungrily looking forward to every involvement. Sometimes you can't find a way to pierce the skin of a game. On other days you feel that you are playing within the big beating heart of it.

I took a catch on my own twenty two that I should have marked but I didn't mark it. This was just three or four minutes into the game. I went off and made a thirty or forty-metre counter-attack that brought us into their half of the field. I don't know where that came from.

Minutes later a fast offload by Stephen Jones stuck to my chest. I was almost stationary but I found some zoom and I took off. Tommy Bowe was outside me to my right. I executed a dummy pass to Tommy and felt myself almost pulled into the channel between two Springboks and over the line in the corner. A try! We converted to go ten-nil up.

Throughout the game I felt an element of being protected by something. By what or whom I don't know but I was getting what I had prayed for.

My catches were good. The game was at altitude and the

Springboks went to the boot when they could but I was drawn to the ball every time, confident that it was mine. Years later, I heard that Fourie du Preez, the South Africa scrum-half, gathered his team around him in the second half and told them to stop kicking the ball at their full back.

Thankfully, though, they continued.

The physicality was ferocious. The pace too was frantic, the sun relentless and Pretoria's altitude sucked your energy. And yet I felt a weird sense of calm in the middle of it all.

I kicked a spiral Garryowen at one stage. It is something you might do in training. They are impossible to catch but you can look like a fool if the execution goes wrong. I would never have tried that in a game before but that afternoon in Pretoria I was somebody else.

Recently that second Test has cropped up a couple of times on *Sky Sports*. I shouldn't be old enough yet for nostalgia but when I watch now as a player, one on the threshold of retirement, I see a different version of myself kicking that spiral Garryowen. I'm asking that young guy, what are you doing that for? You slice that kick, it goes into touch and you're just an idiot. Do you realise that? What's in your head? Why aren't you playing the percentages?

Nowadays I can hardly recognise that young guy. I don't know when I stopped being that bold and confident. When did the risks begin to weigh me down?

I am envious of the kid who had the audacity to try those things. He didn't know his boldness was water seeping from a well. If he had, he might have been more sparing with it. I kicked a few more spiral Garryowens in my career but never on that sort of stage and these past few years I can barely imagine doing it at all.

I was so much at ease with myself as a player back then. The older I have got, the more my game has become a constant worry about limiting my mistakes. Percentages. Percentages. Fifty one per cent defender and forty nine per cent attacker.

As a team, that game was so bruising and disappointing but personally, on a selfish level, it was one of the great experiences. I had come up with a performance that put me on the world stage in rugby terms. I had come up with it in the very game and on the very stage that I would have nominated if life allowed us to choose those big moments. I had played some good games for Ireland before that but this was different.

That is the sweetness of the memory. I will always remember the ending too, though, and how that tasted. When I think about bitter losses over the last fifteen years there are the two World Cup quarter-finals against Argentina and New Zealand to mull over. Yet because those games were decided well before the eighty minutes was up, we didn't have the same whiplash feeling of going from joy to heartache that came at the end of that 2009 game in Pretoria.

The 2009 second Test was the first but not the last of the huge, searingly painful disappointments. There was also the 2013 loss to New Zealand. 19-0 up after eighteen minutes. Thirty seconds left on the clock and we were five points clear. We were also in their half and we had the ball. And still we lost. It was the afternoon of my favourite Ireland try and our most agonising loss. That day and the Lions second Test in 2009 were the two games that just broke my heart.

I was still on the pitch for the last play in Pretoria. Their kick went over. I was underneath the posts. There is a great photograph of me with my socks down just sitting back against the upright, looking completely dejected.

When ROG famously kicked that ball in the dying seconds I'm not entirely sure of whereabouts I was on the field. I think I had just put a big kick into their twenty two. It was two metres short from bouncing out of play, five metres from their line. I had gone to chase my own kick and I was making my way back down the pitch.

Hindsight is twenty-twenty and it comes cheap. It is easy to say that ROG kicking the ball out of play and us getting a draw and going into the third Test to tie the series would have been the ideal scenario.

At the same time, you have to put yourself in that moment and wonder. What if we go and win that ball that ROG launches, then force a penalty at the next breakdown? Then it's one Test each. We are going into the decider with momentum. We are going to win the series. In that scenario, ROG is the absolute hero of the hour.

I'd never blame people for the decisions they make. Was it the right decision? Probably not. Sometimes, though, you roll the dice. You have to. ROG had that ball in his hands as a professional rugby player conditioned to leading teams and to winning with Munster and Ireland. He went for it. It was just unfortunate that it backfired.

I had said a few words at Enfield less than a year before and when we went on to win the Grand Slam those words were inflated into something that they hadn't been. That happens when people search for simple reasons to explain success or failure. In 2009 with Ireland, we defended our asses off and got through games. Other teams made mistakes. We made fewer mistakes than they did. We won through with bits of fortune and courage. Enfield didn't do all that.

ROG got the reverse effect. A split-second decision taken

at the end of an eighty-minute match doesn't explain why we were two Tests to nil down just a minute later. There was a lot of rugby played and a lot of mistakes made before ROG found himself in that position.

Afterwards, in the review, Ian McGeechan said that he was totally proud of the way everybody played. He had no regrets or recriminations. There was no finger pointing. I remember a silence, unbroken for a long, long time in the dressing room afterwards. When Ian did speak, he was gutted and so upset. You could hear it in his voice but he was already building us up for the next week. We needed to win a Test game for the sake of the Lions. For the future of this extraordinary team and also for ourselves as competitors.

Throughout a career, you graduate from level to level. From minis to a school team to the Senior Cup. From the Pro 14 to a European game and maybe then to an international. If you are lucky enough or good enough, there is another step up. You get to go to a Lions training session. To just work with the best players from four different countries is a learning experience. And then you step up again to playing Lions tour games. Every guy on those dusty fields in midweek matches wants a piece of the Lions. And finally there are Lions Tests, rugby at a different altitude to anything you've ever known. Even though we lost that day, I knew that I had found a performance up where the air was, literally and metaphorically rare.

You watch sports people talking about how they can compete with anybody in the world and how they back themselves to do this or to do that. None of what they say matters until they actually do it. Until they have done it they will always quietly wonder if they really can back up the talk with the performance.

Distraught as I was at the end of that second Test, I did a post-match interview with *Sky* and Graham Simmons. They just wanted to talk about my performance. Graham asked me something along the lines of, was that the most perfect eighty minutes of rugby that you ever played?

I gave the stock answer. We lost. Individual performances don't matter. We're all just gutted.

It was all true but deep down that wasn't the only thing I was feeling. When he asked that question I was thinking, yeah, maybe I have just played the best game of rugby I have played or will ever play. I kept parroting clichés while taking this realisation in.

It was an odd feeling. I was dejected but I knew that in a few hours, when I started feeling better, there was going to be a lot to be happy about personally.

After the game Dad and Richard were around, of course. I could never do it now but I went on an almighty piss-up that night with Richard and our friend Paul O'Donnell. Dad was present at the start of that night but, wisely, he went off and found a more suitable diversion. It was a drinks and nightclub until three or four in the morning sort of occasion. A less sedate, more youthful version of the night I would share with Richard and Paul some ten years later in Japan when Ireland's World Cup ended.

Back in 2009, even with the Lions, once you were present and mainly correct at training on Monday morning it didn't really matter how you'd spent the night after the game. That is where rugby was at that time. And that was where I was at.

We won the third Test the following week. We owed it to ourselves having delivered two of the great Lions performances without winning. Lee Byrne never got back to full fitness.

There was a part of me that wanted him to be available and competing for the third Test. I wanted to know that I was being picked on the basis of how I had played and not because I was the only full back available. From having arrived in South Africa as a kid just pleased to be there, that was some change in my mindset.

When the tour ended, I travelled straight to Las Vegas to meet Aonghus, Pierce and a few more of my old friends from Clongowes. I was young, free and single, just coming off the back of this incredible tour. The year 2009 brought the biggest amount of money I had ever earned. We'd won Europe and the Grand Slam and there was a nice Lions tour fee. Some of that money stayed in Vegas but there was enough left to allow me to buy a house to live in when I came home. Life was great.

What happened in Vegas duly stayed in Vegas but what had happened in South Africa stayed within me always.

There's a good reason why clichés attach themselves to sporting careers. They are the easiest shorthand to describe the world which has as its polar extremes the feeling of being 'gutted' and the feeling of being 'over the moon'.

The experience of different sports people has so many overlaps that clichés are inevitable. One day you're touching the sky with your fingertips, the next day you are in that valley where it is dark most of the time. How else can you describe these things in simple terms?

I came home from South Africa in 2009 and what came next was a similar experience to what happened to my mood when I had returned from Australia and New Zealand the year before. In 2008 in those two Tests, I thought that I had made a breakthrough as a full back. I came home to play on

No nonsense: I had my ups and downs with Michael Cheika

Strong hand: Declan Kidney put his faith in me and created a player-driven environment

Iron rule: I would never dream of questioning Joe Schmidt. He took Leinster and Ireland to a new level

Prize scalp: Celebrating with Jamie Heaslip after our victory over South Africa at Croke Park in the Autumn Series, November 2009

Memories of 2011: Training camp in Queenstown ahead of the Rugby World Cup in New Zealand. *(Above, top right)* on the way to a win over Australia in Eden Park, Auckland and *(above right)* with our legendary bagman Patrick 'Rala' O'Reilly

Hat-trick heroes: With *(from left)* Cian Healy and Jamie Heaslip after our Heineken Cup win over Ulster at Twickenham in 2012. After missing the final in 2011, this tasted sweet

Laugh of Brian: With Brian O'Driscoll enjoying a joke at a Leinster training session. We have become great friends over the years

Pride of Lions: *(Left)* with Geoff Parling, Sam Warburton, Ben Youngs and George North in 2013 and *(right)* in action on tour against New South Wales Waratahs

Men Down Under: A chat with Owen Farrell during a training session *(left)* and some down time with the squad at a recovery session in the sea at City Beach, Perth

Ecstasy and agony: Scoring our third try against New Zealand in the Autumn Series match in Dublin in 2013. We were 19-0 up after eighteen minutes and still ahead with thirty seconds to go – and lost. It was hard to take. Dave is directly behind me on this picture

Joy of Six: Celebrating with Chris Henry and Johnny Sexton after scoring a try against England at Twickenham in the winning Six Nations campaign of 2014

No stopping us: A try against Scotland the same year in Dublin *(below)*

Game for a laugh: Me and Johnny have had great fun down the years in training sessions

Bringing it home: Enjoying the moment with fans and the Six Nations trophy at Dublin airport, 2015

Family silver: Me and Dave savour the moment with the Six Nations trophy after our dramatic win in the Stade de France in 2014

Other side of the story: Hooked up to a Game Ready machine, doing rehab on international duty – it's not all about glamour!

Winning run: Skipping away from a tackle in our 29-15 defeat of South Africa in the Autumn Series of 2014

Memories of 2015: *(Top)* one of my proudest moments in an Ireland shirt – singing the anthem with Dave before the France game and behind the scenes wearing our Rugby World Cup caps. *(Above)* saluting the crowd after the win against France and *(below)* end of the road against Argentina

the wing for Leinster. It felt like a reprimand. When I got back from South Africa from a tour which could not have gone better from a personal point of view, Cheika put me on the bench for the beginning of the Heineken Cup campaign. Back in my box.

Circumstances improved but the next two years of my career were bumpy. I went off with a knee injury against France in Paris in February 2010. A medial ligament strain. I recovered to come on as a replacement in the last two Six Nations games. I got to be on the field when we lost to Scotland in Croke Park as our Triple Crown slipped away.

Then I was stretchered off in the Heineken quarter-final against Clermont in April 2010 but I recovered for the semi-final and I got to be on the field when our Heineken Cup defence ended.

I toured Australia and New Zealand with Ireland in the summer. I also got to be on the field when the All Blacks put sixty six points on us in New Plymouth.

Finally, I did cartilage damage against New Zealand in November and didn't play again till the following August in the World Cup warm-ups. That World Cup ended in disappointment too.

I had serious operations on my knee and back. My name when it appeared in newspapers was usually tagged to phrases like 'injury concern' or 'new setback'.

After the Lions breakthrough it all felt as if I was running to stand still for two years.

Then 2012 happened.

10

HAMILTON AND BACK

W hen I think of 2012, I close my eyes and I think of full time in the Clermont semi-final. Normally I would never get emotional on a rugby pitch but I cried after that semi-final.

I won the Man of the Match award in that famous game. Those awards can be a bit random but there was relief in getting that one, given the heroics that Isa had performed the previous season when Leinster had won the Heineken Cup without me.

In the first half against Clermont, I had been drifting a little. Not playing badly but not offering enough. My back was getting sore. I remember in the interval Joe sort of looking at me a little bit askance. I knew I needed to engage a higher gear so, for some reason, I decided to change my boots at half time.

It was just a little mental nudge to remind myself that the second half was a new beginning. Joe said something to me on the way out which he often said down the years. Big players produce in big games.

I felt reset.

Johnny had spoken at half time. He said that the next play he would call was the one where I come through the middle. And he said, with that certainty that Johnny possesses, that it was going to work. Joe was nodding, yeah, this will work. So that was going to be the first play. I prepared myself mentally for getting my timing and my angles right.

That play is called a two ten bag hook. We've used it a lot through the years and we have got great value from it. The 'two ten' means that the two would be twice around the corner. And then 'the bag' would be three forwards running onto the ball. 'The hook' would be a hook ball back inside.

The hook ball will come from one of those forwards on the bag who takes the ball. This time the ball came from Richardt Strauss to me. On the day, Brad Thorn got his role wrong. That was the one thing you absolutely did not do under Joe. Hell hath no fury like Joe Schmidt if you screw one of his moves up. Those moves are planned out with surgical precision and Brad was probably six inches from messing the whole thing up. History often hinges on small unseen things like that.

Anyway, I went through as planned. I made a forty-metre break. Aurélien Rougerie came to tackle me and I just popped it off to my left to Cian Healy, who scored. 12-13 to Leinster.

A couple of minutes later, I marked a ball in my own twenty two. I was hard against the left touchline and I spiralled the ball. That wouldn't be a normal thing to do when up against your left touchline and kicking with your left foot but it was a free-kick off a mark and we were using the Adidas balls back then. They were just the nicest things to kick, they had a much bigger sweet spot than the Gilbert ball. So, suddenly full of pep, I launched this kick and it went over Rougerie's head and bounced back into their twenty two.

I was in my flow then. A few minutes later, the drop goal came. It was something of a gift. Brock James launched a punt from his own twenty two after a line-out. It dropped into my arms, just in from the left touchline about forty six metres out. I had time, I looked up and that was it.

Johnny always slags me that I won the 2012 European Player of the Year award on the basis of those seven minutes. He may not be too far wrong.

After the group stages they had announced a shortlist for the European award. There was a roll call of twelve players and none of those names was mine. It is unusual to come from not having been on the shortlist to go straight into the final five but that's what happened. It came down to myself, Johnny, Stephen Ferris, Ruan Pienaar and Jonny Wilkinson, who was playing with Toulon.

My comeback to Johnny is that I scored six or seven tries that season in Europe and, if he is really so cut up, I'll happily swap the trophy for his World Player of the Year gong! For two guys who played against each other as schoolboys and have ended up playing together in more games than we can count, that's not a bad bit of slagging to be getting on with.

In the final minutes of that game in Bordeaux, I remember Clermont just being camped on the Leinster line. They really should have scored. Wesley Fofana dropped the ball over the line. Gordon D'Arcy had put in a very good half tackle but we definitely thought that he had scored. It was only on the replay that it was reversed. We were good but we were lucky too. That day we were the men they couldn't hang.

My emotion at the end wasn't from relief at winning a close game that we probably should have lost. It was more that I was now finally going to start in a Heineken Cup final for the first time. I had missed out on 2009 and 2011. This was my time.

Or maybe not. We trained on the Monday on the week of the final. When I went into Leinster again the following day I met Jason Cowman, our strength and conditioning coach, who was loitering outside the door. He looked at me oddly. How are you Rob? What is going on?

I knew something was up. This wasn't a chance meeting. I had hurt my back in the Clermont game and I hadn't been able to train at all for the next two weeks. When I had trained for the first time the day before, I had been moving really poorly. I looked terrible and I knew it. I didn't imagine that Joe Schmidt might have been watching me so attentively though.

I just nodded to Jason. Yeah, I'm ok? Why?

I was completely oblivious to what was coming down the line. I'd toughed out worse injuries. Jason looked at me hard and said, Rob if you want to play this weekend you really need to go into Joe now and tell him that you will be ready to go.

I nodded again. Ok thanks.

This was serious.

I went into Joe's office. Straight away he hit me with it. He was pulling me from the game at the weekend. He didn't think that I was fit enough to play. We had a league final the following week and he wanted me to be ready to go all in for that.

This was a sudden blow to the gut. Missing a European

final but being ready for a league final the next week felt like a really bad deal. My whole rugby world collapsed again. This was Leinster's third final. I hadn't started the first one. I had missed the second. And now I had just been pulled from the team for the third.

I looked at Joe and I could sense that he was expecting a response. I knew there was space for me to make a case for myself.

Joe was always quite good in that way. If you told him you would be ready to play he would take your word for it but obviously then you had to deliver. You only got one shot at changing Joe's mind. So I looked him in the eye and gave whatever guarantees I could think of on the spot.

I told him that I was going to Santry straight away to get it sorted. I wouldn't train on Thursday but I would do the captain's run on Friday evening in London. I promised that I would perform on Saturday. He was a little taken aback by my salesmanship but Joe wasn't one to reverse himself into corners for the sake of it. He just said, ok, I'm going trust you on this one.

And right then the pressure was back on me. I went out to the car park, got straight into my car and called the late, great Arthur Tanner, our then team doctor. Then I drove straight to the Sports Surgery clinic in Santry for an epidural. I came home and rested up, waiting for the injection to do its thing. I felt better but still unsure if I could fulfil my promise.

I really didn't feel great on the Friday night. I got through the captain's run but later on I was trying to sleep in a single bed. I'm not sure who I was room sharing with, Dave maybe. At eleven that night I went down to reception in the hotel and got myself a double bed in a new room. It was more comfortable and I got some sleep at least. Next morning, I was still struggling. It was as if there was a clock loudly ticking a countdown in my head. If your body doesn't start doing what you tell it to do, you are going to have to go to Joe Schmidt hours before a major final and tell him. Sorry, even though I said I would deliver, I can't actually deliver.

The longer you leave that chat, the worse it is going to be for you. The real tension lies in the fact that the longer you leave that chat, the better chance you have that your body will begin to feel better. I gambled big on feeling better by the time we got to Twickenham.

As game time approached, I was so pumped with adrenalin that how I was feeling physically didn't matter anymore. I knew that I could play. Of course, only half of that adrenalin rush was excitement. The other half was fear. Over the years I have found that fear can be a really powerful ally sometimes. If I didn't back up the promises I had given to Joe on Tuesday morning, it was going to be detrimental to the team today and very bad for me tomorrow.

Joe is not a cuddly sort of guy. You only get one chance with him in that sort of situation. You have to deliver as promised or you walk.

It was also the case that with European finals you never knew when you were going to get another chance to play in one. That was Leinster's third final in three years. It would be six years before another one came around.

We moved through that final against Ulster on the momentum we had built over the previous two years. It is one of the games that I remember least about. Just the stats. Biggest points total in a final, most tries in a final, biggest margin in a final.

The real satisfaction of the season was knowing that, in 2012, Leinster had become the leading force in European rugby. We had been in a good place when Michael Cheika left in 2010 but we had kicked on to a new level under Joe Schmidt.

In 2012, we had played Cardiff in the quarter-final in the Aviva and we had blitzed them with some sublime rugby. We just tore them apart. Then to go to Clermont and win that game in the manner that we did stamped us as the most complete team in Europe. The final (and, for myself, starting and playing in the final) was the grace note for a great season.

I finished with a clean sweep of five awards between Leinster, Ireland and Europe. There were seasons when I won more medals and seasons when there were more momentous games but 2012 was the season when my game came together in the way I had hoped it would when I had left South Africa in 2009.

All Blacks. Hamilton 2012

I have aways hoped that when my playing career finishes that I will move onto a different part of my life and that I will be able to stop defining myself as a rugby player or as somebody who used to be a rugby player. I've never been an avid collector of souvenirs and mementoes. In my house I have the framed Grand Slam jersey from 2009 with my brother Ross's name on the back. That one is very personal and it is as far as I go in terms of building a shrine to my own career.

I have one jersey from every country I have played against. They're all tucked away somewhere. I'm not sure why. It's like when you're young and wanting a stamp on your passport from every new country you've visited. One of those things that seemed like a good idea at the time. Now that I have them I have no idea what I will do with those jerseys.

It tells me something, though, that I have collected five All Blacks jerseys. An All Blacks rugby jersey is different. It's iconic. You don't like to admit it but it has an aura. I would have more than those five All Blacks jerseys but I would never swap after a loss unless specifically asked to. And there have been quite a few losses.

Also, I've always heard stories about the All Blacks being choosy about who they swap jerseys with and how some guys have been turned away from their changing rooms or been told that, no, he doesn't want to swap. It's bad enough going home with your tail between your legs and your own sweaty green jersey in your bag without risking that additional humiliation.

So I have five black jerseys with the silver fern and I can rattle off the names of the guys who wore them. Joe Rokocoko, Sitiveni Sivivatu, Israel Dagg, Ben Smith, Damian McKenzie.

Two of those five represent wins over the All Blacks. Three represent defeat. In the summer of 2012, Ireland toured New Zealand for the first three-Test tours between the countries. After the first Test at Eden Park, I was surprised when my opposite number Israel Dagg came to me and asked if I would swap jerseys with him. As a rule of thumb with the All Blacks it works the other way round. You ask them if they would be so kind.

I was European Player of the Year though. That gave me a little bit of value in the jersey exchange market. Dagg told me that he had been watching me and that I had been unbelievable all year. Those words from an All Black were like a benediction. It was a great thing to hear and it was the first time I'd felt a little bit of acceptance from a New Zealander. You often feel that rugby is their native language and that they are patting you on the head for your gallant attempts at becoming fluent.

The following week we came within a whisker of beating them in the second Test in Christchurch. We got a bad decision and ended up losing by three points. My reaction was probably typical of the team's reaction. It was a tough game to lose but we had come within three points. It was another reason for me to feel confident after Israel Dagg had come looking for my jersey after the first Test.

What we had actually done in Christchurch was that we had poked the bear. The All Blacks took some heat in their own media. We didn't really notice.

We arrived in Hamilton for the the third Test having spent the week feeling hard done by some of the time and self congratulatory the rest of the time. We had won a moral victory. We had come so close. Three points? Who at home could complain?

If we just turned up again for the third Test in Hamilton we'd rattle them again surely.

Of course, we got humiliated. We were beaten out the gate. Our defence was all over the place. My main memory is of spending a lot of time underneath the posts in urgent team talks. I remember after we went down about forty or forty five points to nil, Brian pulling us all in. He said, I know this is absolutely shit, but what the fuck is going on here? This is even worse than shit. What the fuck?

He didn't even have words to express it. We were all just looking at each other hoping that somebody would say or do something to slow the humiliation.

The All Blacks had spent that same week getting ready to make a point to us in the most emphatic way. The point they made was a sixty-nil win. In an international game. I remember the draining feeling of watching them score try after try after try and seeing that they were never going to lose interest in scoring yet another try.

I remember that Dan Carter didn't even play. I remember Aaron Cruden and Sonny Bill Williams making a series of outrageous offloads as if it were an exhibition match. I remember being sin-binned for an accidental knock-on and sitting there helpless and embarrassed for the first ten minutes of the second half and thinking that it would be no bad thing if I wasn't sent back out there at all.

I remember sitting in that dressing room afterwards and there being no straws of comfort to grasp. I remember that Israel Dagg, whose jersey I would carry home, got a try and a conversion that day. Beware of Kiwis bearing gifts.

2012 was the year when I played the best rugby of my career, the year when the shelf creaked under the weight of the awards I put on it. It was the year when I considered myself to have arrived as a serious player at the top level. And that result stands in the record books as a rebuke to all that. Sixty-nil. Sixty points. That's the sort of beating that the All Blacks handed out to non-rugby nations in World Cup pool games.

For a while, I believed that nothing could be worse than that day. Defeats in close and epic games leave you shocked and whiplashed but the consolation is usually that you have performed. When the music stopped you had the deficit but with another few minutes the ending could have been different. In Hamilton we'd hit bottom. There was no story we could tell ourselves to make it into a positive.

The journey home was always going to be tough. Thankfully I wasn't going home. Myself, Fergus McFadden and Kevin

McLoughlin had booked a holiday in Thailand. We flew from New Zealand to Dubai with the squad but then the three of us split away from the team to catch a flight to Asia. The whole squad was walking together through the terminal in Dubai, then we turned right and they all went left.

When we turned the corner the three of us just looked at each other and sighed with relief. Anything was better than going home with the shame of a sixty-nil defeat around our necks. After such a pumping you don't like going back through Dublin airport. It is a pretty grim place. People are looking at you. You assume that they are laughing at you. Here they are, home. The sixty-nil guys showing their faces back in the country.

Myself, Fergus and Kevin didn't even mention the game among ourselves for the rest of the trip.

In hindsight, Hamilton happened because summer tours were a little bit too relaxed back then, we were too pleased with having come close the week before and the team which had won the Grand Slam in 2009 was running out of steam anyway.

The shame wasn't deleted from the hard drive of our memories. In quiet moments on that holiday I reflected that, as good as 2012 had been, I was still waiting for the perfect year. That year would have to include a defeat of the All Blacks. After Hamilton, though, I wasn't convinced that any Irish player would ever be able to include a defeat of the All Blacks on his CV.

Yet, in 2016, I would find myself having a good chat with Ben Smith in the New Zealand changing room in Soldier Field. I was a winning Irish player. He was a defeated Kiwi. It was hard to absorb. I had gone looking for him and he was as good and as gracious a guy as he is a player. I have his jersey and my own from that historic day framed together up in Cooley. They're not hung up anywhere in the house. They are just gathering dust.

I learned from that and in Dublin in 2018, when I got Damian McKenzie's jersey, a very generous rugby fan donated £15,000 to Crumlin Children's hospital for both our Test jerseys in return.

That last All Black jersey seemed to close off a circle in my career. The mauling we had endured in Hamilton had been a lesson in not being switched on and it had been a flashing warning of the mortality of that team.

When the Six Nations came around in the spring of 2013, we didn't improve too much on where we had left off in Hamilton. We lost away to Italy for the first time in the history of the Six Nations. After that, the writing was on the wall for Declan. Maybe he had run out of steam a little bit also.

Unfortunately for Deccie, at the same time, Leinster were doing unbelievable things under Joe Schmidt. It's tough being in charge of Ireland when a provincial coach is making more waves than you are. In the next few years, if Ireland aren't successful, I'm sure Andy Farrell will hear a lot more than he wants to hear about how Stuart Lancaster does things. That's what happened with Declan. By the end of the 2013 Six Nations, there was a feeling that change was due.

I was grateful to Deccie and fond of him but I would have felt the same. I was in the prime of my career. I was playing the best rugby I'd ever played. Joe was getting the best out of me as a player. I started to get a little bit inquisitive, more serious about taking the success with Leinster into an Irish jersey.

Under Joe, some perspective and some distance was quickly put on the Hamilton massacre. Joe referenced the sixty points a lot in the run-up to the November 2013 game. And when we lost to the All Blacks that day in Lansdowne Road we realised that there were worse ways of losing to them than a sixty-nil pumping. The pain of 2013 burned into us for a long time.

11
—

THE HOUSE THAT JOE BUILT

All Blacks, Dublin 2013

The details are as familiar to me as a favourite horror movie. I know what happens next but I still want to look away. We had got pushed around by Australia the previous weekend and punters, pundits and bookmakers predicted more of the same for us.

The All Blacks were in town to complete the first perfect season of the professional era with their fourteenth win and they were playing the side they had beaten sixty-nil last time out.

When Joe Schmidt had come into the Irish job, there was a sense of excitement within the team. There was also a big element of fear. Players from other provinces would have quizzed us Leinster players a lot about Joe and how he operated. We would talk a lot about an army camp atmosphere. How some of our video reviews with Joe could get rough. How dropped balls or any lack of concentration at training just weren't accepted. How, if you missed a breakdown, Joe would simply go mental. How when Joe went mental with you, it was just a case of taking it on the chin.

And still people wondered what was in store.

From the moment Joe arrived, the All Blacks game in autumn was a huge focus. As a Kiwi and as a rugby man, Joe kicked up another gear every time we played New Zealand. Everything was for that game. We played Australia and we got beaten out the gate. They put thirty two points on us. The All Blacks still loomed.

Australia had felt a little like the Hamilton Test except this time it had happened at home. That seldom happened. Even under Declan towards the end we had held our own at home. It was a shock to the system but in the week of the New Zealand game, there was so much energy that we moved away from Australia quite quickly. We had been speaking about New Zealand for the whole campaign. We knew we had to go out there and put up a big performance.

On the day, we went two converted tries to nil ahead. Then Israel Dagg offered me a gift, maybe in return for the Irish jersey I'd given him. His misdirected pass ended up in my hands. I saw a corridor ahead and I went for it. I galloped from just outside our twenty two all the way till I went over their try line. It was a try you dream of scoring in training, a try I'd never dare dream of scoring against New Zealand. In that perfect moment, the noise in the stadium was deafening.

I was as surprised as anybody when that happened. When

we'd played Australia the week before, I had damaged some rib cartilage and had needed to come off. The injury was painful and I was resigned to not playing against the All Blacks. I met Joe in the corridor on the Sunday night. I was still in a fair bit of pain and he came up to me and said, listen, how is it?

I told him that it was pretty sore.

I wasn't sure if he knew that I was unlikely to play the next week but I decided that I had better tell him the news myself.

I'm not too sure about next weekend. It doesn't look good.

Joe shrugged.

"Ah, that's a pity. Well, just so you know, Dave is playing on the wing next week. It would be a real shame if you weren't able to play with him."

He left it at that. Joe always knew what buttons to push. As he walked away I just thought, oh no, I can't let Dave go out there on his own.

And there was the thought too that this might be the day. It seemed unlikely given that we'd just been freshly hosed by Australia but you never knew. If I wasn't there and we beat them I'd regret it for as long as I played.

How long have people been singing songs and writing books and plays about Munster beating the All Blacks in 1978? You want to be on the pitch when these opportunities come around. You particularly want to be on the pitch if your brother is going to be out there.

So, both Kearneys got to share the numbing sense of death in the afternoon that descended on Lansdowne after the final whistle the following weekend. The All Blacks' second attempt at converting a last-minute try had limped over and the final whistle shrilled. A little half-hearted booing came from the stands but mainly all you could hear was the silence. We'd taken everybody in Lansdowne to the heights and we'd let them drop from there.

It was the most emotionally shredded I have ever felt after a game. I remember coming back to the house and not being able to think straight for days. I had never, never been so affected by a game. We were off for the whole week with nothing to do but wallow in the misery.

On Wednesday, I think it was, I got up and went out and walked around for a while. I just went walking for seventy or eighty minutes. I had no particular place to go. I just had to get out of the house. When you lose a game, perspective usually surges back quickly enough. There's always next week. You'll never be disappointed and sad for too long after a loss. It's another sports cliché but we go on. We do.

November 2013 was different, though. I had never really experienced such proper hurt from a game of rugby. I'd won some things by then and perhaps the biggest thing left that I wanted to do was be on an Irish team that beat the All Blacks. All the next week I thought that our chance had gone. We'd thrown it away.

I wasn't directly involved in that whole drama at the end but, being honest, I think all fifteen of us were involved in some way. We had something like seven defensive errors in that last three and a half minutes of play. Sometimes you might not have that many defensive errors in a whole game. For just one of those errors not to have occurred would probably have been the difference.

There was a penalty given away on the halfway line which they took quickly and, after a tackle was made, we had a few guys who went dipping their heads into a breakdown which they didn't need to do. We needed them to have bounced back up and out. There were a lot of those things, four or five guys doing stuff that if they didn't do we would have won the game. They were exhausted. We were hanging on, longing for the whistle. It was the hardest lesson.

We didn't get together again immediately after that game. The review didn't happen until Christmas time. It was tough viewing. Sometimes it is better to watch those games back the following week. You can take your lessons out of it and consign it all to the memory bank.

That review was painful. Since his appointment, those of us who knew him had been telling the other players how rough a classic Joe Schmidt game review could be. Now they got one for the ages. We had been stewing in our failure for weeks and it would be another couple of months before the Six Nations and the chance to run out onto a field again. Joe made sure that we would remember every lesson and learn something from each one.

He picked apart this error, that fumble. He dissected every wrong option. If this had happened… if that had been done… if this had been held… if that space was closed… we'd have been so far ahead… they wouldn't have come back. No way.

But all that sliding doors stuff was nothing compared to the atrocity of how we defended for the last three and a half minutes. And that's what we took away in the end. That was never going to happen again. No sequence like that would ever be repeated.

Losing and reviewing the loss with Joe were like operations without anaesthetic. The knife cut through flesh and nerves and bone. But losing that game and taking the lessons from it ultimately spring-boarded us onwards.

After that day there was much more emphasis on the bench

coming on and making a real difference rather than just fitting in. Replacements when they came in had to lift the intensity and kick the team on to another level.

And Joe became obsessed with our ability to work through defensive plays for a long period of time. That final, fatal, phase of play against the All Blacks which lasted for those three and a half minutes haunted us for years. Joe personally haunted us with every second of it.

Three and a half minutes became the number that we had to live with for years afterwards. I couldn't guess at how many sessions there were where we had to endure continuous, high intensity defending through periods of three and a half minutes at a time. If we could properly defend a team for three and a half minutes this catastrophe would never happen to us again.

These exercises would come at the end of a Tuesday or a Thursday session when we were tired. We'd just be set up defending our own twenty two and the opposition would have constant ball fed to them. Attack. Another ball. Attack. Repeat. Non-stop for three and a half gruelling, sapping minutes.

And we did it knowing that no error was too small to pass unseen by Joe Schmidt.

A story. My brother Dave's relationship with Michael Cheika was different to mine. Dave was in the academy for a lot of Cheika's stint at Leinster. At that time, I wouldn't have spoken too much with Dave about my dealings with the coach. Cheika gave Dave his first Leinster cap. When a coach does that, you feel valued. I didn't want to poison Dave against his coach.

There was one day when we were training up at UCD and Dave was carrying a quad injury. It was a team session and Dave made a break and then just stopped and passed the ball to somebody else. He had strained the quad again. Then somebody made a counter-break and Dave didn't chase back to try to stop him. Cheika unloaded on Dave.

"Why the fuck can you not run back?"

This enraged me so much that I completely unloaded on Cheika for the first time ever. I'd never stuck up for myself but now I was shouting at Cheika. I told him to shut the fuck up.

"He's injured his quad again and you are fucking shouting at him now."

Cheika was a little bit taken aback at my outburst. He'd never seen this from me. He apologised to Dave the following morning though. To be fair to Cheika, he was good like that. If somebody got into a barney with him it was always forgotten the next day. He was good at just moving on and wiping the slate clean the next day.

The point here is that, in a million years, I would not have turned on Joe Schmidt in that way. Not if he had ordered that Dave with his quad injury should be humanely destroyed like an injured racehorse. To take Joe on would mean that I had, potentially, played my last game for Leinster or Ireland.

You did not take Joe Schmidt on in public. Even if you wanted to question him in some way about something rugby-specific you would need to be very sure about what you were saying before opening your beak. You had to be one hundred per cent correct. Very few of us have that self-belief. That's Johnny Sexton territory. And with Joe, even Johnny would frame his questions rhetorically. "Or it could work this way too, Joe?"

Joe and Johnny operated at the same level when it came to seeing and understanding the game. Joe respected that but even Johnny knew to be careful.

You could go to Joe occasionally for a one-on-one and discuss things with him a little more freely but you would never do it in a room full of players.

Joe was one hundred per cent certain and specific about everything that he wanted. There could be no dilution of the message because the message was always meticulously accurate and on point.

If you wanted to take Joe on in anything, you had first to understand that Joe had thought about it a lot more than you had. He understood it a lot more clearly than you did. He had tested every possible argument you could come up with in his own head before you even thought about how to put your words together.

Before you might challenge Joe, you had to appreciate that Joe had an incredible understanding of how to win rugby games. His understanding was better than your understanding. End of.

Having considered all that, did you still want to challenge Joe?

The very basics like quick rucks, good passing, ball retention, running lines, the real fundamentals of rugby that were important to winning games, Joe understood them really well and valued them highly. With all those things, anything less than perfect would not be accepted by Joe. Those things were non-negotiable.

We might be running plays in training and after maybe a minute of play Joe would stop everything.

Hey, we were missing somebody on the far side in the first ruck on the second phase. Joe Bloggs needs to be six inches more this way and on the third phase Jimmy Bloggs needs to change his angle maybe ten degrees, when Paddy Bloggs is coming around the back. Where other people saw chaos, Joe saw everything unfolding in slow motion and with perfect clarity. Usually unfolding as he had designed it to unfold.

Like Johnny, he is wired differently in how he sees these things. It's not just the photographic memory but the processing power to interpret everything in a very short space of time. Something that I might see in a slow motion replay, Joe would have anticipated in real time before it even happened.

Invariably he was right and if you thought that he wasn't right you wouldn't say it anyway. I would never really have suggested to him even one-on-one that there might be another way.

In my experience, only Stuart Lancaster comes close in terms of his understanding of how he plans to play the game and how the evolution of rugby is changing those plans.

Amongst ourselves we would say that the Joe the public sees is a very different Joe to the one we saw on a training field or in a video room. Physically, Leinster training would be an awful lot tougher than Irish training but mentally, Irish training under Joe was on a whole new level. He would stress us and put us under such pressure that you ended up mentally stronger or you just didn't survive.

If you made any mistake, Joe would let you know but if you erred in one of the non-negotiable areas he would shout at you and call you out in front of everyone. Breakdown work, running lines, working hard, being where you are meant to be. None of those things require any talent. If you don't adhere to the perfect level of expectation, you were going to get blasted.

I got that a couple of times. It would be quite cutting. Sometimes, especially in Carton House, people would come to watch our training. They might be friends of the coaches or people from charities or often other coaches from Gaelic football or soccer teams who had along come to learn something new.

One day, Joe had us doing a drill and the rules of the little game he had come up with were only explained to us two minutes beforehand. I wasn't as quick to pick the details up as some of the others and I screwed up on the first run through. Joe exploded in front of everybody.

"If you don't want to play this game and do what you are supposed to do, just go and piss off somewhere else."

Everybody else's heads are down. The guest spectators are all aghast. You feel two inches tall at that moment, but you would never answer back. You just wonder does he really mean for you to actually fuck off or does he mean you to keep going.

It has happened that sometimes a player has responded literally to the words and thought that he has been told to just go away. He has turned, only to trigger another explosion.

"Where do you think you are going now?"

"I thought you told me to go away?"

Every player would have a story of when they were the target. It's never funny even if it's somebody else. It is such a tense moment. Nobody is laughing or making a joke. Somebody passing you might mutter: right, head up, next ball, get it right next time. No slagging. No banter.

That was Joe's way. He put us under severe pressure all week because if he didn't, we wouldn't survive the weekend. There was method to that element of madness. Many weeks, when Saturday came it was a relief just to be getting onto the pitch.

Despite all that, I knew that it was the very best environment for me. I played at a high level for fifteen years and I put a lot of that down to the environment Joe Schmidt created where nothing less than your very best was acceptable.

For me the best thing about Joe's incredible specificity was that I always understood what he wanted from me as his full back. The media often didn't get that.

For instance, the breakdown for Joe is the heartbeat of the game. The essence of rugby. You keep the ball. You don't let the opposition get a sniff. The quicker ruck ball that you get, the easier it is to play the game. You send two men to every breakdown. It doesn't matter if you are wearing number one or number fifteen, you have a job to do. Get rid of the opposition person, get over the ball carrier, get a man to the right side and a man to the left side. You both have work to do.

If you are not good at the breakdown, you don't get into Joe's team. With so many players down the years, I would hear the media asking why was he not in the team. He's so good at this and he is so good at that. A lot of the time it just came down to breakdown work.

There were a few guys down the years that I am sure Joe probably didn't rate. People would say that it wasn't fair how they were treated but Joe makes it very simple. What he wants might not be the stuff that you or the media think that you are good at. There is nothing more crushing and black and white than Joe pointing at your slouching form on a video screen on Monday and saying, you are walking here, why are you not running? Your job was to hit this breakdown and you didn't do it.

All that was spelled out so clearly beforehand that you have nobody to blame but yourself when Joe comes for you.

Your only viable response is to say that it won't happen again. If Joe says, can you run faster than that, he is right. It is pretty clear on the screen that you can run faster. There is no discussion.

Often when I was drawing media criticism or there were campaigns for other players to be brought in, I was a lot more sure of my standing with Joe than the general punter would have thought. I understood the huge emphasis that Joe put on defence, on all the things you do without the ball in your hands.

With the ball in his hand, Simon Zebo is a really gifted footballer. He can do exceptional things that I can't do and, as I get older, I can't even think about doing. Under Joe, though, what you did without the ball is at least as important as those things.

How you made other players on your team look was very important. Positioning. Covering the back field. Working at the breakdown. If you don't do your job at a breakdown somebody else has to come in and do it. The knock-on effect is that you lose another player somewhere else across the field. Doing those things – and knowing that Joe noticed me doing those things even if the media didn't notice – kept me pretty secure.

I had a lot of pretty quiet international games where my two wingers would perform very well. Without doing anything amazing or flashy when I had the ball, I could enable players around me to have a good game. I knew that was important to Joe.

I always had a really good relationship with Simon but, rightly or wrongly, I knew that I was Joe's first choice whenever I was fit. I just happened to be Joe's type of full back.

The areas of the game that Joe put a huge level of emphasis on were the areas I was strong in and Simon was a little weaker. Simon was very good aerially. No question that he is a better broken field runner and distributor than I am. Simon could try things that others wouldn't. However, those dull things like backfield coverage, fitness and work rate were things that I would have had an edge in. I was just fortunate that those were the strengths which Joe favoured.

The technical workings of his brain never ceased to amaze me. Down through the years there have been so many moves, like the beloved two ten bag hook, that he has devised and taught to us. I can't count how many hours I've spent learning them all and walking through them with Joe's voice in my ear.

The younger lads coming in now are all about opening books and writing things down. Learning and reading. I am more about trying to keep it in my head because I was with Joe longer than anybody else. And I have seen him mellow.

Before games now, I see the guys hunting through their notebooks desperately looking to refresh their brains about the week's moves. In the early days it would have been suicide to do that in front of Joe. First of all, he expected everybody to be as captivated by the science of these moves as he was and he expected that our enthusiasm would have burned the details into our memories. If you were relying on paperwork you weren't learning it all as well as when it is in your head.

Also, when Joe came in first, his caution was much more acute. He hated things being put down on paper. He wanted the stuff in our heads where it was safe. If something was written down, it could get into the wrong hands and into wider circulation. These were things he had worked out in his head and on training pitches for years. His intellectual property. These things were the edge he brought to every job.

He had his furies but it wasn't all stick with Joe either. Sometimes there was carrot. One of Joe's big things with me before a game would be to come up to me and just say, best of luck buddy. No matter how the week had been with Joe, I felt bonded by that. He'd say best of luck buddy and then he'd always add, big players step up in big games. That was a bit of a gee-up. Every time he said that before a game he made me feel that I was one of those big players; I was one of those guys that Joe could rely on.

Before the All Blacks game in Chicago in 2016 I was riven with doubts. For all sorts of reasons I wanted to be somewhere else, anywhere else.

I knew that Joe was eyeing me in the changing room. We had finished the warm-up and we were back inside, putting on the match jerseys and getting ready to go out for the anthems in ninety seconds or so. There was just time for Joe to give me the 'big players in big games' line.

Instead, today there is a subtle variation. He quietly says to me, "We need a big game from you today, Rob. You need a big game for you."

It all happens very quickly. Kick-off is maybe four minutes away, tops, and I'm thinking, fuck you Joe. Why would you just say that to me now before we got out the door to play the All Blacks. You know the way my head is. What the hell?

We're going out here where we may well get bloody well pumped, Joe, and right now you're basically telling me that you've put your ass on the line for me. You've just reaffirmed what doubts I've been feeling all week. You've just told me that I'm in this team by the skin of my teeth.

I had to turn it around quickly in my own head. In the tunnel I was thinking, screw him. If this is my last game for Ireland, I'm just going for it. I don't fucking care anymore. I knew I wasn't fully match fit and that the whole thing wasn't looking too promising and now Joe was pressuring me like this.

I'd had a knee injury for weeks but this was a new day. I hadn't strapped the knee that I had strapped every time during the previous four weeks of playing or training. It felt a little better. I'd decided that, literally and metaphorically, I was going without the strapping. I didn't know how it would work out but I felt free to properly go for it.

A big factor that week had been the public bandwagoning, the lobbying for a change at full back. I knew that I hadn't been playing my best rugby for some time but that general acceptance that you are finished can really get to you. Anything good you've ever done ceases to matter. I needed Joe's imprimatur that I was still a big player who was going to step up for this game.

I played well, out of anger and out of not caring anymore. There was a point in the game when I felt that this was going to be a good day and when the game was over, I remember retreating into that selfish corner.

That's me back. That's a point proved. I've bought myself another eighteen months in the number fifteen jersey.

On the field afterwards, I did an interview with American TV. I don't think there was an official Man of the Match but we did one of those on-the-spot reaction interviews. When it finished and I turned away, Joe was there beside me with that boyish little grin.

"I'll have to say that to you more often, Rob."

Buttons pushed again.

Before Joe came along, life under Declan Kidney had been less stressful for Irish players. Players would never have been afraid of Declan. I certainly wasn't. I was definitely scared of Joe.

When Declan lost his temper, you would get a bit of a fright from it because it was a rare occurrence. I think, like most players, I felt that I had a very good relationship with Deccie on a personal level. He was always very kind and thoughtful towards me and as such it wasn't the odd flash of temper that ever bothered me. It was that I would never want to do anything to disappoint him. It felt like disappointing your father.

Another coach you would say to hell with him but Declan was one of those guys who when you failed him he wasn't angry with you, he was just disappointed.

I definitely got the sense from Declan that he was always trying to help grow me as a person and as a player. He would be feeding me with stuff always, talking about a broader world than rugby.

The Enfield incident probably defines Declan more than it defines me. It was classic Declan creating an environment where things came from the players up rather than from the coach down. I doubt that he knew with certainty beforehand that it would be me who would raise the issue of Munster and Leinster's unresolved relationship but he knew that somebody would and he would have narrowed it down to it most likely being a young and naïve Leinster player who would wander into dangerous territory.

When it happened, he was pleased. That had been the object of the entire episode. I don't know if Marcus Horan had been primed to pick up on the issue as soon as it was in the air. I wouldn't be surprised, though. And I wouldn't be surprised if Marcus wasn't even conscious that he had been primed. That was how Deccie worked.

His team that won the Grand Slam in 2009 was vastly different from the 2018 Grand Slam team in terms of personalities and skill sets. In 2009, we quite obviously revolved around Brian O'Driscoll, Ronan O'Gara and Paul O'Connell. We depended on them to produce. In 2018, the load was more evenly shared.

I'm not sure why exactly we didn't kick on from 2009 to further success. There was room for the younger guys to grow in stature. Perhaps Deccie's more human approach meant that we ran out of steam.

In 2009, at no stage of the season were we allowed to talk about the Grand Slam. We never put that pressure on ourselves. We got through and we won but it was game by game. In 2018, under Joe, we spoke of nothing else. Anything but a Grand Slam would have been failure.

Deccie was still in the job by the end of the 2013 Six Nations when we lost to Italy. We knew, though, that no Irish team should lose to Italy and that change was probably needed.

Quietly in the squad everybody was already talking about Joe Schmidt. The Leinster players were being quizzed about his type of training and his level of detail. We'd go into the national squad and spend time explaining that, at Leinster with Joe, we'd be doing this and Joe would make us do that.

That was dangerous territory to get into. It was unfair on Declan and risky in terms of the ongoing rivalry that you might have had with the other provinces. I remember talking to Paul O'Connell. He was asking about Joe and I was thinking to myself when you have a guy like Paul, with such a growth mindset, somebody constantly trying to get better and improve and to win, is he taking all this info about Joe back to Munster so it can be replicated?

In other situations, if you talked to a Munster player about what we did in Leinster their attitude would be, so what, we don't care, we do things our way. Talking to a guy like Paul, though, you knew that if he thought there was a better way, he wanted to be doing it that way.

It's not unfair to say that Deccie wouldn't have the same coaching nous as Stuart Lancaster or Joe Schmidt. A great coach can have many different strong attributes.

Deccie was happy to delegate. He didn't have to micromanage. As I have said, in 2009 Mervyn Murphy did a lot of training ground work on set plays with us. Huge difference. Deccie also brought in Les Kiss as our defence coach. That changed our whole defensive system. Les incorporated the choke tackle into international rugby. It hadn't really been seen at that time but it was massive for us in that 2009 campaign.

When the team does it, the whole crowd gets behind you. It was such a lift to have the crowd going mental when we were holding a guy up and creating a maul and then getting the turnover.

We practised it so much. You needed a two-man tackle with guys getting under the opposing player's arms so he could be lifted and he has nowhere to go. The tackle is formed by getting your knee to the ground so that you are stopping him from doing that. From the rules' point of view, the key is that it is basically a tackle that is not a tackle. When the maul collapses, we, the defending players, have no obligation to roll away or release the ball carrier so if the ball is not immediately available then it is our scrum.

It worked well for us in that spring of 2009 but we were still learning the technique. It would take perhaps till the Australia game in the 2011 World Cup before we completely perfected the technique and people really began to notice. After that other teams either imitated us or complained about us.

Declan didn't have the obsessive rugby mind that Joe

Schmidt or Stuart Lancaster possess. When he thought about the team, he thought about us as people and how we were growing. That human side probably cost him in the end. Deccie's every waking moment wasn't spent trying to work out how to eliminate our flaws and mistakes and how to stay one step ahead of every other team.

Joe though…

Mum once bumped into Joe in a hotel corridor and he spoke to her for ten minutes about formations and breakdowns. Mum is a woman whose interest in rugby doesn't go far beyond whether her sons are safe and ok.

In the end, it was easier for us not to improve under Deccie's benign style than it would ever be when we lived in fear of Joe.

Late in a career it is natural to look back at the coaches that got you through it all. In school, obviously Adam Lewis had a huge influence on me as a player and as a person. Dad would have had a huge influence also. Apart from support and advice, he has always handled my contracts in a friendly non-confrontational way that has shielded me from stress.

Michael Cheika and David Knox I don't think got the best from me. With Declan Kidney and with Eddie O'Sullivan, I don't think full back play would have been their forte. Eddie was abstract and distant and I never knew him. Declan was different in ways that are obvious and that I have described.

Joe, of course, has been a huge influence on me with Leinster and with Ireland. I have done more sessions and reviews with Joe than anybody else and shared more success with him.

Given all that, I have been surprised at how much I have come to appreciate Stuart Lancaster at Leinster at this stage of my career when I clearly know that I am not his cup of tea when it comes to full backs.

Leo Cullen is the Leinster front man who does the talking. When you are dropped, he comes to you and he explains the rationale. When something different is wanted from you, Leo is the one who asks you for it.

Stuart, though, is fascinating. He breaks games down even more than Joe does. Joe would show us starter plays and things to do. He wouldn't always go into the in-depth of literally all that followed. He'd show us something and say, if we do this we will score. Simple and very methodical.

Stuart will regularly break down entire games. He takes them apart like a composer breaking down a piece of orchestral music note by note. He hears every instrument and understands its place in every moment. He will go through full games where we would watch with him from zero to eighty minutes. Provincial coaches have the luxury to do this given the amount of team meetings we have together. It helps if you are fascinated by the process.

Joe would typically select maybe four or five different examples of a certain team defending in a certain way at different points in games. Or, here are four examples of this player doing this, or watch these three times when he shot out of line. Here I have four times they left the space there and that weakness is why we are going to execute this play. Stuart, though, will go through a whole game. The concentration and depth of analysis is remarkable.

I have always known that the way I play full back is not the way Stuart ideally wants the position played.

The things that Joe always valued in me as a full back, my aerial ability, my kicking game, my reading of defences, my grass coverage, all those are less important to Stuart. He wants a full back who has the ability to be a second playmaker. So Leinster believe that Jordan is more of an attacking threat. They are right.

I can't argue with that.

It is an odd situation. The old non-negotiables which are important in international rugby are not as important in provincial rugby until you get to the semi-final and final of big knockout competitions against the very best teams.

In 2018, I didn't play in the quarter-final of the Heineken Cup against Ulster. I missed a couple of games in the group stages too. Against Ulster, though, Jordan had a mediocre defensive game at full back. He lost a few balls aerially and they got a lot of access in our half through the backfield. I came back in for the semi-final and final.

I've spoken to Leo about this issue of playing less. He asks me, how is my head, what is my frame of mind? I say that, frankly, over the last few years I have come to see that any value I have doesn't come into play until our big games at the end of the season. So I keep training hard and working hard because I feel that opportunities will still come my way.

I like the discussion. I like the back and forth. I know that time is running out on my career and it is good for me to be challenged to get outside my comfort zone. It is useful to have to argue for my own virtues every now and then rather than taking my position for granted.

After the 2019 World Cup when we were heading in to the Heineken Cup with Leinster, Leo said to me, you know that we are judging things off the World Cup? And we think that Jordan played very well for us in the tail end of last year for Leinster.

I knew what Leo meant but I said, hold on a second. Jordan

was on the wing at the tail end of last year. In the Heineken Cup final v Saracens I was one of our best players. Did I not finish the World Cup as the starting Irish full back? That knocked Leo off guard a little bit. When you have these chats with coaches it is very easy for a coach to say, well, that's just what we think. I didn't really expect to change Leo's mind or Stuart's and also my heart is with Leinster and with the idea of Jordan being the best player he can be for the club. It was nice to make the point, though.

There are times too when it is best not to pick the battle. Usually those times have been with Joe. When Joe pulled me aside before the English game in the 2019 Six Nations to tell me that he was picking Robbie Henshaw at full back, there was no argument from me. I hadn't been in Portugal the week before. I had played poorly against Scarlets for Leinster last time out. I just said, that's fine. You have given me the nod so many times. I'll take this on the chin.

At the end, a career is about the medals and the memories and you have better memories from winning. The game is more enjoyable when you are winning. I am not sure how looking back on losing season after losing season would be enjoyable. Winning medals has always been my biggest motivation and playing for Joe Schmidt brought so many medals and memories.

The years 2014 and 2015, as Joe really grew into the Irish job, were maybe my happiest period in rugby. I wasn't getting injured anymore. I was playing well. Joe was managing Ireland and I understood clearly what was wanted of me when I put on that green jersey.

In my mind, those seasons almost morph into one. We were

riding such a crest of a wave. Everything we had done with Leinster, Joe was now doing with Ireland. Us Leinster players were walking around Irish team camp reminding lads from the other provinces that we'd told them all that this would happen. We knew Joe would bring the goods.

If I can separate those seasons in my brain it is because 2014 stands out because myself and Dave were playing together in every game. Myself, Dave and Jamie Heaslip were the only three players to play every minute of every game in that Six Nations.

After we won the championship in Paris we had a little time together upstairs in our hotel room. The five of us, me and Dave, Mum and Dad and the Six Nations trophy. Special.

I think we knew even then that it wouldn't get any better than this. I was 26 or so. Dave was 23. I said to Mum and Dad, let's just enjoy this one. It won't be this happy for the remainder of our careers. It can't be.

When I think of 2014, I think of Dave's intervention in the last play of the game in Paris when he pressured Pascal Papé to make the pass and Papé ended up throwing it forward. Dave's intervention pushed us over the line to that trophy and it is as great a career memory as I have.

That was drama but the next year in Scotland was crazy. We went over to Murrayfield with not much of a chance. The score differential looked impossible. Ourselves, Wales and England were tied on points but England had a points difference of thirty seven points to our thirty three and Wales twelve. Wales were going to Italy. England were hosting France and we were in Scotland.

Perhaps only Joe believed. We had gone to Cardiff in our previous game and we had been so convincingly mediocre in losing to Wales that it was quickly decided by the media at least that this was a crisis point of Joe's managerial career.

On the Sunday night before an international, we normally go through our plays for the next week and have a look at some footage. I remember the meeting that Sunday was just about one number that Joe had written on a whiteboard. I think it was seventeen points. Joe was just pointing again and again at the number and saying that this is how many points of a difference we will need this weekend. All week everything was building towards that number.

By the time we got to the ground in Murrayfield, Wales had pumped Italy in the first game of the day. The number had increased. We needed to win by twenty one just to overtake Wales now. In the huddle beforehand we just said, fuck it, let's throw everything we have at them there.

What will be, will be.

And we had this unbelievable game and beat Scotland 40-10.

We came off the field and next up it was the French against the English. The French were at a low ebb that year. We watched the first half in the changing room with a few beers. Then we had to go upstairs to the post-match function. Outside there were ten thousand supporters still in the stadium watching on the big screen.

We were sitting in the post-match function with the Scots who had just been hammered. They really didn't give a shit about what was going on. A bizarre ninety point game came down to the wire with England knowing that a converted try would win them the championship.

In the frenzy at the end, there was that crazy play when Yoann Huget took a quick tap and ran with the ball five metres from his own line. Lunacy. We couldn't believe it. What the hell is he doing? Everybody had their head in their hands. Why are the French faffing about? Of course, they didn't care or understand anything by that stage. They were lost in the madness of a twelve-try game. Finally, Rory Kockott just kicked the ball out and the craziest ever day of Six Nations rugby ended.

There were so many big, big days like that with Joe. In those earlier years, he always seemed a little bit apart from us when a trophy was delivered. In time, he softened.

On a few occasions he has even had a few drinks with us. In Chicago I remember he loosened up, had a bit of craic. A Kiwi who had just plotted to beat New Zealand. That was a different level for Joe.

And there was a night in Australia in 2018 when we had won the series down there. We were on our summer holidays when the final whistle blew and the night was bound to be boisterous. I remember us back in the team room at the hotel with Joe at two or three in the morning and there were a few cigars and some bottles of whiskey going around the tables. We had a rugby ball in the team room and we were doing some of Joe's drills and ripping the piss out of Joe while he watched. I thought, this could all go badly wrong, but Joe was loving it. He could laugh at himself at times like that.

By then he had the right to a few nights like that. He was unimpeachable as the greatest coach the Irish game had seen. Every time we had a big game for Ireland or before that with Leinster, he upped the ante for us in the week beforehand. That gets harder to do over time. I listened to Joe's voice for nine years of my career. I was as afraid of tuning out at the end as I had been at the very beginning. In those years he drove us to levels that we couldn't have imagined.

At the end of Joe's time, there was some grumbling that

the 2019 World Cup had tarnished his legacy a bit. I don't agree. All teams, even at their peak, are disintegrating in some way. 2018 was the perfect year. With a larger pool of players than Ireland will probably ever have, some guys would have been quietly rotated out of the 2018 team making way for oven-ready replacements.

Joe didn't just up the ante for us on a game by game basis, he changed Irish rugby forever. If somebody ever surpasses Joe's achievements in Irish rugby, then and only then can there be a serious discussion about Joe's legacy. Not before.

I don't see another coach doing that and, if they do, they will have begun their work by standing on the platform that Joe built.

12

SANTRY TO SOLDIER FIELD

The clear highlight of the 2015 World Cup was the win over France. We had planned for that game for months and on the day we got everything right. That game also carried the seeds of the defeat to Argentina the next weekend.

We will never have the depth to absorb the loss of players like Johnny Sexton, Paul O'Connell, Peter O'Mahony and Sean O'Brien for a World Cup quarter-final.

Argentina rampaged through us at times. Down the years we used a go-to cliché whenever we talked publicly about a forthcoming All Blacks game. If we play to our best and the All Blacks are slightly off, we can beat them. Argentina could say that about most of the teams perceived to be above them in world rugby. They played great rugby that day. We were off our best.

It was a World Cup that we began as back-to-back Six Nations champions, a World Cup played in familiar venues and comfortable weather.

For me, losing to Argentina marked the end of the sublimely happy period of the previous two years. My body started to rebel again. Through the 2015-16 season, I was really struggling with injuries. I was picking up a series of minor hamstring injuries, grade one strains which I was getting even without doing a huge amount of work. I would just be running multi changes and not even sprinting and, damn, something would pop.

I would rehab the injury. A week or two later, I was back in rehab again. In the season after the World Cup, I barely put two games together back-to-back. The frustration was made worse by there being nothing concrete to suggest why it was happening.

We played Connacht in the Pro12 final in Murrayfield at the end of the season. Taking a break from a persistent pattern of hamstring problems, I managed to strain my ankle ligament (a grade two strain) two weeks before that. I wasn't going to play in that final. Isa should have been full back but then he broke his arm in the week beforehand. Suddenly I was back in the team.

I was in no way fit enough to play and it really showed. I performed really badly. We lost and I copped a ton of shit for my performance in the media post-mortems.

Still, there were consolations to consider. I had been selected for Ireland's tour to South Africa that summer. The day before we were due to fly out, Dave got ruled out of the tour with a grade two calf injury that he had picked up in the league final. The next news was that Johnny was ruled out with a shoulder problem he'd picked up in the same game. I was the last one standing, even though I wasn't feeling too good myself. At best I was coping, getting by. I was thinking I'd get on the plane to South Africa and I'd get myself back to match fitness over there.

We had a session in Lansdowne Road the day before we were due to fly. We were running the bag hook play and I made a clean break. I was sprinting through to the line to score when I felt the familiar little dart in the hamstring again.

I went for a scan that evening. The night before the tour and I still wasn't sure if I should be packing. The scan report grounded me. This was bad news for yet another Kearney. Dad had booked his flights and hotels the week beforehand and was looking forward to seeing his sons playing for Ireland on tour.

He ended up as one of two Kearneys touring South Africa that summer. Team manager Mick Kearney and himself but neither of his sons. His old friend Chris McCann saw more of Dad than he had bargained for.

I was now carrying two separate strains in the hamstring. I was told that two tears is very unusual. I didn't really care about the improbability of my situation, I was just nearing the end of my tether with my body.

Ciaran Cosgrave, the Leinster doctor, sensing the effect it was having on my morale, suggested that I needed to get to the bottom of the problem once and for all. He suggested that I spend some time with Enda King in the Santry Sports clinic. The list of people that Enda has worked with serves as its own recommendation for how good he is. Dan Carter had come over from France to work with Enda. That was good enough for me. I made the call.

If I could take one day back from my rugby career and live it differently, it would be the day when I was working on weights in David Lloyd's gym in Riverview when I was nineteen years old.

It's still a painful live and learn story. It was one of my first sessions with the seniors. Girvan Dempsey was lifting with me. Girvan was doing ninety kilos and I felt that, if I was to be one of the big boys, I should do that too.

I had no business doing a clean and jerk of ninety kilos. I was young and slight and inexperienced but I wanted to show that I could keep up with Girvan. We had done some upper body weight work in school but that was different. I had never really been taught how to lift correctly with Olympic weights.

So I got into my position and did precisely what you are not meant to do. I lifted the whole shebang with my back. I felt a pull on my back straightaway. That one mistake has caused so many other things. Eighty per cent of my soft tissue injuries for the next thirteen years happened because of that one moment.

My preparation has been affected for years. My commitment to weights programmes and leg strength has been compromised ever since that day because of my inability to commit to a full gym programme because of my back. I haven't squatted in maybe ten years. The squat is an important exercise in your gym programme to keep you strong and fast and powerful. I have always had to try to find other ways to do that.

That initial back problem kept me out for about six weeks at the time. I was young and I wasn't really clear about these things. I was in an awful lot of pain for the rest of that season but it was my first real injury and I had no understanding of the human anatomy. I wasn't sure what pain you were meant to play through and what pain you were not meant to play through. So I toughed it out.

That set the pattern. I would go on to have multiple epidurals and nerve root blocks down through the years. We are talking maybe ten to fifteen of them. Looking back now, that is maybe too many but you can be so desperate at times to feel like an athlete again.

In November 2010, I had my first serious operation for a micro-fracture in my left knee. That was the biggest injury that I have had. I was out for nine months. It happened against South Africa in the Aviva, not a tackle, just running and I opened a little fissure in my cartilage. When the injury was described to me, I was asked to imagine plaster on a wall. The plaster is there and it looks fine but when you get so much as a little crack in it the plaster will just fall off.

When you have a micro-fracture it is actually more serious than an ACL, although doing the cruciate is the injury that players traditionally dread. The surgeons can go in and fix up your anterior cruciate ligament. With a micro-fracture you lose some of the cartilage under the knee cap.

Ray Moran was my knee surgeon. When he operated, he drilled holes into my kneecap. The blood flow from this is meant to reinvigorate new cartilage growth. Ray was very reassuring at the time but he told me later that basically, as a surgeon, you are drilling holes into somebody's bone and you never really know if the cartilage will actually grow back.

If it does, you don't know to what extent it will grow back or how the body will adapt following the procedure. It was only after talking to Ray in other consultations down the years that I came to realise that the knee injury had been a career-threatening moment. Ray told me later that he hadn't been sure if

I was going to play again. Thankfully, he did an incredible job on me.

Through all the time since I had injured my back in that weights room, I had been playing with various levels of discomfort or pain. I finally underwent back surgery in October 2012. I was hitting a bag in UCD when I felt another tug in the same spot. I'd had enough. For six months prior to that, I had been in a huge amount of pain. On the New Zealand tour that summer, I was literally hobbling back to my bedroom after training. I still don't know how I even played in those games. My back was in a dreadful way by the time I went under the knife.

Before heading out to Santry in the summer of 2016 to work with Enda King, I took a two-and-a-half-week holiday. Usually we take four weeks at the end of the summer but I was so fed up with my body that I needed some time away with my partner Jess, who thankfully is the most positive person I know. By the time I headed out to meet Enda on the first of July I was in the right frame of mind, if not the right physical state, for a few weeks of intensive work. Mentality makes a big difference in my approach to these things. I badly needed some positive energy. Jess is infectious in that sense and Enda, as it turned out, is a very positive person too.

Since my back surgery a few years previously I knew that what I was experiencing was most likely neuropathic symptoms coming from my back. When you delve into the anatomy of nerves and discs it all gets complicated very quickly, especially for the layman. So I had started to convince myself that there would be no way out of this. My body was just not able for it anymore.

The thought of a premature end to my career knocked my morale down a bit further. When I had the knee injury back in 2010, I had been out of the game for nine months and it had been pretty much touch and go for my career. There was a chance that I wasn't coming back from that one but I only appreciated that fact a little bit later on.

When you do recover and you get some good seasons under your belt, you forget very easily. You begin to take things for granted again. Now, in 2016, if it was all going to end, I was in no way prepared for a life after rugby.

Enda was unbelievable though. He said that he was going to find the problem and fix it. As simple and as positive as that. I believed him because I was desperate to believe him.

The first thing that he did was a comprehensive assessment that lasted sixty minutes. He deposited me on a physio bed and checked my hip mobility, ankle mobility, my ability to squat, my thoracic control and lumbar control. We did simple tests like an overhead squat, a lunge, a dead lift. He wanted to see what way my pelvis and trunk were working, if they were in tandem, if there was anything that was out of sync.

There were no X-rays needed. I'd had so many MRIs on my back over the years that Enda had a full album of pictures of my disc trouble. We did some 3D biomechanical testing which gave him even more of a clear picture.

From a one-hour assessment, Enda pinpointed seven or eight different deficiencies that I had. That was the good news. Some answers at last. The bad news was the amount of work I appeared to have ahead of me.

The key areas of focus for Enda were hip control, lateral hips, hip extension, thoracic control and lumbar strength. We devoted most of the attention to these. I could sense that my body was a car that was badly failing its roadworthiness test. It was going to need a lot of repair work.

Enda takes the view that, within the body, everything has a knock-on effect. You rob Peter only to pay Paul. Some part of the body is doing a lot of work here because another area is weak and inefficient.

The surgery I'd had on my lower back a few years previously had involved part of a disc being shaved away to relieve the pressure on the sciatic nerve which runs right down the leg. My hamstring troubles ever since had their source in my lower back problems.

There were fundamental anatomy flaws inside of me that needed addressing as opposed to injections.

For two or three years before I went to Santry, I'd experienced back pain every morning when I woke up. Ok, I told myself, you have a bad back. This is the territory. Deal with it because this is how it is going to be. After two or three days with Enda, I could feel that pain in my back start to go away.

I had so many weaknesses in my body that had never been taken care of. Things as basic as muscle weakness. My glutes weren't strong enough. My quads weren't strong enough. If the quads and glutes aren't up to it then your lumbar spine does a lot more work. And if the glutes and the lumbar are getting sore then the hamstrings have to work harder. My hamstrings were really testing strong when the club did tests but I was straining them regularly because they had no back-up.

For a long time, the answer to every problem had been that it must be my back. Why? Because my back was getting sore too. So we kept injecting my back.

It's a tricky situation. Rugby is a very high attrition sport. You are going to be sore. You will take bangs and bruises. After a game of rugby, you will be in pain. Your joints will be inflamed and anti-inflammatories are going to be useful to help you get over that. Did I take a lot of painkillers and anti-inflamms through the years? Yes. I took my fair share of them. If I didn't take them, if I sat out games whenever I was in pain, I would have played half of the games that I did. That's not a stat you want to bring into your contract negotiations.

The work with Enda brought almost immediate pain relief and four or five weeks later I was a different athlete. I was running differently, I was applying force through the ground differently. I wasn't waking up every day stiff and sore.

Enda retuned me with exercises aimed at strengthening the neglected areas of my body. The sessions were grindingly tough. I was shocked by how tough. For the first ten days working in Santry, I was technically still on my summer holidays. It felt like anything but.

The week would begin on Monday morning with a 10am assessment in 'control'. Written down, that could be mistaken for a little pre-rehab type of thing. Definitely not. I almost drowned in my own sweat after those 'assessment' sessions.

I had my own room in the sports clinic for the three-week period. Most days I would go out to Santry for eight in the morning and have my breakfast there. I would do the 10am session and then take a much needed shower. Then we'd have a linear session at 1.30pm, focussing on running mechanics. I could be on the track in Santry on a summer day running around carrying 20k barbells over my head to stop my thoracic rotation. We might be doing work planting on plates in the gym to get my ground contact stronger, just working on putting more forces through my leg. Whatever it was, it was always tough.

Then usually there would be a lower body strength session at 4pm. Late in my career I was learning that you can have all the strength and all the muscles you like but to get the value, you need to be able to control them and have the right type of movement between them.

I wouldn't finish until 7pm in the evening when I would grab another shower and then fall into the car one hundred per cent knackered. The intensity of those days was like nothing I had ever experienced. I never knew that you could get that tired from just doing gym work.

There were a couple of times when I didn't even bother going home. I just stayed in Santry. Having a shower in the room at 7pm meant that it was half seven by the time I was ready to hit the road. I had to be coming across the city again at 7am the next morning. So I'd just give up, stay in Santry and use the hours I'd gained to catch up on my rest.

With Leinster, meanwhile, the pre-season work was starting up while I was still toiling away out in Santry. I called up Joe and told him that the work that I was doing was transforming me as an athlete. I wanted to stay in Santry for another week while Leinster were back at work. The IRFU were paying the bill for my time with Enda. I had a long-term contract so it was worth the investment. Once Joe gave the all-clear, Leinster were just told that they wouldn't have me around until the following week. I would be returning as a much improved version of myself though.

I was fortunate that Karl Denvir, one of the Leinster physios, came to all those Santry sessions with me. Karl learned a huge amount from Enda at that time and he brought it back to Leinster in order to work with me. Some people in jobs like Karl's would be defensive and territorial about things like that but Karl viewed it all as a professional learning experience. In the years since then, he and I have had almost daily early morning sessions where we apply the lessons of Santry.

Karl's dedication and his specialist knowledge of what makes my body work and what makes it stall have added years to my career. I am indebted to Enda King for those three weeks of repairing me and enlightening me and I am even more indebted to Karl who took control of my maintenance for the next four or five years.

When I got back to Leinster training after Santry, I felt like a new athlete. I felt as good as I had in years. Physically I had lost a little bit of explosiveness but my body was in the best shape I had ever been in. And I had Karl, who had the manual for keeping it that way.

Then, in a not too surprising plot twist, I went to Glasgow and did my knee on their brand new all-weather astro turf pitch at Scotstoun. I was chasing back, trying to make a tackle. There was nobody around me but I went down and my knee just hit the ground. I think they may have laid concrete as the base beneath the pitch before all the other layers went on top. The outcome was a grade two rupture of my posterior cruciate ligament. It kept me out for five weeks.

The November internationals were approaching. After all the sweat and pain of the summer, I was back to the familiar race between my broken body and a clock ticking down toward an event that I badly needed my body to be mended for.

All Blacks. Chicago 2016

The dressing rooms in Soldier Field, Chicago are big spaces made for big herds of big beasts. A few minutes before we were due to go out on to the field on Saturday, November 5th, 2016, I was feeling the size of the occasion a bit too much and the surroundings were suddenly dwarfing me.

I was sitting beside Andrew Trimble. We looked at each other and I said, if there was a plane outside this stadium right now, I would go straight out and fly back to Dublin. It wasn't the most reassuring thing that a full back had ever said to a team-mate but Andrew looked at me and said, I'm so glad you just said that. I'm feeling exactly the same.

I'd come back from the knee injury just before the European Games in October but mostly I was on the bench. While the Irish team was in camp for a week's preparation before Chicago, I was sent back to sit on the bench again for Leinster against Connacht. Something with the knee still wasn't fully right. I played twenty minutes, heavily strapped, and the knee was still a little sore. I went back into camp, trained on the Sunday. We flew to Chicago on Monday after a training session.

The knee was still worrying me. I was short of match practice. In training, myself, Garry Ringrose and Jared Payne had been swapping around, inter-changing positions a little bit. Joe would have Garry Ringrose go to thirteen and Jared Payne go to fifteen. Normally you get a fairly good inkling what Joe is thinking but before Chicago, I wasn't sure. It triggered alarm bells in my head. I wondered was he losing faith in me.

We trained on the Sunday and watched a video that night, then trained again early on Monday morning in Carton House before heading straight to Dublin airport. Joe told us the team on Monday morning before going out to training. I was relieved to be picked. At least somebody who matters wants me to play. I took a little bit of confidence from the fact that I wasn't at my best but he was still trusting me.

Being picked was reassuring but I wasn't certain I could repay Joe's faith in me. I had been feeling more self-doubt than usual. There was an idea around the place that I was done, a bit of a beaten docket. Every mention of me in media or social media seemed to be in terms of it being time to put me out to grass. Tiernan O'Halloran was playing very well for Connacht. Jared Payne was playing very well in Ulster. Simon Zebo was playing very well for Munster. Even at home with Leinster, Isa was playing very well at full back whenever I was injured. Everybody had their backers. Everybody was playing well except me, apparently, and it felt like nobody was fighting my corner.

When I had originally been named in the travelling team, I realised that a big part of me didn't really want to play in the game. I wasn't fully fit. I'd been getting so much heat from everywhere that my confidence was low. Also, there was a good chance that we could get beaten by twenty points in Chicago.

It was the All Blacks so yes, there's always a chance of that. Playing the All Blacks, you believe that on your very best day you can beat them. It has to be your very best day, though, and their performance has to be not their best. If it all went badly I knew that, as had become the custom, I would be one of those carrying the can. One of the lessons of Chicago would be that it was long past the time to stop picking Rob Kearney.

The All Blacks were in that phase where they had gone eighteen games unbeaten. They had conceded five tries in the whole rugby championship. We knew that we were basically there to sell seats. AIG was rehabilitating its image in the US and was sponsoring US Rugby as well as the All Blacks. They wanted an occasion, a spectacle that would sell out the stadium. So who else were they going to call? New Zealand were the lions. We, being honest about it, were cast as the Christians whose followers would buy the tickets and hope for the best. Of the Christians I felt that I was the one most likely to get at least a bad mauling. Or at worst be completely devoured.

That week Joe had a very clear game plan though. He wanted to throw the kitchen sink at them. We were going to attack them from everywhere. We would fight them on the beaches, the fields, the hills, the streets and so on.

The subtext to this was the loss in Dublin three years earlier. We had stopped attacking that day and we had just stood back to absorb their pressure. Joe was adamant all week. It couldn't happen again.

We went to the Chicago Bulls training facility on Wednesday afternoon; a massive building close to their home court in the United Center. It was the most incredible facility you could imagine. Two full courts, the Bulls offices, sixty thousand square feet, full of state of the art equipment. Locker rooms with hydrotherapy pools, an analysis room that is a full cinema, weights and cardio rooms and embedded technology that collects players' stats for instant analytics. They even have crowd sounds that can be pumped onto the practice courts. It was a galaxy and a half away from getting changed at the boot of the car in Old Belvedere.

As we were leaving the building, the All Blacks were coming in for their own tour. You rarely have those encounters and it was quite awkward to bump into the opposition like that just a few days before the game. There were no friendly exchanges. We knew that, in a couple of days, we were all going to be kicking the crap out of each other.

Early on the Thursday morning, I went up to the gym on the top floor of the team hotel. There was nobody else around.

I was just going up to do some of my usual switch-on stuff. Joe was up there. It would be unusual to see him up there and more unusual still to actually have some sort of a dialogue. Normally with Joe it would just be, good morning, how are you? Sleep ok? This time though he was telling me that he needed me to train really well today. He was talking about quick feet, giving me little cues.

That was fine but training was pure shite that day. A really poor session. The pitch was a college facility at the University of Illinois but the quality of the surface was really poor. Waterlogged, mucky and with uncut grass. It was mid-afternoon, a day or two after Hallowe'en and, at one stage, we thought we heard bullets go off.

As always on the Thursday morning, we had worked on our restarts. Beforehand, Joe puts up a piece of paper showing exactly where all the opposition players are going to be set up on the field. It's just numbers on a piece of paper showing where we expect they will all be in their half of the pitch. Then he will put three circles on that sheet of paper. These are the three places where they are weakest, where they are under resourced or where Joe thinks that we are strong.

One of our strong areas was straight down the middle. Seeing this gave me a jolt of confidence. Historically I would have contested a lot of balls right down the middle of the field. I was understanding a little better the strengths that Joe still saw in me.

Apart from that, Chicago was up there in rugby terms as one of the worst weeks of preparation we have ever had for an international match. Maybe the All Blacks would say the same about their week too.

For other reasons it was amazing to be in Chicago on that

week of all weeks. That evening, the Chicago Cubs ended a one-hundred-and-eight-year drought and a local curse to win the World Series in baseball. On Friday, we went up to the very top of the Trump Hotel to watch the victory parade. We were on top of the second tallest building in Chicago the day before our game, watching a city and a team celebrate something that people had long thought to be impossible.

Conventional wisdom said that the Cubs never win the World Series and that Ireland never beat the All Blacks. Now there was this epic river of five million people oozing down Michigan Avenue to celebrate the romance of sport, illustrating the fact that anything is possible. Conventional wisdom had taken a beating. I had never seen anything like those scenes.

Better still, as we watched it all, we learned through social media that the All Blacks were down there, right in the middle of the celebrations. They were down there for a few hours. We'd always said that, on our best day, we could beat them if that was a day when the All Blacks fell short of their own best. The Cubs had been failing to win the World Series since 1908. Ireland had been failing to beat the All Blacks since they first played each other in 1905. Maybe tomorrow we would be at our best and the All Blacks, for reasons relating to the Cubs, would come up short.

The self-doubt was still eating at me though. Fear is a funny thing. You can either go into your shell or do as we did the next day and go out with the mindset that says, fuck it, let's just throw everything at this and see what happens. I could sense that the team were approaching that mindset. I didn't know if I was capable of going with them.

There were a lot of excuses I would be able to make if things went badly but thinking of those excuses in the countdown to a game was problematic in itself. I sensed that Joe had been treating me a little differently all week. On the night before the game, I asked Enda McNulty if we could have a quiet coffee together in the team hotel. I would speak to Enda once or twice a year but never around game time, our conversations would always take place a week or so out from a game. If a sports psychologist is asked by a player for a sit down the night before a big game, I suppose they know that something is up.

I wanted to see Enda because everything was getting to me. This was different to the normal pre-match pressures. The seed had been planted in my head during the week that this was the first time that I hadn't really been sure of my place. The public and media scrutiny was at its very highest and I wasn't playing overly well. I knew that myself but the constant reminders were bothering me. I would always be pretty self-critical but around this time I knew that things just weren't happening for me.

I said to Enda, listen, I am just waiting for something to happen for me. I need that spark and I don't know where it will come from. You say these things hoping that the other person will hand you back some pearl of wisdom that instantly returns your universe to its rightful state. That never happens.

Enda said, fuck that. He asked me why I was waiting. Why didn't I just go out and make the spark happen for myself? I hadn't become a bad player. My job was not to wait for things to happen. I was better than that.

It reaffirmed something in my own head for me. Go out and do something to show yourself that you can still play. Be that kid you were in Pretoria in 2009. Make the spark.

They started well. Waisake Naholo made a line break and

came one on one with me. The odds were all with him. A big powerful winger coming from midfield is close to impossible to stop. I missed the tackle. That's one of the annoying things about being a full back. No matter how exposed you have been and how powerful the winger was, it goes down on the slate as your fault. They went on and scored the try by George Moala. Five-three after four minutes. Straight away, I've forgotten about creating my own spark.

Here we go, back to getting pumped by the All Blacks. Business as usual.

Then the sparks came…

Just before CJ's try, I made a really good line break of my own. I stepped Aaron Cruden on the inside and moved away from Kieran Read. He caught me at the ankles, just short of the line. It was a twenty five or thirty-metre break. Against the All Blacks. That was the moment I was looking for.

Simon Zebo had come behind me and he'd caught their eye-line as Johnny faked a pass out the back and hit me a short ball. They'd been watching Johnny's eyes and decided that if somebody was looming out the back, he was going to pass out the back. It was a really good pass from Johnny to me. I hit the line and made the break through. Then we scored.

I remember running back and saying to Johnny, thank you so much. And Johnny was looking back at me confused. When did we start doing formal acknowledgements to each other mid-match?

I missed another tackle in the second half which I should have made. This time on Scott Barrett when he got his try. The gap narrowed to four points. I felt a shiver of the old déjà vu. Was this the start of their comeback? Is this Dublin 2013 again? And always the personal dimension. I missed the tackle.

I am going to get so much shit for that they'll need a pressure hose to clean me up.

That try was the high point of the All Black revival though. You have to bully the All Blacks for eighty minutes-plus. Not seventy nine minutes. We'd learned that the hard way. All those crazy intensive defending sessions at the end of training, working for three and a half minutes at a time with Joe in our ears. We'd been hardwired with resilience.

When our big half time lead was being nibbled away, I had thought back to Dublin as we all had. We were constantly referencing that haunting post-match silence in Lansdowne Road 2013. If we don't attack, we told ourselves, we will end up defending and eventually they will score.

We gathered ourselves and went at them again.

Chicago was the most creative performance that we ever produced. We bullied them and we won enough turnovers to make even Joe happy. More importantly, we scored five great tries too. They hadn't conceded five tries in total during the entire Rugby Championship. Our lead was the greatest half-time deficit in All Black history. Seventeen points.

After the game, the changing room was one of the happiest I have ever been in. The release of pressure, the sense of huge relief, the strange idea that the little bit of history we had all longed for had happened now and it couldn't be changed. It was done. No Irish players were going to have to go into pre-game press conferences to mouth the empty formula about believing that on our best day, yeah, maybe…

And, for me, in that selfish corner of the brain where you weigh the personal impact separately from the collective, I knew that I had bought myself another year or eighteen months in the Irish jersey. Two hours beforehand I hadn't been sure if this wouldn't be my last game for Ireland. I was thirty years old. A rugby player at thirty has had a good innings. People are saying goodbye to you, looking over your shoulder to see who is next in line. We had beaten the All Blacks, though, and I still had a career.

There was a great group photo taken in that changing room, beers flying around, everybody a little crazy. David O'Siochain, our PR guy, came into the craziness and put the arm on me. I knew what he wanted. I hadn't done much press and generally he would never ask me to. He senses these things and leaves you be. This time, though, he said you will have to come out Rob, they will want to speak to you.

I said, Dave, you can tell each and every one of them to go do one.

He's a good guy and he would do anything for the team but he wasn't going to do that.

"You have to go out there. This will be good for you. Go out there, talk. They'll be saying good things about you again."

"Ok. Grand."

He was right. In the mythologising of a great win, the two missed tackles which would have been hanging offences on any other day were forgotten. I was declared officially viable again.

We had a quick function with the All Blacks after the game. Sometimes you are not sure about their level of humility and losing is such a rare experience for them we were watching them like hawks for signs that they were taking it badly. We could feed off any bad grace they might show.

In fairness, they were pretty decent in defeat. One of their players had been quoted as saying forlornly that they were going to go down in history as the first All Blacks team to have lost to Ireland. That was fair enough. They were. We were on the happy side of that same equation. If it felt momentous to us, it had to feel the same for them but in the negative.

They gave us no reason to complain. That evening was the first time I felt that we'd wrung a little bit of respect out of them. You don't get that until you have beaten them. Beating us was their normal. There were no parades in New Zealand for beating Ireland. Not losing to us would have been their single biggest motivation. Avoiding historic humiliation.

So coming to Chicago and losing in the style that they did was apocalyptic. Just wearing the magical black jersey was supposed to protect them against Ireland, some sort of positive juju. On the days when they had narrowly escaped from us, they'd never believed that the reprieve wouldn't come.

In Christchurch in 2012 when Dan Carter kicked the late drop goal in a game that, again, we should have won, Richie McCaw gave an interview after the game, just thanking Ireland for a good game today. We were thinking, c'mon Richie, it was better than a good game. You should have lost. Richie wasn't thinking that though. Of course they had won.

After the Lansdowne Road game a year later, he'd said that they had known all along that they would get one more opportunity. They'd just needed to make sure that they took it. That mindset is annoying in ways but very admirable too. Being unshakeable is part of what they are. We'd had the game in our hands and we'd made mistakes and lost. They just kept doing everything right. And afterwards they made that point, knowing that it would gnaw at us. They are always getting inside your head. Sometimes I think they don't even know they're doing it.

So we watched them in Chicago but they were gracious and humble. Steve Hansen came around and shook a lot of hands and offered congratulations and 'well dones' to everybody. There was an element of we'll see you in a couple of weeks. That was natural. Even after the game we'd been joking around about that ourselves. Oh no, we've really gone and poked the bear now.

Mum and Dad were in Chicago. It was a late decision. I had done some ambassador work for Aer Lingus and I'd got an email on Wednesday. They had a few seats on a plane if my parents wanted to go to Chicago. Mum and Dad didn't need to be asked twice. I remember saying to them – as I'd said before every All Blacks game I'd played in – that this could be the one. You wouldn't want to miss this one.

So, after the match, I spent most of the evening with them back in the team hotel just nursing two beers. I was shattered. Mentally it had been one of the toughest weeks of preparation that I have ever had for a game.

It meant a lot having my parents there. The shit you get is tough to take at times but knowing that my family are affected by it can really get to me. You feel responsible that they have to read these things and hear them. In Chicago, I could just see my own relief reflected back in their eyes. They had travelled all over the world through the good times and the bad and this was one of the best days.

The Chicago aftermath was made even more memorable by the intervention of a more distant relative. Myself and Dave had actually been to America a few months earlier in 2016 on his invitation. It was suddenly a lot of contact from a guy who, for years, never wrote, never called.

In June, I had been on a sunny beach when my phone rang. A man on the other end introduced himself as an assistant of Enda Kenny's. That got my attention. He said that US vice president Joe Biden would be in Dublin the next week. Biden's people had done some sort of family tree investigation and they'd hit the absolute jackpot. He turned out to be related to the Kearneys of Cooley, County Louth!

Enda Kenny's assistant informed me that Joe Biden was my sixth or seventh cousin and that the Taoiseach himself would love it if myself and Dave would come to Farmleigh House in the Phoenix Park for a lunch with Biden and a small number of people the following week.

I thought at first that it was a piss-take. The beach I was sitting on was in Barbados and I was sure that this was somebody winding me up. I was either being recorded or I was on speakerphone for the benefit of a room full of amused rugby players.

I called Dave next. He'd checked it out. The next week the two of us went to what was a pretty small lunch. I remember that, beforehand, Enda Kenny had myself and Dave sitting in his office for about an hour before Joe Biden and his full entourage arrived. Just myself, Dave and the Taoiseach having cups of tea and swapping small talk.

By the time lunch started, we were just about drained of our small talk resources. There were forty or fifty people spread over different tables. We were at the table next to Biden's table. At one stage, Enda Kenny came over with a young lad around ten years old, who was introduced as Joe Biden's grandson. An even closer relative of the VP! No wonder we were a whole table away.

Joe himself came over then.

Ah, so you are the Kearneys!

It was all a little surreal. He knew the family. He had already met Mum and Dad and Richard and Sara when he'd gone to Cooley a couple of days beforehand. Next day, there we were on the front page of the *New York Times*. Myself, Dave, Joe Biden with Enda Kenny behind us and Joe Biden's grandson taking a photo.

Joe said, you guys have gotta come to the White House.

We said, yes that sounded good.

It sounded more like one of those exchanges you have when somebody says, you must call in and you say, I certainly will if I'm passing. Neither of you really means anything by it. But later, Dave and I decided that yes, going to the White House did sound quite good. We would be those distant relatives who actually do call in.

We flew out in August. Jamie Heaslip was having his stag in New York at the time so we killed two birds. After New York, we stayed with Joe Biden's brother, Jim, in Philadelphia for a night and then stayed two nights in a hotel in Washington.

We had to negotiate a huge level of security at the White House. Being relatives of Joe didn't speed things up at all. We had to bring our passports, we had to have our phones scanned on the way in and we were told that anything we typed or texted from there on would be recorded by somebody.

We got the full tour of the whole place. We weren't allowed into the more secret rooms but we saw the networks of tunnels, the florist shop, the chocolate shop, the dentist, Joe Biden's office, the Oval Office. Barack Obama was out (so they claimed anyway!) but we got to have a little peek around. A memorable day.

So, back to Chicago. At the post-match dinner, I get a call

256

History makers: At Soldier Field after we had beaten the All Blacks for the first time in 111 years

'**Big players produce in big games**' . . . I felt ready to go after what Joe said to me just before I went out on to the pitch against New Zealand in Chicago

Victory roar: Celebrating a Jacob Stockdale try against Wales in the Six Nations at the Aviva in February 2018

Another step closer: The smile says it all after a Conor Murray try in our win over Scotland in Dublin

Feeling grand: I've never felt so relaxed before a Grand Slam decider at Twickenham as I did on Paddy's weekend in 2018

Memories of 2018: With Mum, Dad, Jess and Richard. *(Far right)* a selfie with my great friends Pierce *(left)* and Andrew who I spotted on the lap of honour

Our year: *(From left)* Tadhg Furlong, Johnny Sexton and Jack McGrath with the Pro 14 trophy and European Champions Cup

Trash the Bridge! *(Left)* with Sean O'Brien, Noel Anderson and Dave – the trophies always came back to the Bridge bar! *(Above)* with Rory Best and more silverware

Perfect summer: Lifting the Lansdowne Cup after the third Test against Australia in Sydney in June

Rolling the dice: I risked a critical injury against the All Blacks in our famous victory in Dublin in 2018

Foursome: (*Left*) with Dad and my brothers at Royal Down Golf Club and (*above*) Richard's 40th with my sister Sara

Blues brothers: With Dave and Luke McGrath. It has been great to see Dave enjoying a glorious Indian summer in his career after being unlucky with injuries. This was my 200th cap for Leinster and Luke's 100th

Shoulder to shoulder: I will never forget the emotion of standing with my team-mates for the anthem

Come in number fifteen: Our number 14 Jordan Larmour can go on to have a glorious career

Uncle Joe's office: I thought it was a wind-up when I was told that US Vice President Joe Biden was related to the Kearneys of Cooley! We took him up on his invitation to visit the White House

Spark: With my fiancée Jess – she is smart, ambitious and the most positive person I know

With a little help from my friends: *(From left)* Andrew, Aonghus, Charlie and Pierce. *(Below)* with Sara, Richard and Dave before my godson Archie's first day at school

This is the end: Leaving the Tokyo Stadium pitch after our Rugby World Cup quarter-final defeat to the All Blacks in 2019

Changing times: Some socially distanced Leinster training with Johnny in July 2020

Happy ending: It was a proud moment to lift the 2020 Pro 14 trophy with Fergus McFadden

The future: I'm already looking ahead to the next challenge

from a private number. The phone has been hopping mental for the whole evening so this is just another call that I ignore. Then I get a text message from Joe Biden's brother, Jim.

Uncle Joe wants to speak to you. Call him on this number.

So I call and the vice president of the United States answers.

He said, hey, I am sorry I couldn't call you but the Russians have hacked all our phones and they are listening to everything. This is the secure line though.

I thought, what exactly is going on here? Any line that I have the number for can't really be such a secure line can it?

Joe Biden said that he had watched the game. He thought it was an amazing thing that we had beaten the All Blacks in Chicago on the week that the Cubs had won the World Series etc. It was a short conversation but on the day that was in it, a nice call to get from a relative.

I think we all know what's happened to him since!

Two weeks later in Dublin, as we expected they would, the All Blacks came at us with furious physicality. I felt throughout that game that we were absorbing so much, whereas in Chicago we had exerted so much. There was definitely a little shift in the momentum of the game. They came out just to kick the crap out of us. And they did that. Probably illegally a lot of the time. We didn't play badly, though. They just played very well that day.

I still think that when Joe Schmidt had planned the autumn of 2016 he intended the ambush at the pass to take place in Lansdowne not Chicago. Joe being Joe, though, he took everything he could from that two-game series. There were things he wanted to illustrate from our win and lessons he wanted to apply from our loss. The whole business had an unfinished feel to it. The next time we would play the All Blacks would be the true test of both teams.

That series against the All Blacks felt like an emphatic way to put a line under the difficult period which had begun with the World Cup calamity against Argentina. As a team, we had pulled out of what threatened to be a nosedive. As a player, the work that I had done in Santry with Enda and continued to do every day with Karl had transformed me as an athlete. I hadn't been bullet-proofed against the injuries that professional rugby inflicts on the body as a matter of course but I was confident that I was done with all the irritating breakdowns of my own body which had been costing me so many games.

Of course, life doesn't work that way. I just started collecting rugby injuries at a greater rate. First, I tore the posterior cruciate ligament in Glasgow. Soon I added a broken small bone in my ankle and a ruptured bicep. 2017 was to be a Lions tour year. Would I have got in? I don't think so but I wanted to give myself every chance.

Had it been a year later, in 2018, when I was really getting the full benefits of Enda and Karl's work with me, it might have been very different. In 2017, though, I tore my bicep in the second Six Nations game against Italy. I decided to tough it out. I'm not sure how I even played against France and Wales. I wasn't able to pass from left to right and I couldn't tackle by grabbing.

I was just so obsessed at that stage with getting international caps I refused to give up. I hurt my knee again in the Wales game and finally I had no choice but to miss the last match of the campaign against England. That, of course, was the one game that Lions coach Warren Gatland came to watch in

Dublin. Jared Payne came in at fifteen, his first game of the championships. He was back from an injury himself and he went pretty well.

I wasn't confident about the Lions. My involvement in 2013 had been pretty peripheral but the following week I called Éanna Falvey, who was our former Ireland doctor and the Lions doctor at that time.

I told Éanna that I needed to make a decision whether to get my bicep operated on. After a rupture, you have a five to six week window of the surgeons being able to operate by using your own tendon to re-attach the muscle back down your arm. If you wait longer than that, the tendon sticks to your muscle and gets lost in the muscle. Then you have to use a cadaver tendon. I was prepared to take that risk if it meant going on the Lions tour.

I asked Éanna if he could ask Gats a question. Where was I in his thoughts? Knowing where I stood would help me to make this decision. Éanna called me back the next day and said, listen, you're pretty close but you're carrying an injury and Gats has said that he is only taking two full backs. Most likely Stuart Hogg and Leigh Halfpenny. And he is going to use Liam Williams as cover.

Éanna was perhaps being gentle in telling me that I was pretty close but that was the decision made for me. I knew that I had to get the bicep done. It was a blessing in disguise. In hindsight, travelling with a busted bicep would have been a crazy thing to do. It was giving me such pain and the subsequent surgery turned out to be so much more complicated that I'd anticipated.

At the back of my mind, though, was the thought that 2017 would be my last chance, that I had an understanding of the type of game that New Zealand play, that they kick a huge amount of ball and that I have always been comfortable with that.

I did feel that I could have added value on that tour. Yet when I look back at the way 2018 unfolded, I know that I was blessed to have had the decision made for me. I got knee surgery on March 26th, my birthday, and then the following week I went over to Manchester to get the bicep surgery done.

So I was out for the remainder of that season. No Lions. No summer tour. Just focussing on getting myself back and ready to go for the start of the 2017-18 season. Back for September 2017. I think it was maybe only the second time in ten years where I had played pre-season warm-up games with Leinster. I had always been coming off the back of summer tours before that. I felt that I was ready for a new beginning.

One of my first games back in September was the first home game of Leinster's season. Cardiff at the RDS. A modest occasion. I got another huge hamstring tear. A high grade two tear, which translates to six to eight weeks out of action.

For the first time in my career I thought, that's it, you've had it now. You have done all this work. You fixed up every deficiency. Your body is telling you that enough is enough. Heed the message. You are done.

13

2018 AND ALL THAT

It was January 2018. I'd had the Christmas off. I was back home in Cooley on the couch, just stuffing my face and keeping an eye on the lads who were playing down in Thomond. It was an ordinary enough game in so far as the Leinster versus Munster tradition goes. Then, with eleven minutes to go, Jordan Larmour took a catch deep in his own half and set off. He left a trail of red Munster jerseys tackling fresh air behind him. He didn't stop running and jinking until he had scored the try that made a dull game instantly memorable.

Oh, for Christ's sake, I thought, here we go! Jordan Larmour has just ruined my Christmas and my new year. Fully ruined the holidays! I had to laugh. Jordan!

The media hit full messiah mode. I woke up the next day and

every report was essentially saying the same thing. We have seen the future and its name is Jordan Larmour. His wonder try has redefined the limits of human motion. Blah blah blah.

I know that Leo Cullen and Stuart Lancaster were reading all these reports over their porridge and purring to themselves. With Leinster, Stuart and Leo have been very keen on bringing young lads through and the morning headlines would be a strong affirmation of their faith. They like to give the young lads as much experience as they can give them and I fully embrace that culture, except when it applies to the number fifteen jersey.

What a start to the new year! I knew that Stuart and Leo still hadn't got the 'Joey Carbery as full back' experiment out of their systems yet. Until recently, Joey had been playing at fifteen occasionally and Stuart had really enjoyed those games.

Having triumphantly declared myself fully repaired after Santry in 2016, the next season, 2017, had brought the bicep rupture, the knee injury, the ankle problems. All unfortunate rugby injuries, but my absence had created the chance for Joey to play full back for Leinster in the Heineken Cup quarter-final against Wasps. On the day, Wasps weren't great but Joey was superb. He took the Man of the Match award.

Leinster then went to Lyon and lost to Clermont in the semi-final. Joey was as good as ever when attacking but he had a tougher afternoon defensively. It was an experience which I hoped wouldn't have softened his view of the full back position. Leinster had needed to catch a late restart to stay in with a chance late on but had lost possession and Clermont just played the phases and ran down the clock. Gavin Cummiskey, no fan of mine, wrote that 'Rob Kearney probably would have caught that late Clermont restart.' I'd wondered if the sentence was supposed to begin with 'Even Rob Kearney...'

It seemed, though, that the version of Joey which Stuart had seen against Wasps was the one which Stuart was choosing to place his faith in. And I was injured again, so why not? I was in the midst of yet more rehabbing, Leinster were now going a different way and that was how the 2016-17 season had ended and the following season had begun.

Leinster wanted to be a modern team where the full back operates as a second playmaker. Saracens, when they had been the team to beat, had Owen Farrell at fly half and Alex Goode at fifteen. Two playmakers. And Stuart and Leo liked that set-up a lot. If Joey stayed at Leinster, he could be playing fifteen if he wanted to. I knew, though, that Joey really wanted to play fly half. I was quietly hoping that Joey would go to Munster to do precisely that. It's tough losing your jersey at the best of times, but losing it to somebody who's only half interested in wearing it?

One evening, I had heard Stuart on the radio speaking enthusiastically about what great players Joey and Jordan were, how they were both superb fifteens. I was thinking, well, blow me down, I'm really up against it here now. Not one but two of them are breathing down my collar.

It was hard to hear Stuart saying that. Joey had no real experience at full back. He hadn't played a huge amount of games but Leinster were putting him there. His style fitted Stuart's game plan and, in the short term, it also solved the problem of getting Joey the game time which he wasn't getting at ten.

I rested my hopes on Joey's desire to play ten. I knew that Joe Schmidt was telling Joey that he needed him to be playing out-half and that Joey was fighting for the Johnny Sexton back-up role with Ross Byrne but not getting picked ahead of Ross too much at the time. So the pressure was on for Joey to go some place that would play him as a ten and not a fifteen. That was fair enough in my view. As the national coach, Joe wanted his back-up out-half to be playing ten every week. Playing full back wasn't going to get Joey picked.

Now Stuart was on the airwaves rhapsodising about both Joey and Jordan. The club had apparently come to see the number fifteen position as a round hole and me as a square peg.

Jordan was just fresh out of the academy and had only signed his first senior contract that January. Anybody who had seen him since his schoolboy days knew that he was going to be a serious player. I hadn't reckoned on him putting together a highlights reel quite this fast though.

Suddenly it felt as if everybody would be happier if I just faded away gracefully. With the amount of injuries I had been having, people may have been under the impression that was what I was doing anyway.

On the plus side, in January 2018 I was still the Ireland full back. I felt like that man who is forgotten but not gone. Until I was actually gone, I had some hope.

When I got the grade two hamstring tear, I naturally called Enda King and asked the obvious questions. What is this? Why is it still happening? I had convinced myself that these injuries were a thing of the past. Now I was completely down about it all. There was no light at the end of this tunnel.

Fortunately, Enda King and Karl Denvir are two incredibly positive people. Deep down they may have been thinking the same things that I was thinking. He's done all this work and this has still happened. Maybe his time has come. He's permanently crocked.

I did a lot of work with Karl over the next few weeks and I went back to Santry for more slog with Enda King. I managed to get back for a game for Leinster against Ulster in Ravenhill in October before the November internationals loomed.

I was still very much on the back foot physically and mentally. If I actually was in decline and my body wasn't able for it, that meant the end of my career was coming at me very quickly. I wasn't braced for that impact. As regards Ireland, Tiernan O'Halloran and Jared Payne had possibly moved ahead of me. At the very least they were breathing down my neck. Tiernan had been excellent for Connacht in the Pro 14 final when I'd stunk the place out.

I had got a call from Joe on the morning that he was announcing his squad for November. He said he probably wasn't going to be including me. Naturally, the hamstring injury cropped up in the conversation. Joe told me that I needed to get my body right. That was all I needed to be concerned about for now.

In that situation, it's hard to know if you are just being let down gently. Was Joe saying, well, he's done all his specialist work that he asked for extra time for last summer and now he's broken yet again? Was Joe just letting me come to the realisation myself that I was done? I'd miss the November games and I'd be old news by the time the Six Nations came around.

Towards the end of the conversation, Joe asked me how my rehab was going, how far along I was. I'd had these chats with Joe several times over the years and I sensed the opening.

I said, it's funny you should ask that Joe, because I've only just sprinted at ninety per cent of my top speed.

In the next couple of seconds of silence I could almost hear Joe thinking to himself. Maybe...

I don't know what his lines of communication were into the club but the session had just happened and it had gone a lot better than I'd hoped it would. I'd felt good. I was back sprinting again.

So Joe reversed course and he put me in the squad for the November internationals. I played my comeback for Leinster that Saturday against Ulster and then I was named to play full back against South Africa two weeks later, having only played maybe two games in the previous five or six months. Joe had backed me again. I felt like I still had a career.

Over the Christmas break, I had rationalised the Joey Carbery situation. As happy as it made Stuart and Leo to see Joey at full back, Joey's greatest potential lay with what he brought to the number ten spot.

I could survive the threat of Joey because Joey didn't necessarily want to be a full back threat. Jordan, even before his new year wonder try, was young and gifted but I surely would be able to hold him off for a year or two as he developed. Thankfully, Jordan wasn't a one trick pony. He could be used on the wing for a while as I had been while I was apprentice to Girvan.

That left Leo and Stuart and the style they wanted the team to play. That style, I felt, involved not picking me in the team. Whatever explosiveness I once had was ebbing away with age and injury and I had grown more conservative about full back play anyway.

The 51 per cent goalkeeper, 49 per cent attacker ratio didn't suit a Leinster side who were now very much all about attack, attack, attack. Whether or not I was playing for Ireland was immaterial to Leinster. Leo and Stuart only cared about their team doing well and they were right. I started to feel that my face may no longer fit.

The main thing to emerge from all that festive introspection was a huge shift in my own mindset. What would be, would be, I could only look after my own peanut stall. I could only control the controllables, as they say. Having reached a dead end with worrying about what everybody else was doing, I decided to just go out and really enjoy my last couple of years of playing the sport that I'd always wanted to play.

In 2018, every international game that I went to I consciously reminded myself to appreciate it. I knew what it was like not to be involved. Every game could be your last game, so just enjoy it.

With Joe, I always knew that I would get picked – not because of the things that I do well but because I would always have the lowest error count among the available alternatives. When the margins are tight, errors are the enemy.

Joe would pick me because the full back's work is mainly done while everybody else is watching the ball. You prowl behind the play, cutting off one option while anticipating the next. You shout to get the other two thirds of the back three to the places where they need to be. That's the bread and butter.

I had become more cautious in how I played the game but that was rational too. I didn't have the resources to be cavalier. For two years, every time I'd burst with the ball in my hand, I was waiting for a hamstring to rip. So I steered away from those explosive moments. When I watched Jordan gallop through

Thomond Park, I envied him his youth and his hamstrings but I knew that I would have to continue with doing more mundane things with a boring consistency. I didn't care about the tepid reviews because I knew I was doing what would get me picked for Ireland.

And, with Leinster, I meant it when I said to Leo that my value only came into play toward the end of a season. We happily play an all-out attacking game with two playmakers when the stakes are lower. Against the big boys, though, there is a chance I will get called in. We grow more conservative when springtime rolls around.

Ultimately, Joey's career would resolve itself without any reference to me. He was serious about challenging for Johnny's green jersey and he had to find the stage to develop those skills. Johnny would sense that in his own time. It comes with the territory. When you are past thirty, you see your own successors standing right behind you. It would be bizarre if you looked over your shoulder and saw nobody at all. That was all that was happening with myself at Leinster. I had once fidgeted impatiently behind Girvan. Jordan was only doing what I had done but with better grace.

So I learned to stop worrying. I'd gamble on doing what I was good at and just see how 2018 unravelled.

I wrote some notes in the sunshine of Dubai in the week after we had won the Grand Slam. On the Tuesday, Jess and I had flown out in the company of Conor Murray, Peter O'Mahony, Keith Earls, Rory Best and all the plus-ones.

We just had a week of drinking Peronis and playing cards on the beach. Pete got engaged to Jessica in the pizzeria on the last night before we went home. There was a feeling of quiet happiness among us all week. We had shared something unique. These were some of the lads I would have been close to throughout the campaign and Dubai was a great way to write the postscript. For some reason, I wanted to scribble a few words down. In my career, so many occasions like this have passed by without me paying attention.

I wrote about the strangeness of how Paddy Jackson and Stuart Olding's trial in Belfast had cast its long shadow. I wrote about the week of preparation we took as a team in Spain when we had just chilled for a couple of days before the Wednesday morning, when the coaches nailed up our plan for the season. We set out to win a Grand Slam and agreed not to be shy about it. No more doing what Irish teams do, saying we would give it a lash and we'd see what might happen. We planned to win it all. That was a very distinct switch in mindset for an Irish side going into a tournament.

In Paris on the very first day, we could have come undone. It poured with rain and we were playing with a slippy ball but somehow we were able to execute those forty-odd phases before Johnny hit that stunning drop goal from forty metres out to win at the death. It was an incredible moment. If you give that same team one hundred more of those opportunities, how many of them would we take? Very few but we met the moment. We applied the lesson we had been learning ever since New Zealand did something similar to us in 2013.

After France, we knew that we had used up one of our lives. We had been very, very lucky. France were the better team and for all our talk back in Spain in the awful conditions we hadn't got out of first gear. Having survived brought us clarity though.

In twelve campaigns, I had never known a group to be as close as that team. Our togetherness was incredible.

Often people ask how it compared to 2009. It's difficult to make a comparison. 2009 almost happened organically. We had no great expectations in our heads or in our discussions. We never looked beyond the next game. It was my second championship. Declan Kidney's first. The team rested on the three girders of O'Driscoll, O'Gara, O'Connell.

Nine years later, we had a different culture and the whole game of rugby had changed. The ante had been upped but we did exactly what we had planned to do. Giving it a good lash was never going to be enough. The load was spread more evenly through the team. In 2018, Joe was Joe. In 2009, Deccie was Deccie. Each the right man for their time.

The game with Italy was a routine day. We were comfortable within ourselves and gathered ourselves for the Welsh.

Wales was the biggest game, the hinge of the season. We had the most intense week of prep ever. I remember Andy Farrell building us up at 9pm on the Wednesday night before the game. I had decided I was going to enjoy every game but that week I was beset with huge nerves.

Wales didn't get out of the blocks, though, and we allowed ourselves a mid-tournament piss-up. A brilliant night out. We had the Beast from the East howling across the country at that time. There was snow on the ground. Conor Murray and Bestie were among those who couldn't get home. They wound up staying in my house that night.

For Scotland, the weather meant that we had very limited prep. Two days of training on half a field. We were staying at Carton House and the groundskeepers from the golf course pulled the snow off half the pitch so we had a little space to work with. It limited preparation a little bit. We knew, though, that if we won that game the championship was probably ours.

To their credit, the Scots brought their A game. They attacked but we had been working on a good defensive set-up all week. Their best laid plans came to nothing every time. I ended up with a Man of the Match award.

England lost to France a little later on. Not for the first time, we found ourselves sitting with the disappointed Scots as our fate was being decided somewhere else. Our focus on the Grand Slam was so intense that not one of us celebrated or even acknowledged the scoreline.

It was as impressive as anything we did on the field that spring. There we were at the post-match reception with the Scots in the Aviva suite. Sponsors, guests and committee members were milling about in abundance, watching the English game and being raucous after a good day.

England's loss meant that the championship was ours, regardless of what result we might achieve in Twickenham. The room burst into life with hundreds of people celebrating. The Irish and the Scottish players just sat there, completely impassive as if we had both just received some disappointing news.

Not one Irish player acknowledged the championship, let alone celebrated it. We were so focussed on going to Twickenham to win a Grand Slam. Anything less would be a disappointment. That was uniquely 2018. Two hours after playing a Test match, we were already dialled into the next week. I was sitting at a table with Rory Best, Keith Earls and Jess, Jodie and Edel. I'm not even sure who the others at the table were. The events in Paris meant nothing to us.

To London on Paddy's weekend. I kept asking myself where my nerves had gone. I have never felt so relaxed before a game, let alone a Grand Slam match in London on Paddy's weekend.

My confidence was high. I was playing well. All the worries I had carried into the new year were gone. Some of the other boys were telling me that the jitters were the worst they had felt in years. Keith Earls and I played up the old soldier routine, announcing the night before the game that if we won we'd hang up our boots the next day and happily vacate the scene.

The game complemented my relaxed mood. We were 21-5 ahead at half time. Forty minutes away from the history books. I'd never counted chickens before they hatched but I found myself quietly thinking that I had started twenty out of twenty of our four championship wins. An Irishman in Twickenham counting his chickens and his blessings. Luxury undreamed of.

The end was just a surge of adrenalin and relief. The pressure we had created for ourselves was gone. The weather put paid to the idea of a reception in Dublin so we dallied the next day in London. Probably the best craic that we have had in a long while came the morning after the game. Everyone came down to the team room in their suits at 10am, ready to fly back for the homecoming. There was an announcement that the flight was delayed indefinitely. We now had no formalities to attend to in Dublin. I just remember it being a long morning at a table with Conor Murray, Peter O'Mahony, Johnny and Rory. The day began with us drinking espresso martinis at ten in the morning.

There was a sing-song and music blaring in the team room. Coaches and staff were all involved. Everybody got up for a song. We hadn't hit our beds the night before till four in the morning. We'd just been singing in the hotel basement bar for hours.

When we arrived home on our delayed flight, the fire engines were out on the airport tarmac spraying their hoses in the air so that, in the evening light, they made a rainbow arc to honour us. We stayed in the Shelbourne that evening. Christy Moore came in and played to the whole squad plus family and friends. Another great sing-song till we were hoarse.

There was a little dancefloor in the banquet room. The trophy was left in the middle of the floor with most of the team dancing happily around it. One of those unique moments I will always remember with a smile.

It had been a very different week. We were in Carton House in our own room until Thursday when we flew over to Richmond. In the hotel we stayed in, we all had our own rooms as well. Jess came over on the morning of the game and she stayed in the hotel that night. Everything felt different about the week as if we had at last learned how to be at ease with expectation.

It was all a revelation for me. As a veteran, you shouldn't feel newness but I got so much out of the entire season. I enjoyed the big occasions much more in 2018 than I ever did before. The first five or six years of my career, I took the big days for granted. The next few years I worried myself into dark corners about injuries and performance level and what everybody else was doing.

I had changed a couple of things for 2018. I shifted three kilos of weight. I would have historically played at ninety three/ ninety four kilos but, in 2018, I was around ninety/ninety one. The older you get, the more you want to be a little bit lighter. The game was changing and, at Leinster especially, I was going to have to do a hell of a lot more running due to the style we were playing.

After years of tampering, the changes I was making to myself physically were paying off.

After Dubai, we got down to the business of club rugby again. Rumours circulated about Joey being wooed by Ulster and then Munster began courting him. He was well-liked within the group but there was an acceptance that Joey would have to do what was best for him.

After all the worry, I was in the fifteen jersey for all the European games that season. We had an unbeaten Heineken Cup season and the knockout wins over Saracens, Scarlets and in the final, Racing, were an affirmation of all the work that Leo and Stuart had been doing to build a powerful franchise. In late May, we played Scarlets again in the Pro 14 final and finished the season with another trophy.

The theme of consciously enjoying this late career renaissance continued for me. Our Heineken Cup celebration was maybe the most enjoyable night of celebration that I have had as a player. It was the most fun. With the provincial team-mates, it is usually that little bit better than internationals but 2018 was especially good.

The principal scenes took place in The Bridge 1859 Bar in Ballsbridge. It was one of the most loose nights out we have ever had. We took the two rooms upstairs in the bridge and we went mental. There was lots of raucous singing and jumping around with abandonment. I thought that the roof would collapse on the place.

It is important to note that The Bridge is one of the pubs that myself and a few of the lads co-own. The other is the Lemon and Duke pub in Dublin city centre. For some reason, anytime the lads go The Bridge or the Lemon and Duke, they always have this idea of trying to trash the place. This is amusing to them. They get a real kick out of it.

Picture the scene. We were walking to The Bridge that night, forty celebrating rugby lads. Pretty much everybody without a financial interest in The Bridge is cheerfully chanting "trash The Bridge, trash The Bridge." They are half joking and half not joking. The enjoyment of my night hinges on which half wins out.

So, beset by common sense even on the big nights out, I'm calling up the others involved and I'm getting onto our manager and another co-owner Noel Anderson, wondering if we might need security for the party I am with. I don't know what is going to happen here, I tell Noel, suddenly soberly conscious that I am taking the team to our bar and asking for security for our visit.

The Bridge still stands.

One of the great things when you celebrate a win is having the trophy in the pub with you for the night. It's an inanimate object but its presence lends a different and brilliant sort of feeling as when we danced around the Six Nations trophy for half the night in the Shelbourne.

When you are all in the bar and the trophy is there in the middle of the mayhem and it is being passed around or danced around, it feels unique and tribal.

When we got to The Bridge that night, it was noticed that the trophy was missing. On these occasions, a certain man called Johnny O'Hagan always looks after the trophy. He's the bag man for the team and in many ways he is much more than that. He has been around the club for God knows how long, certainly long before I was ever there. He is the longest-standing member of the club by a long shot.

Johnny is also a very single-minded man who does what he wants to do or what he needs to do. He gets everything done his way. For instance, he looks after all the gear and the balls. He has a Portakabin for storage down in Donnybrook. We always joke that it is full of old gear and rugby balls and all the stuff he never gave us over the years. Sometimes we are training with balls with no grip, balls that are losing their shape and Johnny will be telling us that there are no new balls, no new balls.

Then, in May, with the season almost done, he might bring out forty new balls. He is a serious hoarder and he has been an integral part of Leinster through all the good days and the bad days, somebody that everybody has a huge amount of respect for.

He is one of those characters that is an awful lot more powerful than their job title suggests. There is a lot more to what Johnny O'Hagan does than giving out the gear and getting things ready.

But, on this night of celebration, both Johnny and the Cup are missing.

Myself and Johnny Sexton began calling around to find out where the trophy we'd won was. Word came back through Leo. Johnny O'Hagan has the trophy in Kiely's of Donnybrook. Best of luck trying to get that back!

Kiely's was Johnny's local. He was loyal to the place. This was a solid lead.

Detectives Kearney and Sexton said what the hell and commandeered a taxi to take them to Kiely's. The trip might take Detective Kearney's mind off the pending destruction of his pub.

Into Kiely's and there they are. Larger than life. Johnny O'Hagan and the Heineken Cup. Negotiations follow.

We won the trophy, Johnny. It's our trophy as well. Please give us back the trophy.

No, get out of here. I've been here longer than the two of ya together and I'll be here after ye're gone!

But Johnny. You've had a go of the trophy.

The trophy is commandeered. Last words.

Now piss off to that shithole The Bridge, he joked, and drink the expensive drinks that ye can't hold and ye overcharge for.

As I said, Johnny was extremely loyal to Kiely's!

We were gone for about twenty minutes, half an hour. That's how long it took us to finally get the trophy back. We'd played matches for it that were easier. Johnny wasn't happy. This was serious business. We knew we'd be playing with misshapen rugby balls for some time as a consequence.

We took the trophy back into The Bridge. Up the stairs, and when people see it arriving, everybody goes ballistic. The trophy is here. The trophy is here.

No thanks offered to Detectives Kearney and Sexton.

The night is such a happy blur. My final memory is a moment of brief conflict between the old rugby culture that I started out in and the new professionalism.

Noel Anderson is proposing that he'll fill the cup with spirits. There are calls for vodka, for rum, for whiskey, whatever…

And in the midst of the mayhem there comes an anguished voice.

No. No. No.

It's Jordi Murphy. He's pleading for good sense.

– We've to play Munster on Friday. Just fill it up with beer.

Quote of the evening.

Footnote. Those nights are strictly team-only. As an unwritten rule, nobody brings outsiders.

In the aftermath, though, word spread through the network of significant others that good times were had in their absence.

The pressure was on and two weeks later when we won the league and there was a movement toward another night back at The Bridge, the girls got invited along. The experiment was short-lived. After two or three hours, the women decided as a group to evacuate and (with another quote of the evening) "leave you animals to yourselves."

I was operating in some sort of dreamland in 2018. I was playing every game through the season, having had years when I couldn't put together two back-to-back games.

In the summer, we went to Australia for the three-Test series and I played every game down there too. When the year was tallied up, the first Test down under was my only experience of losing all through 2018.

This remission from injury and worry began to feel like pure luck. It changed my perspective in a positive way. When I took a bird's eye view of my career, the games I had missed would broadly have been the ones that I would have elected to miss if I had been handed a list and forced to choose for myself the day when I would be marked absent.

I wished, of course, that I had met Enda King and proceeded to work with Karl a few years earlier than I did but I had only to glance across at my brother Dave and the damage that injury has done to his career to know how lucky I had been.

It was indulgent to even consider it but I needed my body to do me one last favour in 2018.

All Blacks. Dublin 2018

Between traditional rugby injuries and the accelerated wear and tear the professional game inflicts, most players learn more

278

about how their bodies are put together than they ever wanted to. Most of my career memories are of events which happened on grass but if I needed to, I could produce a memoir about the other life spent on physio tables and in operating rooms and in rehab sessions.

For me, 2018 was the greatest season that I have had. I know that I played better rugby in 2012 but I was young and I had a different body back then. For me to have been able to play really good rugby in 2018 was the result of a lot of hard work and mental resilience. I had put my body back together bit by bit in the two or three years beforehand. Playing at all was a relief. Having a season like 2018 just gave me a huge amount of satisfaction.

I strung long sequences of games together as we won another Grand Slam, another Heineken Cup and triumphed in Australia. The year was a series of wishes ticked off and everything built incrementally to the November showstopper in Lansdowne Road when the All Blacks would come to town. We would be challenging them for the number one spot in the world rankings. A few weeks beforehand, Leinster travelled to Italy for a Pro 14 game with Benetton. I came off early in the second half. The papers noted for the umpteenth time that I was an 'injury concern' for the November series. A shoulder problem, they thought. Another anatomy lesson was on its way.

Pay attention now. You have your AC (acromioclavicular joint which connects the clavicle/collarbone to the highest point of your shoulder blade, the acromion) and you have your SC (sternoclavicular joint which connects your clavicle/collarbone to the breastbone/sternum).

The SC and AC joints keep the shoulder stable. The clavicle

is the only long bone in your body which lies horizontally. So if you are a cyclist and you come flying off your bike, you will often injure the SC or AC, usually the AC. Also, if you are a rugby player and you get really smoked from the side in a tackle, you may be in trouble with your clavicle too.

I got smoked in just such a tackle against Benetton in Treviso and I subluxed my SC joint. When your joint is subluxed, it feels like the word it almost rhymes with. You feel completely subluxed. It is basically a partial dislocation and it was without doubt the most painful injury I've ever had. There are apparently three ways of subluxing your SC joint. Anterior (popping it forwards), inferior (downwards) and the rarely seen posterior subluxation.

I suffered the rarely seen posterior subluxation which means that the joint got displaced in a backwards fashion. The entire joint shifted backwards by forty per cent. When it shifts in this direction, it threatens all manner of vital parts from the oesophagus, to your trachea to some key blood vessels like the vena cava and the aorta. It's very dangerous and it hurts like nothing else I have experienced injury-wise.

There was a new doctor with Leinster for that game. Stuart Flanagan was the new guy and it was his first away trip and I got this rare injury. The trouble became apparent when my voice began to go after I had been taken off the field. Stuart was immediately thinking of rushing me to hospital in Italy straight away. Leaving a player behind in hospital is a big decision, though. Stuart phoned the head of the Leinster medical team, John Ryan. I was handed the phone to try to speak to John who asked me a few questions and told Stuart to bring me home. That was October 28th. Ireland were playing New Zealand on November 17th.

I knew that I had no right to play in that game. I knew that if I was smart, I wouldn't even think about playing in it. I had a very dangerous injury that had no chance of healing fully in time.

I turned up at the Irish training camp on the first week of November. Ciaran Cosgrave, the doctor, wanted to send me home. He told me straight, you won't be playing rugby for some time.

The problem was that with the joint being so close to key arteries, nobody wants to go near it. There was no talk of pain medication for this one. If the injury is traumatic enough and any of those things which the clavicle shields is compromised, the treatment is often immediate surgery.

Ciaran is a really trustworthy doctor who will always put the players' health first. Although I would sometimes have put a lot of pressure on Ciaran to allow me to return from injury earlier than advised, a decision is made following detailed discussions. Sometimes, if the risk is low enough, the medical staff relent. Sometimes, if the risk is deemed too great, the decision stands. The decision is always made jointly between, player, medic and sometimes the coach.

I wasn't in the category that required immediate surgery thankfully but I was told that if I got hit again and the joint got displaced further backwards, there was a danger of pressing on the blood vessels linked to the heart.

A couple of days later, Leinster headed off to South Africa to play Southern Kings without me.

I went to see Hannan Mullett, one of the leading surgeons dealing with this type of injury. I wanted to know if I would need surgery and if getting surgery would speed things up. Hannan told me that he doesn't like doing those type of surgeries unless fully necessary. When he does them, he needs to have a cardiothoracic surgeon standing beside him at all times in case there are any complications. His advice was that he didn't want to operate on it. The joint would slowly recover with rehab and the right sort of bracing.

I was impatient. I knew that I was putting my desire to play against the All Blacks ahead of my welfare but I couldn't get the game out of my head. They were one, we were two. This was our chance to swap positions. It was billed as the rugby game of the season and the deciding rubber of a series that began in 2016.

So I asked Hannan Mullett if he thought that I could play. I basically wanted him to sign me off to play. He said he'd sign me off but I should know the risk. On the other hand, he thought it was academic anyway because he really didn't think I would be able to play.

"If you really, honestly feel as if you are able to perform your job on the field, then you can play. But I don't think that is likely."

Back in Ireland camp, Ciaran Cosgrave was more cautious than Mr Mullet. He just didn't want me to play until he was one hundred per cent confident about my safety.

In the meantime, Ireland were to play Italy in Chicago. I announced that I was feeling better, mending well. I wasn't fine but I wanted Joe to keep me in the squad.

He had a panel of forty two in Carton House for the November series and only twenty six were travelling to the US. If I dropped out of the 42, my season was over. If I could stay back and keep working while they were in Chicago, then I had a chance. Jordan scored three tries over there which was a little worrying. I was still unavailable the following week, so

Jordan kept the fifteen jersey for the more demanding game against Argentina.

There were other conversations going on around me. I will never forget the conversation with Mum on Thursday the week of that game. She didn't want me to play. Herself and my fiancée Jess were having conversations during the week. Jess didn't want me to play either. She would never interfere when it comes to games or injuries but this was different and the two of them were having their own chats.

He can't play.

You have to tell him not to play.

Somebody will have to tell him he can't play.

Myself and Dad were having conversations too. Mum would tell him to tell me not to play, that it was too dangerous, but Dad knew to leave me to my own devices.

I took to ignoring calls a little bit during the week. At the start of the week, I had intimated that I wasn't playing but later I was having second thoughts. I knew it was too painful and potentially dangerous if I got another tackle that pushed the joint back further. The doctor and the surgeon weren't fully convinced yet.

Then, on Thursday, I had to tell Mum that I had decided to roll the dice. That was one tough telephone call.

Senior rugby players get to know their physio pretty well, and vice versa. Karl Denvir knew more than anybody how much the game meant to me. Karl had gone away and done a lot of research on the injury. It boiled down to the fact that in thirteen years of professional rugby, I had suffered one tackle like the one I took in Treviso. The chances of getting another one just three weeks later were slim. The odds were long on getting the same injury again but the price was very high if

I did. If I could endure the pain and live with the risk, Karl thought I should play. If we won and I watched from the sideline he knew that I would always be paying a different sort of price for a long time.

We trained on Monday which would have been a non-contact day. It was ok for me. Bearable. My mind was switching back towards playing. On Tuesday morning I was named in the team. Straight away there was huge pressure on me to play at the weekend. Named in the team, I was the only one who could change that. I would have to go to Joe and pull out. I might forfeit a chance at another camp. On that Tuesday, I could see him watching my every move, but not having any specific sort of dialogue with me. Maybe neither of us wanted to have that conversation.

I remember having a talk with Ciaran Cosgrave on that Tuesday afternoon after I had been named in the team. I said, listen, it's improving but still a little sore. I was trying to understate things a little so I could gauge his reaction. It was actually worse than 'pretty sore'. It was very painful. I was still in two minds about playing. I suppose if Ciaran had heard the words 'pretty sore' and marched off to Joe and pulled me out of the team then it would have been out of my hands. By not telling him that I was in a lot of pain, I convinced myself that I was medically approved to play.

Ciaran stood with me and put me through a pretty rigorous contact circuit to make sure I could perform my job. Once he could see me take repeated contact and the joint was stable, he was happy that further risk was minimal.

On the morning of the game, Richard and my godson Archie came into the Shelbourne to collect tickets. Archie was five years of age. He saw me and jumped up to give me a hug.

When I held him, I could feel this awful tug and I dropped him to the floor. I noticed Richard just staring at me, concern written in his face.

I wasn't feeling pain, though, when we were standing for the anthem. The usual adrenalin flowed through me for a few minutes. I love those moments when the anthem is being belted out in Dublin before a huge game. Nothing would take away from that. After that, though, any sort of movement that turned my shoulder just sent a crazy voltage of pain through my body. Had it been any other game, I absolutely would not have played.

Any time the game demanded my involvement I just had to brace myself mentally, throw myself into it and deal with the pain afterwards. I remember at one stage going up for a high ball and landing down on that shoulder. That was bad. Contact like that would mean that a sharp pain would come for ten seconds or so and then I just had to get up and carry on again. Fortunately, the opposition would never really target an injury out on the field, particularly as they couldn't see the strapping under my jersey. On the other hand, the All Blacks don't tend to be gentle with you either.

I played well. I came off after sixty five minutes. It was too painful by then and I couldn't continue. I had done more than I wanted to do. I just kept thinking of the history books. The first Irish team to beat New Zealand on home soil. I had needed my name to be on that teamsheet.

Against New Zealand that day, our ability to keep them try-less was incredible. Everyone will tell you Jacob's try was straight out of the Joe Schmidt play book. Everyone is right!

That is where Joe's great value as a coach was. Breaking down opponents. For all the criticism that some of Joe's teams

– especially toward the end – lacked shape in the phase play, we won so many games and so many trophies on the back of his ability to think up power plays. That day against the All Blacks was the high point.

Beating New Zealand in Lansdowne Road! I will always remember the changing room after we beat them in Dublin. That was an incredible occasion. If we had caught them off guard in Chicago, we proved ourselves this day when the cards were all on the table. The big room filled with a huge sense of shared achievement.

It's the togetherness I loved. In those moments, we are all on an equal level. There's something very endearing about that. It makes the idea of the team special and the feeling of winning after great sacrifice that little bit richer.

They have a massive jacuzzi in the changing rooms of the Aviva. I remember after that game in particular – but some of the euro games for Leinster that year too – going into that jacuzzi with a bottle of beer in my hand. The water is warm, the beer is ice cold and you are hurting so much. It is the greatest moment. Life at its most perfect. The muscles and the bruises are letting you know that they are there and your mind just says, later, later.

You have forty five minutes to an hour of bliss before you have to go off and do media and sponsor stuff. That time is precious. Before the game, you are full of nervous energy jangling you. During the game it's battle. Then the jacuzzi, a beer and the shared sense of a job well done.

I won't miss the eighty minutes of playing rugby. I will miss the national anthems and I will miss those moments in the changing room with your team-mates right after a win. I'll miss the mad celebrations in the pub that night. They are the things I know I will miss when I think of rugby. Not scoring a try or pulling off a tackle but the moments after a victory.

Why do it? It is more than just a competitive desire, this willingness to put success and history ahead of health. I probably wouldn't have done what I did for a Pro 14 game but that day was special.

Was it worth it? Yes.

I take a huge amount of pride in that game. More than I do from days when I have had better performances and won Man of the Match awards. What we did as a team and what I went through to be part of the that team is a great highlight for me. We'd finished 2018 as the number one team on the planet going into a World Cup year.

Moving through Christmas and into 2019 was an entirely different experience than I'd had twelve months previously. I knew that I was in the bonus years of my career and unable to justify asking for more. I would take more if I could get it though.

If I had been told to hang my boots up after the New Zealand game in Dublin, I probably would have been happy to do it. By January, though, I was feeling the desire and the hunger to be at the World Cup. The heart sometimes wants what the body counsels against.

We were the number one team in the world and, for me, 2018 had been the best of all seasons. To have been able to play really good rugby in 2018 and to have found the resilience to turn my body around gave me a huge amount of satisfaction.

The environment had changed too. The celebrations were good but different and maybe better for their rarity.

When I started out on the final weekend of the Six Nations,

you played on Saturday and after the match you would attend the usual function. You were tired and not up for too much. But the next day was traditionally Super Sunday. That was always the day when you cut loose and went out to have the good craic. Even if we didn't win the Six Nations, we always had a Super Sunday at the end.

It's been seven years maybe since that ceased to be a tradition. There might be a quiet pint or two but it's back to the bread and butter business of being a playing professional straight away. So 2018 was different in that way, even if we debated filling the cup with beer instead of spirits.

Also, I felt more embedded and integral to the teams I played in. I'd felt a bit surplus at Leinster for a few years but now I was grateful for the challenges that Stuart and Leo had thrown at me and grateful to the club for having given me a space where I could be at that level for so long.

It was all good. The selfishness of the professional player eventually washed over the mellowed gratitude. 2019 was a World Cup year. I knew that everything that had happened in 2018 gave me a little credit going into the New Year. I'd be retired for long enough.

What's next?

14

THE CIRCLE

Twickenham in 2018. Another team bus on the way to another famous rugby ground for another huge game. If we beat England this afternoon, we win the Grand Slam.

Today I am conscious that I have reached a stage of my career – after so many injuries and some heat over my performance level – where I am consciously looking for every scrap of enjoyment that I can take from these days. Every medal, every big game, every great day like this is a bonus.

There won't be many more and I regret all the ones I consumed without even tasting them. For years, I was just mad to immediately get onto the next thing. I was too young to know better.

Outside the bus window it's a familiar scene, this great mass of people wending their way towards the stadium. Thousands and thousands of faces. When I was younger, I would have shut all that out but now I scan the faces looking to feed my adrenalin with their excitement.

To my amazement, I lock eyes with two of my best friends. Andrew and Pierce are wearing their Irish jerseys and sauntering along in the flow as our bus pokes its way toward Twickenham.

As this is the Irish team bus and obviously they know that I should be on the bus, they aren't quite as astounded as I am when we spot each other. Seeing them makes me boyishly happy. Because there is the window at the back of the bus and I sit on the back row, I can turn around and maintain eye contact with them as they fade into the distance. They look happy and up for the game. I give them the thumbs up.

The other people meandering toward Twickenham must think that I have gone a little mad as my excited face looms at the back of the bus but, for me, it's just a lovely little moment between mates. We were schoolboys together but our friendships have endured through the real world that the guys live in and the strange bubble that I live in. The older I get, the more I appreciate that being able to share these moments is a huge pleasure of my career.

Afterwards, with the game won, we players find ourselves down on the Twickenham grass dwarfed in the cathedral of English rugby. We are doing a lap of honour. There is no need to remind myself to savour this part of the day. I spot the two lads again. They are down by the touchline and I jump the hoarding and we wrap each other in hugs. They both tell me that the moment is one of the most special memories they own. For them to feel that makes it extraordinarily special for me as well.

You have so many times in a professional sports career when

you absent yourselves from the big events in the lives of the people you love. You put your career first. Everything else suffers.

For instance, eighteen months previously, I had missed Andrew's wedding. We were playing Treviso in the RDS. I was to be a groomsman and I had given Leinster six months' notice about the date. They'd said that everything should be ok. The week before the wedding, Leo called me. It would send out the wrong message if we let one guy go away for his friend's wedding...

So it wouldn't be surprising if people around you grew tired of it all. Your priorities always being placed above their needs. They could wave away your bad days as first world problems and meet your successes with a handshake and a distant 'delighted for you.'

But little moments like that embrace in Twickenham confirm how strong your friendship is. Something so important to me meant as much to Andrew and Pierce. Maintaining those friendships through everything is one of the happiest outcomes of fifteen years of pro rugby.

The guys were on one side of the ground and Mum, Jess, Richard and Dad were the other side, so I got to see them as well. The same feelings. Matches are just matches. They fade and your memory of them gets blended with the memory of what you saw later on the TV or in video analysis. Those other moments are what you really remember. The times when you can pay back a little bit of the love and support you have received just by acknowledging that it wouldn't be possible or worthwhile without those people.

I remember Andrew and Pierce coming up to my bedroom a few hours before the French game in the World Cup in 2015.

For a long time, the match was being built up to being our biggest challenge of the World Cup. All the speculation and pundit chat for months before that World Cup focussed on France, France, France.

I was rooming with Dave and the two lads came up to get their tickets from me. They found the Kearney boys staring blankly at a cartoon show in the bedroom. Truth be told, both of us were shitting it.

The lads were in Cardiff for this hugely-hyped World Cup game and they were looking forward to it. They remember leaving the room having got a glimpse of the flip side of World Cup 'glamour'. They said to each other that they'd seldom felt so sorry for two people. We were like men waiting to be led to the gallows.

As they left the room, I gave each of them a hug before they were gone. They said that I almost made them feel guilty for having to leave. That's most likely true. I think I just wanted them to stay in the room with us for the rest of the day.

Aonghus Smyth, Andrew Lynch and Pierce Casey are my three closest pals. In Clongowes, Aonghus and myself were inseparable. Pierce was the first boy I had met in the school when I arrived and we played together right through to Senior Cup in our last year. Andrew, meanwhile, was barely on my radar at all. He wasn't particularly sporty and he was a bit of a messer who would push the boundaries a bit, so I think I tried to avoid him a little.

When we left school, Andrew lived just up the road from me in Dublin, though, and we quickly fell into a friendship. He would have been the guy from school that I saw and spoke to the most and that would still be the case over the last five years or so, since we started a recruitment firm together called Mason Alexander.

Of the three of them, Aonghus would be the one who is the most brutally honest with me. At school, he was a very competitive sportsperson and he was very good at any game he turned his hand to so there would be no bullshit. If I say to Aonghus after a game that I thought I had played poorly he is likely to say "well, to be frank, you've actually been pretty shite for a couple of months." The other two lads would never do that. They would put the arm around me. You need that searingly honest pal like Aonghus though.

Aonghus is a Man United supporter and the two of us would have gone to Old Trafford a lot over the years. His dad Ray, a well known GAA man with Mullingar Shamrocks in Westmeath, brought the two of us to Old Trafford when we were still in school. It was my first time there. We were seventeen and we had to make up a bogus excuse just to get out of school. An absence for a football game at Old Trafford was unthinkable, so Ray rang Clongowes to say that he had something very important happening family-wise and he thought it was critically important that Aonghus should have his friend there with him through it all.

We stayed in Manchester and, bravely, Ray gave us free rein out on the town that night. We were young men going out in a big city for the first time. We'd never experienced anything remotely like that in boarding school and we hit Manchester as if we'd crawled through a long tunnel and out of Shawshank.

Ray went to check on us in our bedrooms at three in the morning. No sign of us. He checked a while later. Same story. He started to get a little bit concerned about having to make a phone call to the Kearneys of Cooley and the Jesuits of

Clongowes. We stumbled in sometime after four o'clock in the morning, much to his relief.

The Enfield business in 2008 is typical of Aonghus's role in my life. The two of us had chatted quite a bit about the whole Munster situation in the weeks leading up to the Enfield gathering. It was those conversations with Aonghus that had spurred me to say my little bit in the group. Afterwards, when I got back to my room, I was in a bit of turmoil but I didn't call Mum or Dad which would have been my habit back then – before I realised that I was just stressing them out by laying all my worries at their feet. I called Aonghus.

– It's all exploded. What have you got me into here, pal?

Aonghus was nonplussed.

– Fuck it, you were honest. It needed to be said. Just go and roll with the punches now.

He has been a great supporter of my career. I used to go to see him play Gaelic football with the Shamrocks but Aonghus has gone a few miles further to see me play. He came all the way to South America to see me win my first cap in Argentina. That's friendship.

Before he had a family and kids, he would always have worked his summer holidays around mine. Players get a very specific two to three week window in the summer for holidays. Aonghus always saved his own holidays for those weeks and we would head off together for cultural explorations.

As for Pierce, the two of us would have been very much the rugby pals in school. He was the out-half on the team that I played on and there was a connection between us from our first day in school. Our paths diverged for a little bit after school days when Pierce went off to work in London for four years but the great thing about those relationships is that they can pick up exactly where they left off. Pierce came back to Dublin and our friendship fell into its old easy rhythm.

Pierce and Andrew provide the optimistic influence in my life. Aonghus balances things with shots of reality.

We have our moments. When we all play golf, myself and Andrew can't be paired together. We get into heated arguments that accelerate from nought to sixty very quickly. I'll never get into rows with the others but myself and Lynchy just know how to push each other's buttons.

To be fair, Andrew is a bright guy but when it comes to golf he is always wrong. He's the sort of person who will interject to give me the exact line of my next putt. If for some reason (better judgement maybe) I don't follow his suggestion and I miss the putt, he'll be very unhappy.

– I told you that was where the line was!

I'm thinking (but, naturally, would never say it) mate, you're playing off twenty two, please don't be telling me where to putt the ball! Do you think you're off scratch?

Andrew played a little rugby on the senior fifths or sixths so he is also qualified as a professional rugby analyst. When he is rowing against the tide and telling me that I played well when the world is telling me that I stank, I genuinely appreciate Andrew's underrated punditry.

On a more serious level, there is always an intelligence in what he says. He is one of life's unshakeable optimists. When things are going badly, you appreciate having that sort of guy around you. The recruitment office is close to where I live, so I pop in a lot just to bend his ear. He knows me particularly well by now and he is a good and patient listener. He spends many hours just sitting there listening to me and then talking things through and fleshing them out for me.

When a game finishes and I switch on my phone, I always know before it comes to life who the first few texts will be from. Andrew, Jess and Dad and Dave – if he wasn't on the field with me. Makes me smile every time.

Some part of the memories from my career are forever tied up with what the lads were doing at the time. After the first Lions game in 2009 when I came on, the three lads decided to go up to Belfast for a weekend to watch the second Test there. They'd completely lost their heads after I scored the try and I remember being in South Africa with them sending me video updates of themselves in ever-deteriorating condition in the bar that night. They were on cloud nine or possibly cloud ten and it felt like I was sharing it with them as well as with the team-mates around me.

I don't know if it is a legacy of feeling isolated as a kid in primary school but I tend to value the friendships I have and I take a lot of strength from them. Surrounding yourself with good people gives you a lot of joy and insulates you from so much unnecessary stress.

My manager David McHugh is another person whose friendship I really value. David was the team manager of the Leinster rugby team when I first joined and he always kept a close eye on me from day one. David has been my manager for fifteen years now and like my close pals, he is someone who shares in the players' ever-changing rollercoaster of emotions – the biggest compliment I can pay to David is that he always puts the player before himself, which is an unusual trait in somebody in his line of work. He cares more about the person than the player and is constantly making sure his athletes upskill themselves to ensure they cope with the transition out of sport better.

There is the odd row or moment of conflict but generally I like things in my life to be simple and steady. I like a quiet existence without tension. I think the only time I have been involved in any sort of physical altercation off the rugby field as an adult was an incident a few years ago at Electric Picnic down in Stradbally.

There was a dust-up in front of a large audience, none of whom thankfully filmed the scrap on their mobile phones to provide instant internet content.

Luckily, too, Jamie Heaslip was at hand and when he got over his shock, he stepped in and put an end to the fisticuffs.

Life is simple as a player and it is best to keep it that way. Apart from the three musketeers who have been beside me since schooldays, I have my team-mates, most of whom I have shared great and memorable occasions with and some of whom have become good friends. And, of course, I have the family.

The least spoken about Kearney – and the one who probably likes it that way – is my sister Sara. I can't imagine what it has been like for Sara growing up as the only girl in a house where sport in general and rugby in particular might often be the only source of conversation for weeks on end.

Dave and myself have been happy to define ourselves as rugby players. Sara had almost no choice about being cast as a 'rugby sister'. Her general interest in the nuts and bolts of the game wouldn't extend any further than Mum's. She likes to make sure that we are safe, is happy when we win, has perspective when we lose and knows enough to provide broad answers to all the general queries about how her brothers' careers are going at any given moment.

Through all that she has carved a life, skills and an identity for herself. We don't come with thousands of strangers to watch Sara work and we don't read dissections of her performance in the papers but to the rest of the family, her substance and her abilities are as celebrated and meaningful as any Grand Slam win.

Sara is brilliant with Richard and his wife Sarah's kids, Archie and Isla, and despite them having two amazing and amusing rugby-playing uncles, she is the clear favourite in their eyes. It feels right that she is embarking on starting her own Montessori school. We know she will be brilliant and she knows we will be very proud of her.

On the Venn diagram of family, friends and team-mates, there is one name in the area where all three intersect. My brother Dave.

Where to begin with Dave?

Dave is apparently the nice Kearney. Generally, people describe Dave to me with rapt expressions and words of wonder. He is such an easy-going, laid back sort of person, they say. They've met him and Dave really is the salt of the earth and the light of the moon. Just the soundest young lad you could meet.

I get it all the time. I think I am being told something in a not very subtle way. Dave is so lovely. When they met Dave they were so surprised. Why? Well he's the complete opposite to you, Rob.

Dave is the loveable yin to my grumpy yang. I can't argue. I have no 'shocking dark side of Dave Kearney' stories to relate.

As kids, our older brother Richard was away at Clongowes and only at home for two or three days a month. Richard was never really in the picture as Dave and I were growing up and a lot of the time for me, Dave wasn't even in the picture.

I was generally a very busy young guy. I had something on every single day from Gaelic to soccer to swimming or golf. Mum's life mostly consisted of driving me around County Louth to some sort of sporting activity or other. I barely took notice of Dave and what he was doing unless I had to. There were times when the weather threw us into each other's company or vacant afternoons when Dave and I just messed around in the garden. Sometimes we went out in the farm to be useful to Dad by firing spuds at each other. At that age, though, the few years age gap made a difference. Then, when we each arrived at the right age, we headed off to Clongowes ourselves.

Dave is generally described as being one of the most laid back creatures on the planet. Nothing bothers him too much. I do remember at an early enough age that I began exploring the limits of Dave's easy-going nature. There had to be a switch somewhere and I wanted to be the one to find it.

One day we were playing on the PlayStation, as we often did for hours if the weather kept us in. Pro Evo football was the game of choice and not wanting to be immodest about it, I was beating poor Dave up a stick. I was winning game after game and really rubbing it in in classic big brother style. Gloating. Fake sympathy. Commentating on my own excellence. Goading Dave to try again. Just winding him up.

And nothing.

Dave just kept coming back for another beating and then another until the whole process was starting to bore me. And then, out of the blue, bingo. Paydirt! After one especially sore loss, Dave just stood up and punched me square in the eye and walked off.

There is a first time for everything!

I had found a limit to his good nature and it didn't feel great. I was a fair bit bigger than him. I was around fourteen and he was eleven. After all the button-pushing, he'd caught me so off guard I just took a bit of a metaphorical step backwards.

I didn't hit him back but, as the most evil of the Kearneys, I knew that I had found the boundary. I didn't push him too far after that. It was a good punch to be fair.

On another day, some time before that, Dave and I were having a potato fight in the shed one day after school (yes, that's farm life. It's either PlayStation or potato fights). Dave jumped over a bale of straw to fire his spud at me and he suddenly let out a mighty yelp. He'd felt a sharp pain in his leg. When he examined the spot, the pain had also left a black mark. I looked him over with my expert eye and solemnly told him that he'd just been bitten by a rat.

All hell broke loose. Dave went running back into the kitchen screaming. Mum gathered us for a trip to the hospital. Just before we sped off, Mum called her own father, Danny, who asked if Dave had had anything in his pocket. Dave was frisked. The lead from his school pencil and not a rat had attacked him. Perhaps the punch was less to do with PlayStation and more to do with payback for the rat bite hysteria.

The real closeness between us only developed in later life. At home, before Clongowes, we were thrown together a lot but the age difference mattered. In Clongowes, Dave had arrived as a first year when I was in fourth year. He had his own friends at Clongowes and I had mine. I think Dave experienced more homesickness than I had when he arrived. He had been a happy young lad through primary school days and he hadn't laid huge store on Clongowes being a whole fresh beginning in his life.

After school, when I was with Leinster during the reign of Michael Cheika, I shared a place with Richard, our older brother. When Dave left Clongowes, he was playing with Lansdowne and studying. I wouldn't have seen a huge amount of him then either.

I bought the place in Ranelagh off the back of the 2009 season and when I moved in there, Dave moved in with me. We lived together for seven years or so from then on.

As had been the case with Richard, I was amazed at how there could be such an underlying blood bond with somebody you hadn't spent a whole lot of time with while growing up.

When Dave and I moved in together, all of our chat was about rugby. We watched games together. Went to training and back together. We parsed and analysed everything together. We were very open and honest with each other about what was expected of us or about what either of us should have done in a particular situation. We were working together, holidaying together, eating together. Every decision I made in my daily life through that time would have involved Dave too.

Like me, Dave had an incredibly good ear for knowing what Joe Schmidt wanted from him. If you understood that and applied it, you had a very good chance of getting picked. Consequently, Joe liked Dave. When Dave took the ball into contact, he always made ground and never lost the ball. It always comes back to the ruck for Joe and when Dave was in there he always came out with a plus sign.

The fact that we played different positions was important too. We have never competed for the same jersey. That might have changed the dynamic a little, especially during the few years when we were both being picked every single week. Those were the greatest days for us.

I would single out the game against France in the World Cup of 2015. That anthem in Cardiff was the proudest moment I have had in an Irish jersey. We were on a World Cup stage. Two brothers from Cooley. As always, we stood beside each other, shoulder to shoulder for the anthem. The roof was closed and the Irish in the stands were going mental. The place almost vibrated. Ireland had to deliver on our potential that day and Dave and I were together through it. That stands out as a very proud day.

There have been lots of bad days for Dave, though. So many times when he was going through such miserable times with injuries. If I could have traded places with him, I would have. No question about it. It was hard to watch him go through those times.

He had a number of years where the only luck he got was lousy luck. He played in the 2014 championship which we won under Joe, he was on the field for every minute of those five games. Myself and Jamie were the only others to do that. Dave had been a cornerstone of the team but then he did his ACL at the end of that season and missed out on the entire 2015 championship.

He got back for the World Cup where he played really well until the Argentina game. That was the afternoon where the whole team just crumbled and Dave bore the weight of our general awfulness in defence. He was left with so much work on his left wing and all their tries came from there. He copped a heap of criticism after that. He will always say that Argentina was by far the most disappointing day of his career.

In 2016, he got picked for the Six Nations away in France and Guilhem Guirado absolutely minced him with a first-half clothesline tackle. Dave was ruled out for the rest of that Six

Nations as well and beyond that for about two years he got no proper injury-free run. He should have been at the peak of his career. Joe was still there and wanted him to play but Dave was never fit.

Living together, there were so many days when I could see the impact it was having on him. Injuries and selection issues can really have a bad impact on players. You are living and breathing this game. It is all you do and all you want to do. It's hard to imagine how tough it is when your body keeps breaking down and your brother and housemate is going off to training every day, playing games every weekend, heading away on tours.

Dave was bursting to play. He needed to escape the endless rehab. And, by and large, I was playing away. A lesser man would have resented me. He gave me nothing but support.

Strangely there is no competitive element between us. We are both competitive people but there is nothing of that nature between the two of us. There are always comparisons being made between us which must be frustrating for Dave when he has had so much down time with injuries. I have won things that he would certainly have won too if it wasn't for bad luck. I'm not sure if our positions had been reversed that I could have dealt with his success with the good grace and support-iveness that he has shown on those days. How he has handled himself throughout his career has been the biggest thing that I admire in him. He is one guy who would have a licence to be a little bitter or resentful but there is never a trace of it in him.

With Dave, as I am the bigger brother, I do feel a little respon-sibility to care a bit more for him. In bad times, I would never have unloaded any sort of stuff on him. He has experienced worse than I have and he didn't need that.

I remember that famous game down in Thomond, the incident when Paul O'Connell accidentally kicked Dave in the head, a huge incident at the time. Joe was still coaching Leinster and he went absolutely nuts over that incident. It happened some time before the Lions tour and the thing sort of got swept under the carpet.

I was glad that I didn't see the incident at the time. I was over the other side of the field and missed it all. When I saw the replay, I didn't know how anybody could say that it wasn't reckless.

I didn't know that at the time, though. I saw Dave being driven off on the stretcher alright and I don't know what I would have done had I actually seen Paul's kick. When something happens to your younger brother on the field you have a little bit of a switch inside your head. You think you are going hard in games but I have experienced so many times where Dave might be under pressure at the bottom of a ruck or might not be getting the ball back and I have felt that extra little bit of madness that I can use.

A few years later, I saw him being carted off a field again and I got a little insight into Mum and Dad's life through our careers. It was 2017, when I had ruptured the bicep against Italy and then damaged my knee against Wales in the Six Nations.

I'd had two surgeries in the space of five days and I was rehabbing. Mum and Dad were in Portugal for the Easter break and I went down there for a few days to hang out with them.

Dave had been through another really bad injury spell too. A toe injury in early season had cost him eight weeks. He came back in April for a game and now we were down in

Portugal watching him play. There was a group of about fifteen or twenty of us watching the game in the Cheeky Pup on the Algarve. Dave's first game back. Leinster against Connacht in the Sportsground.

We were around people and, in those situations, I don't like to be too animated watching a game. I noticed, at the top of the screen, Dave going into a tackle. The play moved on but Dave stayed down on the ground. Mum and Dad both noticed straight away. They looked at me. Is he ok?

Regardless in these moments, even if there has been gunfire, I am always going to say, ah yeah, just a bang, don't worry.

Thirty seconds later, the camera panned to Dave and they had the oxygen mask on his face. I will never forget Mum and Dad's faces. It turned out that it was less drama than it appeared when we saw the face mask.

Dave had broken his ankle but that was the end of that season for him. When Dave and I are both retired, those will be the moments that Mum and Dad will never miss. There we were in a happy pub in Portugal and Dave is on an oxygen mask in Galway. Mum started to get teary and Dad was upset too. And at the same time there were a hundred people in the pub constantly glancing over at us.

Dave is thirty now and having this glorious Indian summer in his career. As I was back in 2018, he is playing the best rugby of his career. To really shine he just needed to be injury-free and for a coach to pick him week in and week out. He needed somebody to invest a lot of time in him.

And now, Dave being Dave, a man who (at times) if he didn't have bad luck would have very little luck, sees the season grind to a halt due to a once-in-a-lifetime pandemic.

The season will begin again, of course, and I hope that this year will be the one that will change the way that he looks on his career. Hopefully Leinster stay on the same upward curve. When Dave is back in the Leinster European cup team as a valued starting player, the bad days will seem distant.

He has shown an insane amount of resilience. That will stand to him. Even when he was fit last year (and for some time before) he sometimes wasn't getting picked for the big games. He played very well in the Heineken Cup quarter-final against Ulster last year. Played really well and Jordan, it would be fair to say, probably didn't have his best game at full back.

The next day, I came back into the team and Jordan moved to the wing. To accommodate the shuffle, Dave had to be dropped. That was very tough on him. As a result of me coming back in, Dave found himself locked out. The two of us are in the gym together when we find out about the team. Me happy to be playing but also gutted that Dave was the one to have missed out.

That day at Electric Picnic about five or six years ago? It was Dave and I who were fighting each other. We were living together at the time, on top of each other all day, every day and we were having a few drinks down there in the off season with a few others players: Jamie, Cian Healy one or two more, maybe.

We got a lift down and a lift back. And for reasons too embarrassing to go into (well, full disclosure. Dave walked off ahead of me somewhere and I said, you didn't wait for me. It was something as simple and as stupid as that), myself and Dave got in this monster fight. We were both playing on the national team at the time. There were maybe fifty or a hundred people watching us. I started on Dave. He came back at me.

Poor Jamie had to jump in between us and break it up. It was one of those mad all-out fights that only two brothers could have. Easily the worst thing that ever happened between us.

We were driving back to Dublin that evening and there was no chat in the car. We'd had to leave Electric Picnic early. When we got back to Ranelagh, I walked straight upstairs and into Dave's room where I started packing his bags.

"Get out of my house and don't ever come back here again."

When I look back at the melodrama, it is all mortifying. Thankfully, Dave stayed. Maybe just to spite me. It had been such a bad day. If I hadn't tried to throw him out, he probably would have left happily! It took a day or two before we could both look at each other and wonder what that was all about!

They were great days sharing the house and our careers together. We talked for thousands of hours about rugby and played hundreds of hours of PlayStation without a blow being struck.

When Dave finally did move out, Jess moved in. The PlayStation gathered some dust. Grown-up life had begun.

Jess is from Dundrum. We met through social circles on a night out in Dublin, seven years ago. I was twenty seven. Jess was twenty. There was a fair age gap there. Probably a little uncomfortable for me at first. By now there are times, especially when I am on the verge of having to live and work in the real world, when she seems a lot older and more sensible than I do.

I was out with Dave that night. I don't remember where we were, which is an unromantic confession to make. It was in town. We chatted a bit and, in the new age of social media, I was able to find her Instagram account and we began messaging a little from there on. The rest is history. Our own history. Jess is definitely the most positive person I have ever met. That is infectious and it brings me back around to my point about surrounding yourself with really good people.

When we sometimes appear in the social columns, Jess is sometimes presented as some sort of wag-like accessory to a rugby player. That's a little embarrassing. She is an incredibly smart woman. Pharmacy isn't an academic pursuit for dossers or bimbos. Jess came first in all her exams down the years.

She is ambitious. She will set up her own pharmacy some day. She will succeed on her own terms when I am just some guy who they say used to play rugby.

She is a great family person, always kind and positive. People fall for each other pretty randomly but if you made out a list of all the really great attributes that you would want in a partner to spend the rest of your life with, well, in my case, I would be describing Jess. That there is such a spark between us is just more good luck in my life.

I suppose early on I wondered a little about the age difference between us. After a couple of years, though, it was very evident that we would be having a long future together. I found myself quietly thinking, well, the difference between a fifty-year-old man and a forty-three-year-old woman seems like nothing.

We got engaged in New York on New Year's Eve, a few months after the Japan Rugby World Cup. At the end of rugby, life with Jess feels to me like a pretty exciting prospect. There'll be a wedding when the world is doing weddings and social occasions again and there'll be a new life after that. I'm apprehensive about my place in the world after rugby but at the same time very excited about the future. That's down to Jess.

She is not somebody who has ever been too into rugby or

who has ever wanted to understand much about it. I would never talk to Jess about the game. She is one of those people in my life whose interest in my rugby career has never gone much beyond how I'm doing injury-wise. She wants to see me happy down through the years after rugby.

There have been so many things that I have been absent from in the years since we met but Jess has always had a huge understanding of the selfishness needed to keep a professional sports career going. Because she understands now doesn't mean that she won't be glad when that part of our life ends. With rugby, you either can't commit to things or else you commit to them and then have to pull out.

I am sure Jess has lost count of the amount of weddings she has had to go to alone or how many family events she has been to when all her sisters would have had their partners with them and she has spent the day explaining to people where I am. That has happened so much through the years and it can't have been easy for her.

Who you are in mid-career, having somebody who understands and makes space for that makes an incredible difference.

There will be many years to make up for all the absences.

15

NO FAIRY TALE

O ur warm-up series had encouraged us. Prep had been
meticulous.

In good spirit we left for Japan on a Wednesday
afternoon and arrived in Tokyo at 3pm on Thursday. We went
straight to Chiba, to the south east of Tokyo Bay.

We had travelled business class. We had an in-depth sleep
protocol to beat the jet lag. We slept for the first five hours then
Jason Cowman, the team's strength and conditioning coach,
came around and woke everybody up. A few boys nodded off
again. Jason came around and woke them again. Jason was
meticulous with his preperation.

Still, I struggled for the first four days. We were one of the
last teams to arrive out there. Humidity emerged as a big
factor. South Africa, the eventual winners, were the first team
to arrive in Japan. Hindsight is great.

In the warm-up series our loss to England had been a

pothole, causing the mood to temporarily drop off a cliff. We'd been in Portugal for the week before the game. The sun shone and the sky was blue. We weren't on holiday but we needed a little stress to sharpen our edge. We trained unbelievably hard in Portugal. I actually woke up sore on game day and asked myself how I was going to play a Test match against England that afternoon.

I had been so jaded after the captain's run the day before that I went for a two-hour nap. I never nap. The heat had taken a lot out of us in Portugal and continued to do so in London.

Twickenham. Saturday, August 24th: England 57 Ireland 15. Crazy.

The mind will be led to where the mind needs to be. We played Wales the following two Saturdays.

Principality Stadium. Saturday, August 31st: Wales 17 Ireland 22. A huge game for us.

Home to Dublin then and our second win over the Welsh in a week returned us to the top of the world rankings. Before the game Wales were number one.

The usurping of Wales was the final home game for Rory Best and for Joe Schmidt. We put out a strong team for their farewell. The Welsh were strong too, short just three players.

As it turned out the Welsh game in Dublin wasn't just Bestie and Joe's final home game. It was mine too. I scored a try, the first that I had scored for Ireland in nearly four years.

The *Irish Times* said that 'another definite boon was the performance of Rob Kearney. Much better than at Twickenham under the high ball with a couple of confidence boosting early takes but again demonstrating his passing game, Kearney looked sharp, fit and quick. He saved one try, helped to prevent another and ended a run of 25 Tests dating back to the pool deciding win over France four years ago with an excellent finish.'

It all helped. The team doesn't get picked on scoring tries but I had put a little pressure on myself. I knew that I could get picked without scoring tries but not scoring them just niggled. And you know it is there in people's minds. It's in the conversations. It's in print.

Big picture? We had won and everything was rosy again. The England game was just a blip, we said. Aviva Stadium. Saturday, September 7th: Ireland 19 Wales 10. We were back.

There were bells tolling in the distance but we didn't want to ask if they were tolling for us. The Six Nations and the England warm-up had suggested some decline in us. Against Wales in the spring we barely played. Against Italy we made strings of errors. Against England we got bullied twice. Once in the spring, once in August. But when we beat Wales in Dublin, we chose to genuinely believe in ourselves again. Going to Japan we were thinking things are good. Really good.

World Cups weigh heavy for me. We've never really had a successful World Cup, just disappointments with scattered good days. For the last while through injuries, criticisms and disappointments the World Cup has, for me, been that light at the end of a tunnel. Suck it all up and get to another World Cup. Then whatever will be will be.

Now, right on the eve I was surprised to find myself almost dreading the tournament and the pressure and scrutiny. There was such expectation about the team and I felt the weight more than I ever did as a younger player.

On squad selection day I had been freaking looking at

the phone hoping that Joe's number wouldn't come up. If Joe was ringing it was to have 'the chat,' the bad news chat. Will Addison had played fifteen the weekend before in Cardiff and he had played well. You never know. One of us would be getting 'the chat.'

The game against England had been bad for everybody but Joe had opened me up with a scalpel in the Monday morning review. He had things to say about my work rate. I had been bolloxed tired but that was not an excuse.

Being disembowelled by Joe only takes fifteen or twenty seconds but it feels like forever. When he was done with me Joe said that we needed to park it, that we all needed to move on.

There was some joking about it at lunch. He's really going for you today! Players are selfish. Nobody cares who is getting the treatment once it isn't them. That morning it was me.

I didn't see the humour. Will was coming in for the Cardiff game. Maybe Joe had decided on Will already? Maybe he had decided on me but this was shock therapy. Maybe I was overthinking things.

In the afternoon Joe brought along clips of the game. Shit! He hadn't parked it at all. He opened me up for the second time in a matter of hours. For both sessions I was one of the players who he came down on hardest.

This has been a trend and I thought I understood why. I was a bit older and Joe knew that I could take it. If he goes after an older guy it lets Joe show something to the young guys without damaging their confidence.

Also, a pattern had developed. Joe would fillet me and I would play well in the next game. If he heaped shit on me I'd crawl out and play well for him at the end of the week. There were times, though, when it felt straight up unfair. I'd stare straight back at Joe wanting him to know that this wasn't ok. Joe knew though that I would suck it up and just get on with it.

So, on squad selection day my head was a mess. In Twickenham I had failed Joe on the non-negotiable stuff, especially work rate. Failing on a non-negotiable is usually a non-forgivable.

Dave called. We'd been on and off the phone most of the day. He'd just had the bad news chat with Joe. He wasn't going to the World Cup.

He'd reckoned he was probably just outside the thirty-one. On the other hand, Joe was a big fan of his and Dave had enjoyed an unbelievable pre-season. He'd trained well and backed it up against Italy.

He was meant to play on the wing against Wales away but Jacob went poorly in Twickenham the week before, so Joe played Jacob again. Typical of Dave's luck.

He'd learned, though, that Will Addison was not going either. I was disappointed for Dave but Will being out could only mean…

Later when Joe named the team for the Welsh game in Dublin he went through the line-up from one to fifteen. So I was last named.

– Fifteen, Rob Kearney. Now there are some boys who are playing this week who we weren't happy with in Twickenham. You've got to up your game.

He didn't need to look directly at me. I got the message loud and clear. I was still under pressure. I headed to Japan feeling good. I didn't feel that Joe was seeing a question mark over my head every time he glanced my way.

We're not staying in great places. Chiba is soulless and there is not much to do. Hotel selection at the World Cup is based on coin tosses and rankings. We're obviously losing a lot of tosses. We would prefer to be in the heart of a city, rambling out for cups of coffee and food. With traffic Chiba is seventy to eighty minutes in a taxi to Tokyo. Not optimum but we need to be close to our training base to avoid long journeys to and from training every day.

I room with Robbie Henshaw for the whole World Cup. We're close. How it works is you put in a rooming request beforehand. Robbie and I would have roomed together over the last few years so our request was accepted. This is heartbreak for Bundee Aki who would always want Robbie as a roomie too. There is a bit of a love triangle there.

In the old days Declan Kidney always mixed and matched us as a social experiment. You were never with somebody from your own province. It was good. I roomed with David Wallace and with John Hayes a few times and I got to know them both well.

When you start off it can be uncomfortable sharing rooms. My very first roomie experience with Leinster was way back. We were in Cork playing Munster in Musgrave Park. I was late up to my room, getting food or something and Eric Miller was in there just lying naked on the bed watching television.

I was nineteen years old and Eric, the British and Irish Lion, was stark naked, stretched out and oblivious. I'm thinking, what the hell! This is awkward. Six years of boarding school and I never encountered anything like this.

There was very little chat. I brushed my teeth for maybe two hours. The TV was on. Eric was under the covers when I emerged with my bleeding gums. We watched TV for a while and then Eric picked up the remote, turned the television off and went straight to sleep.

Eric was quirky but as you got to know him you liked the quirkiness. He was a good guy and a great player. I was just some young buck he had to share with.

No such problems with Robbie. He's usually been my Leinster roomie too.

As the competition unfolds our room will take on the feel of an A&E with Robbie and I the permanent residents.

Was the room cursed or were we?

Friday is the first full day. Team walk at 9am. Headshots for World Rugby, all the photos between ten and twelve. Then a walk through at twelve o'clock on the tennis court in the team hotel.

Joe gets angry. Our first time together in Japan is an opportunity for him to lay down a marker. Joe gets at the group by picking on individuals. If you have your head dropped at the breakdown or you are in the wrong body position he is in your face. It gets everybody on edge straight away.

We attend a World Rugby integrity session from one thirty to two. Some guy tells us that there is no betting. Neither will we be allowed mobile phones sixty minutes before the game. For the Spotify-dependents this means no music.

In the afternoon there is a welcoming ceremony from three to four thirty in the Mihama cultural hall in Chiba. Another tick-the-box exercise. We each get our cap and medal presented to us by Gareth Davies on behalf of World Rugby.

A spinning session ends the day. Good crack in a dark room with disco lights and pulsing music. A Japanese woman leads us and she is great. In forty-five sweaty minutes the mood lifts.

We slept like logs.

Saturday morning: Hydration tests, body weight checks etc. We monitor everything three times a week. How well you slept. Any niggles to report. We do hamstring tests, calf and ankle tests, groin and hip tests. We have all had markers set for us throughout our careers and if the scores are a little bit down we will be notified. It's an early alarm system for the medics, prevention being better than cure etc.

Alarmingly it takes fifty minutes in traffic for the bus to get us to training. Not good.

On the field the idea was not to go balls out. We'd ramp things up. I did a few accelerations in our ten-minute warm-up. No real problem.

Five minutes into the session I felt a sharp pain in my leg when I accelerated. I had felt a little something earlier but I'd always go on and give it one more go just to check. On the second acceleration I got a sharp pain under my big toe, in the back of my foot and up into my calf. I knew it was something very different. My first FHL injury.

Flexor Hallucis Longus tendinopathy, as I would learn, is when pain emanates from the collagen fibres that compose the FHL tendon. The pain comes at three spots along the tendon. Back of the ankle, under the mid foot and under the base of the big toe.

The pitch wasn't good, a very uneven surface with a huge amount of give in it. Lots of lads complained about that pitch during the week. I went straight over to the physios. They were listening to my woes when literally thirty seconds later Robbie pulled up with a hamstring.

I wondered if my injury was related to the nerve blocker I had got the previous week. The incidence of these had dropped massively since my time with Enda King but with the travel involved I'd got the procedure. Alternatively, maybe we were training too soon or the fifty-minute bus journey or the pitch had done us no good? The sad fact is that I am sometimes easily broken.

One of the physios was treating me right after I got injured and he wondered out loud if today shouldn't have been just a walk through. Hindsight is 20:20.

Myself and Robbie and Ciaran Cosgrave, the team doctor, and Shino Kusunos, our Japanese liaison officer, spent the evening together at a hospital some thirty minutes away. Shino did all the registration forms and all the communicating and her presence made things easer.

I had no real idea about my injury. Foot and calf injuries were new territory.

Robbie had done a hamstring though and he was very down. He had shrieked when he pulled up. The shriek was an indication. Grade One, you pull up slightly. Something is a bit tight. Grade Two, is a jump up and grab it straight away job. Maybe a yell. That's a two or a three. A definite three feels like a shot from a sniper. Big jump. Big roar. That was Robbie.

My scan said: FHL grade 2, grade 2 perineal and grade 2 calf. So, the trifecta. On day one. Three injuries in my first five minutes.

Back in the hotel Joe was waiting. He is unbelievably 'next thing' focused. If a player gets injured in training Joe is not asking for medical details. If you're out, then you are out. Joe is thinking of the next man in. Nothing personal but life continues. You will be looked after but Joe's job is dealing with who is next.

Joe speaks to Ciaran. Ciaran had already told me that this

was all three of the things that he had hoped it might be just one of. I wasn't going to be fit for Scotland and I'd be fifty-fifty for the Japan game.

Robbie's situation is worse. Best case scenario is the Samoan game (in the end though Robbie did very well to actually get back for that).

"Not a great start to our World Cup," I say to Joe. I am fishing for comfort. I hope Joe will say, listen lads it's fine. Get fit. It will be ok.

Joe says, you could both be going home. You'll be no good to us if we don't get to a quarter-final.

It's simple. Robbie and I are out. So are Keith Earls and Joey Carbery. If one more back gets hurt, myself or Robbie or both of us will be sacrificed in order to get replacements out.

And I'm haunted again by Jordan. Against Scotland if Jordan plays out of his skin it may not matter when I get fit. I lose control. I want things to go well for Jordan, just not too well. That's not a conversation for the team room though.

Joe tells the media that I am progressing well. I actually can't put any weight on my big toe but that's Joe being Joe. He loves certainty. If he gets an opposition team a day or two in advance, he can help us prep for those specific players. He assumes that all coaches are the same. If Scotland think that myself and Robbie will both be playing, they will prep on the basis of us being there until a day or two beforehand. Joe is trying to get his one per cent edge.

The plan is for me to train on the Tuesday of the week of the Japan match. The team will be picked that day. Sometimes the medics will tell you that you will be alright for Tuesday, hopefully. Joe will hear that in his head as 'yes definitely you will be training on Tuesday.' He needs that certainty.

The Game Ready machine is pretty much a state-of-the-art recovery unit. It offers compression and cryotherapy at the push of a button.

We have two Game Ready machines in our room. The novelty wears off fast.

Our first World Cup week is spent in our room held hostage by injuries. Bundee swings by full of the joys of the healthy player visiting the lodgings of the damned.

How are my two boys?

We look at him in disgust. His health and happiness inappropriate. Hey Bundee, I say to him, this is too good a photo for you not to take. The picture sums us up. Not happy. The machines are Game Ready. We're not.

Robbie will miss the Scotland, Japan and Russia games. He missed the opening two games in 2015 under similar circumstances. It's rough but at least he hasn't been put on a plane home. That would be a long and lonely journey.

We spend two to three hours a day with the machines on our legs. We just chat and watch box sets. We've watched *Money Heist*. We've watched *Top Boy*. We've watched *Peaky Blinders*. Being attached to our Game Ready machines as we binge watch is a glum twist on Netflix and chill.

Chiba lasts for eight long days. On Thursday to Yokohama for the Sunday game with Scotland.

The night before the match night we had a match jersey presentation. That's something which we never do but we did it because this was a World Cup. Andy Farrell spoke and he was incredible. He gave a great team speech. He spoke about the time he played for England against Ireland in Croke Park.

Our two team masseurs David Revins and Willy

Bennett presented everybody with their jerseys. A nice touch. The two lads have been in the system for so long just working their backsides off. They got suited and booted and walked into the team room like two bouncers. They presented the match jerseys and it was very emotional.

The jerseys just went to the people who would be playing but we all felt something in the heart.

And Andy's speech had been a revelation. That day Bundee had summoned a friend from Tokyo. You can't get a decent haircut in Japan for love nor money. We looked in on barber shops to see atrocities being inflicted on hair. The Japanese do a lot of things well but haircuts aren't one of them. Lads were beginning to despair.

So Bundee called his friend to travel down from Tokyo to give some mercy cuts. He came in and did everybody's hair. I went into Bundee's room which was serving as our salon and Andy Farrell was sitting in the chair getting a blade one tight fade while playing his guitar and singing a song. This is our next coach! Not one element of this situation would appeal to Joe!

It was a moment when I saw the two guys as polar opposites. Andy playing Oasis on his guitar and having a skin fade in a players' room? He's a big Oasis fan and he can really play the guitar. He has sung for us a few times. He won't change. That's who he is. Players will want to play for him, as in a different way they wanted to play for Joe.

Scotland is the start of Ireland's World Cup and I'm sitting in the stand, in my civvies, with Robbie and with Sean Cronin.

On days like this you are always conscious of the cameras. You know that the camera is going to pick you up for reaction shots every now and then, so I try to be quite expressionless while watching games. Poker face no matter how well Jordan plays.

Of course, Jordan plays well. Mentally I try to pick out the things that he might have done better. It's not a long list. With ten minutes to go Keith Earls leans towards me and says we might not get back in for Japan at all. Keith's only half joking. Andrew Conway has had a great game too.

The team blows Scotland away in the first half. Then the rains come in while Scotland were chasing and that was that. This was perceived to be the big game in our pool. Maybe it gave us a little more confidence than was good for us.

Yokohama. September 22nd: Ireland 27 Scotland 3.

The Japan game is in Shizuoka. A new hotel on the Monday, a native Japanese spa type place in the remote countryside. We have the hotel all to ourselves. They serve the greatest food I have had anywhere. They have the traditional hot tubs and the hotel follows the Japanese tradition of no shoes indoors. We are all barefoot while walking around or wearing special indoor slippers.

Tuesday is judgement day for me, Joe is watching me train. He needs to see me go at 100 per cent pace. I know how to manage that and get around it. Accelerating from a standing start was the move that I got injured on so I make sure not to do that in training. I'm always moving about and slowly building up. My top end speed is good. How I got to top speed is a different story but Joe sees the speed and is reassured.

The Tuesday session went pretty well. I'd hardly slept the night before, just worrying about it but when Joe named the team, I was in.

Collectively we underestimated Japan. Afterwards players would say that Joe had spoken about Japan endlessly in training but you have to say that after a game, don't you?

All week I had a foreboding. I felt we weren't aware of just how good they had become in the previous few years. I wondered if we'd had a proper test against a limp Scottish team.

We were complacent, whispering among ourselves about maybe playing South Africa in a quarter-final. We fell into precisely the same trap that we fell into against Argentina four years previously.

We had been spoiled and detached in our lovely hotel out in the middle of nowhere. There was no buzz that begins on a Test match Thursday when you move into the city.

On the day in terms of intensity, collisions and pace, playing Japan felt like playing the All Blacks.

We had no reserves. There was nothing extra there when we went looking. We were shocked by the humidity and then shocked by Japan's intensity and then shocked that we had no response to offer.

We'd started ok. We had two tries and when we went 12-3 ahead we thought, ok, a bit of breathing space now.

It was 12-9, though, when we went in at half time. Japan were hoovering up penalties. There was a little shift in the balance.

I was exhausted at half time. The heat and the humidity were crushing. We have cooling strategies for the first three minutes. Ice packs on our necks for a minute, then putting our forearms into a lovely cooling bin of ice. Thirty seconds each arm. We had done lots of this through pre-season to get us prepped. We take ice slushies in little cups. Three minutes of getting the heart rate down and the core temperature down.

Joe spoke for two minutes to the team. Andy did the same. Backs split off. Joe spoke to the backs and Simon Easterby to the forwards. Andy Farrell jumping between the two.

At half time the message was to stop giving penalties away. Our discipline had been poor. Everything had been basically poor. We were to take an extra yard in defence. Don't go for the ball on the ground. If they don't have penalties they won't have access to a win.

The intensity. The crowd. The ref. Everything seemed to be against us. Japan were very fit and they were playing a better style of rugby than us and their handling was excellent. When they had the ball they didn't give it back. They got to the edges while we played narrow between the fifteens. Too narrow.

In the heat we'd planned to put them under pressure by pumping the ball down into their half as often as we could. They weren't bothered. They simply played their way upfield any time we kicked the ball to them. Their ball retention was incredible. And for us it was exhausting.

They were moving us around the field all the time. On video review you see our guys walking, walking, walking. We are bolloxed. Static. Waiting for them to come onto the ball.

At half time we had trudged towards the changing room as the Japanese ran past us like spring lambs. Coming back out for the second half we were still catching our breath when the Japanese came out into the middle of the field and did a gratuitous little ten-metre sprint. A message. We have loads of energy. How about you boys?

We can read each other's body language pretty well. You look at a guy and he's not saying anything to you but his walk, his posture tells you he is tired. The second half was grim reading.

I came off in the 67th minute for a HIA and I just went

straight into the medical room. Michael Leitch had just come on and I got the brunt of his frustration at having been left out. First ball and he absolutely smoked me. I stayed on but a little later I'd had a forearm into the head.

When they took our baseline measurements for the HIA in Portugal a while before it was the evening time and we were chilled. We were asked to memorise a series of letters and a series of numbers and then do a balance test closing the eyes. No problem.

After running around for sixty minutes in a World Cup game in air as thick as soup, with adrenalin pumping and the heart rate up it's a different story.

I got my numbers right and my words were perfect. My balance was off though. I knew my game was over.

I went back out to watch the dregs of the game. Keith Earls made a tackle under the sticks and I didn't get to see much else. We were on our own try line until Joey kicked the ball out of play. Rightly so. All Japan needed was a penalty to deny Ireland the bonus point. We weren't going to get back down the field. End it.

I remember coming off the field, walking with Keith Earls. What the fuck just happened? he asked. Shizuoka. Saturday, September 28th: Japan 19 Ireland 12.

It's 10am on a Sunday and we know that Joe has been up all night watching the game over and over. He never makes any secret of the in-depth forensic analysis he does.

We haven't slept much. We have been beaten, the adrenaline is up, and we are sore.

After the game, in the devastation of the dressing room, Joe had given us an earful. That was unusual. Earfuls are generally issued at half time if at all. Joe had made reference to the Irish team that went to Japan two years previously and won two out of two. We knew that was a different Japan. We said nothing though.

Now Joe has to rebuild morale. He says that we did so many things that aren't us. He says that we missed so many opportunities. If we want to win this thing he says, we can't do this again.

We watched ten to fifteen minutes on the big screen. So slow to breakdowns. Not protecting ball for that third guy in on the breakdown, poor ruck speed, discipline. All those things that have been so good to us over the years.

Joe knows that we are in a shit fight now for the remainder of the tournament. We have five days till we play Russia. We know there will be changes. We move on. Another game. Another hotel.

My run of luck continues. One evening and we're going up to dinner on the rooftop. There are six or seven of us in the lift and we are all pushing each other a little bit and messing about. Somebody pushes me from behind and I feel a bite in my groin.

I had a dead leg from the Japan game. I'd picked it up in the first minute in a tackle. A dead leg only gets sore when you have cooled down. Sometimes it will be the next day before the full effect hits you. As such I wasn't fully right going into the Russia game but I just hoped to get through it. I scored a first-half try but early in the second I kicked a ball and pulled up with a groin strain. I knew it was related to the horseplay in the lift and to the dead leg.

Another scan revealed a grade two aductor strain. I was out of the Samoan game and I would be touch and go after that for the All Blacks game. My feelings were uncomplicated. I really could have done without this.

I missed ten days training in Japan. This was yet another chat that Joe had to have with the medics about me. What is it this time? Will he definitely be fit for a quarter-final?

Again I got the reprieve and I stayed on. For now we had dealt with Russia though. Kobe. October 3rd: Ireland 35 Russia 0.

When we play Samoa on October 12th we have been away for one month. It seems much longer than that since we set off as the number one ranked team in the world still patting our bellies after two warm-up wins over the Welsh.

Our World Cup has been well planned but the Japan game jolted us. Small problems now weary us. We wonder did we arrive in Japan too late. How did we get the raw end of the hotels carve up? We dwell on things.

Against the big units of Samoa though we scored seven tries. Jordan played well and scored a try. Media thinking was that Joe might remedy our 'one dimensional' attack problem by retaining Jordan for the quarter-final.

The following day's game between Japan and Scotland in Yokohama was being threatened by a typhoon. Whether it went ahead or not we were in a state of acceptance about our fate. We would be playing the All Blacks in Tokyo in a week's time. It could be the end of everything or the day we were reborn. Fukuoka. October 12th: Ireland 47 Samoa 5.

All Blacks. Tokyo 2019

Maybe I was a fraction too early and should have entered the channel wider.

We know this move and it hinges on timing. The thirteen runs a short line and the nine passes behind the thirteen to the ten. The ten has the blindside winger on his inside or the fifteen on his outside.

Getting the timing wrong is the mortal sin of all mortal sins in Joe Schmidt's catechism.

When Johnny took the ball behind the thirteen he had the inside option to Keith Earls and the outside option to me. Often a defender will jump at Johnny and he'll only have a split second to get it away. Johnny took the outside option. What has happened is that Johnny has delayed for a fraction of a second and he has been hit by Sevu Reece.

The ball spilled. The All Blacks went haring after it to the other end.

I have had to turn and chase. Beauden Barrett and I in a foot race I can't win. I chase and hope for the ball to take a bobble so that Beauden might break his stride to take it. No such luck. No bobble. He's just run straight onto it and over the line.

That's their third try. Twenty-two-nil now. Just over half an hour gone. This is my last World Cup game and probably my last international match. New Zealand are pasting us.

Now we're under the sticks just waiting for the conversion attempt and Johnny and myself are just looking at each other, both wondering who was at fault. We don't swap angry words. Johnny just gives me filthies whenever I look over at him. I have learned over the years it's best not to engage. That just makes it worse for both of us.

You don't stop Johnny in full flow. You might look up at the big screen waiting for the replay to see exactly what happened. If the big screen vindicates you, well then you might come back with a defence. You never come back on Johnny though until you are very sure of your ground.

This suddenly feels like an ending and Johnny's rage is a fitting soundtrack for our fade out. I'd miss his voice if it wasn't in my ears right now. We've played together for eighteen years, since we were in a Leinster Schools group at fifteen or sixteen years of age when he was good but not yet special.

When I first knew him Johnny hadn't yet become Johnny.

We became friendly when we were around seventeen or so. We went away to Welford Road to play Leicester in a game for Leinster schools and we got on well together. He was starting to shine a bit and getting a little bit more starting time.

When he came into the Leinster Senior squad in 2008 or so, you saw his self-confidence develop quickly. I had been in the squad for two years at that time and I was still pussyfooting.

Then one day Johnny had a go at Brian O'Driscoll in training. This was something never before done, let alone done by a young wet-behind-the-ears fellow just in the door. Johnny, though, was able to see things that other players couldn't see. So he had a cut off Brian. Something about running lines. Johnny wanted something done and Brian hadn't done it. Brian fought back. He was the god of Irish rugby then. He was expected to fight back.

We looked on with open mouths. This was really something. We were having a bit of laugh. He's called out BOD! What next?

There were a few comments along the lines of "fair play to him" but mainly lads were muttering, "Jesus, what does he think he's at?"

So now against New Zealand I'm distracted for a moment by thoughts of all the bust-ups with Johnny over the years. On the training field. In reviews. In games. We've never swung at each other but we've come close to it a few times. We might not speak for a few days afterwards. You just get on with it and things heal.

So, if it is going to end it seems right that it is like this. Brian O'Driscoll had the perfect fairytale of an ending in Paris in 2014. For the rest of us mere mortals the script is put together a bit more carelessly. If losing to the All Blacks with Johnny raging in my ear is the manner of my own farewell, I'll take it. New Zealand, Johnny Sexton and heartbreaking quarter-finals are career-long threads.

Training last week wasn't perfect for me. The niggles were always on my mind. I lost my focus on the game a little bit. I was thinking about how my groin felt more than how the All Blacks would feel. If there is one team you don't want to blur the focus on…

Colm Fuller, the physio whom I have worked with for the last couple of years, has worked miracles at this World Cup. He got me onto the field, first for Japan and now for New Zealand. I know, though, that needing Colm's services so much during a World Cup isn't ideal.

Our week of prep was actually brilliant. I could not fault Joe, although it would be popular to do so in the following weeks. Before the All Blacks, the old confidence had flowed back into the group. We hadn't been playing particularly well and knew that this was our World Cup final. This was the day we had been subconsciously holding ourselves back for.

At warm-up time when we noticed the river of green filtering into the stands as we went about our business, we were suddenly much encouraged. When the anthems were played Irish voices sounded with elemental unity. Even more so during the haka when we heard Irish fans cranking it up. At that moment our spines tingled, and our hairs stood on end. It was one of the greatest moments of my career.

We had never really done much thinking about the haka before Chicago. In Soldier Field we had formed ourselves into a number eight in memory of Anthony Foley. Since then we have always had some sort of response. Today we locked arms because Irish teams always speak about collective ability and how that can always overcome individual talents of other teams.

Then the *Fields of Athenry* came rolling across the grass like a giant wave, it flowed around us and lifted us up in its swell. We didn't hear a single syllable of the shouting from the sacred haka twenty yards away. Everybody in the stadium, every Irish fan, everybody within our own group felt there was something unbelievably special about this, it was going to be our day. The last thing that Bestie said to us in the huddle was to look around, to listen up, to hear that sound because this was it, this was our night.

Until kick-off everything was as close to perfect as you could have hoped for.

And then?

Nothing.

We never fired a shot. Robbie Henshaw and Garry Ringrose clashed heads just a few minutes in. Garry went off for stitches. Robbie didn't go but he needed stitches later. Jordan came on and played centre after ten or fifteen minutes. I think Keith Earls moved into the centre but it was all too frantic to notice. The tone was set.

The first try of their seven was Aaron Smith under the sticks. They kept moving their point of attack and carrying into our soft shoulders. We were absorbing all the pressure and going backwards.

Nothing fell for us the way we needed it to. We were thirty four to nil down before we even scored. By then there were only twelve minutes left.

The last whistle sounds and we know that this has been more than a World Cup quarter-final defeat. The era of Joe Schmidt is over. Some of us will never play for Ireland again. More of us will never play in another World Cup. For me it is certainly the last time I will face the mesmerising black jerseys. The sight of them lining up against us was always a reminder that you had reached that altitude where it was going to be tough but if you didn't want it that way you weren't worthy of your own jersey.

Afterwards no All Blacks player summons me from the gloom of our dressing room looking to swap my last Irish jersey for another All Black souvenir. I would love to have traded with Beauden Barrett. He made his debut for the All Blacks against us in that 60-0 game in Hamilton back 2012.

This has, most likely, been my last Irish game and I've seen him grow into an All Blacks legend. He has the little bit of Gaelic football in his background also and he knows the happiness of sharing a pitch with a brother or two. I liked the symmetry of a swap but we have lost and I'm too upset to go and ask.

This is an Irish rugby story after all. It's not Hollywood and there is no fairytale ending. No last act redemption either. The new normal of lockdowns and distancing awaits. The end isn't neat or without loose threads. So be it. Something gritty and realistic seems more appropriate anyway.

Epilogue

MORE THAN THE NUMBER

Myself and my brother Ross share the same birthday. We were both born on March 26th. So, always on my birthday Ross is there with me. Every year when I wake up on that day Ross is the first person that I think about. It is a bittersweet waking.

Growing up we would often go to visit his grave, five minutes up the road from home. On my birthday we would go up there as well. We still do after Sunday mass when we all go home for a weekend. The headstone is black and plain. Mum and Dad chose a short and perfect inscription: you will always be with us. All these years later those words ring true. I still feel that our lost brother is the one who has glued us together as a family. I still feel that he has always been with us through the adventures ever since.

I have always accepted my own identity. As the next brother along I have never tried to be a replacement for Ross in Mum and Dad's eyes. There are so many times, though, when I have just wished that he would have been able to share the moments of the last fifteen years with myself and the family.

I look at Dave and how the two of us went on to play for Leinster and Ireland together. When we stand for an anthem I don't think, if I was Ross would I have got these opportunities? I do wonder, though, what it would be like if he was with us. Would he be standing shoulder to shoulder to shoulder with Dave and myself as we girded ourselves to play? Would he be up there in the stands with Mum, Dad, Richard and Sara to watch us?

And now that my career is fading out, would I be looking forward to days when myself, Richard and Ross would walk together to Lansdowne to see the last dramas of Dave's career or even just to watch games with no family interest at all?

It is easy and true to say that life would have been better if Ross had been with us all through. Nobody wants the emotional scars that Mum and Dad, in particular, have borne but it is true too that our lives have been good and on those birthday mornings and other occasions I thank Ross for that.

When I came home from the World Cup I had a clear idea of how I hoped my career would end. I would have one more season on a considerably smaller contract but it would be a withdrawal process from rugby rather than the cold turkey of a sudden break. I knew that I couldn't go to a World Cup and then come home and simply never play rugby again.

I would play some games for Leinster and, in all likelihood, watch quite a few more games from the bench. With any luck I might make Ireland's Six Nations panel to bring some experience into what would be the early stages of the post-Joe Schmidt transition.

I would look around at all the faces which are so much fresher than my own and realise that the Leinster dressing room is far healthier and more inclusive then the one I walked into fifteen years ago. A dressing room where everybody gets on really well without any sort of a hierarchy.

I would use the time to figure out the rest of my life and to enjoy rugby and the professional life for the sake of it, as I once did before I learned to start worrying and stressing about it all.

It hasn't gone entirely to plan. For one thing it has been a sharp descent. It feels odd when the Irish guys are away from Leinster and I am left behind. I was in Eddie O'Sullivan's Six Nations camp before the 2007 World Cup and had been in every one of them since, bar when I was injured in 2011.

I have a few friends left behind at Leinster in those quiet weeks but the majority of the guys available are academy lads or recent graduates. They are twelve or thirteen years younger than myself. I can't remember if when I was their age I even noticed the guys who were as old then as I am now.

I find too that I have a lot more free time to do things. I never had that before. I don't know what to do with the time. I went skiing one week. In season. All my career I would have been too afraid of injuries to do that. I don't know if that's a sign of not caring as much anymore or of transitioning to post-rugby life in a healthy way.

And I find that I had so many conversations with myself and with others debating whether I would have been better off with a clean break after the World Cup. Just saying enough is enough. But I realised quite quickly that's not what I wanted.

The bit of pride keeps you going too. I don't want to start training really poorly, not caring about games and playing shite some weekend and making a complete show of myself. That is driving me on too. I'd like to think that I am still as hard a trainer as I was fifteen years ago.

There is a coffee shop five minutes up the road from the Leinster training ground in UCD, a place called the Thru The Green Coffee Company. It's a drive-thru setup and the lads always go there during the day in the gap after the pitch session and before the weights. We jump into the car and it's five minutes up the road. It's good coffee and a very interesting way of seeing who you are friendly with.

Everybody gets on in the dressing room but you would only jump in the car for coffee with somebody whom you actually want to go for coffee with. It's not a long time to spend with somebody but you have to enjoy the company as much as the beans. Some days in the car it would be Jordan and myself.

It's not mentoring. He's way beyond that. I enjoy his company and we get on well. He's carefree and a very funny, good-humoured lad. And there is a lot of humility to him given the stages where we are both at now.

After the two Northampton games where I had the epiphany that Jordan was the future I moved into a state of acceptance. What amazes me about him is that he is so young, has so many caps and so many incredible tries and there is not the slightest trace of entitlement in him.

I first noticed Jordan in a Six Nations training camp. Joe had called him in for training. I knew nothing about him. Was he just out of school? He looked young enough. He came in and straight away he was side stepping all these lads, left, right and centre. But he did it with this very likeable demeanour to him. Some kids do that and the old guys will be putting the hits on them. There was none of that. I remember that I was just thinking good feet, good step. The real stuff starts here though. Then later there was his try in Thomond Park! I said, fasten the seat belt, there is some competition here now. I wasn't yet thinking here's the lad who will probably take over but he was very much on the radar.

He doesn't need my help at all but I would like to think that I can pass the jersey to him with the same grace that Girvan Dempsey showed to me years ago. And, of course, it is much easier for me to play the role of Girvan because Jordan has never given full-of-himself press conferences telling everybody that he wants to be the fifteen while somebody else was still warming the jersey.

I like to think that I once had a little bit of what Jordan has when I was younger. The confidence of not worrying about mistakes. The hunger to want to make breaks. The older you get the more you worry. That happened to me, definitely. I'm not sure if it doesn't happen to most sports people as they understand more the relevance and importance of events. When you know less you fear less.

With Jordan we'd have a lot of non-rugby chat. We rarely talk too much about the game. Just normal stuff that people talk to their mates about. Holidays or golf or what you did at the weekend. Life. Nothing ground-breaking, a relationship just built on solid friendship.

From a selfish point of view (being a professional athlete is to have a selfish point of view), Jordan's emergence makes retirement a little easier too. I'll enjoy watching him with Leinster and Ireland for the next decade. Having got so much from my time in the blue and green jerseys I am happy to just be a fan.

Small pleasures like the coffee runs have made the last season more interesting but, of course, the year has all unfolded in a way that nobody could ever have expected.

As we approached the business end of a rugby spring we broke up for the intrusion of real life. Pandemic. Lockdown. Life and death. The game just ceased to be played. If you wanted some perspective heading into retirement that was it. Rugby can just stop when the world has more important issues to worry about. People dying slowly of this unforeseen plague made any complaints about big losses and unlucky injuries feel mildly obscene.

The gratitude for the last fifteen years just grows and grows.

In the meantime there is a final season to be finished, a postscript still to be written on my playing days. The end of the great 2020 lockdown brought a new normal to all parts, even to rugby. The last months of my rugby career will be so unlike all that went before that there is no danger of the memories all blurring together.

We resumed playing with a Pro 14 game against Munster. That's called getting back in at the deep end.

We did a three-week block of pre-season as rugby resumed in the new environment. We were living in a world of Zoom meetings and safety webinars, strict guidelines and PCR testing. Sports science was making room for more traditional science in determining the run of our days. So many matters hinged on issues we'd never given thought to a few months earlier. Our contacts, our transport, our precautions. We would get back to contact rugby on a strictly graduated basis.

In the week before our actual match week began the plans were well thought out. On Thursday the main feature of the week was scheduled. We would play a short full contact game amongst ourselves in an empty RDS.

The day would incorporate team meetings in small groups and in the evening there would be a social event out in UCD with Christy Moore coming to play for us in the gym. We would have the following day, Friday, off creating a long weekend before we went into the routine of a full match week and the rest of the season.

We had been doing little bits and pieces of contact but the Thursday game was to be twenty minutes of full contact, with a referee present, experiencing the echoes of an empty stadium. The starting fifteen names that morning would play the best version we could create of the team which we thought Munster would field the following weekend.

I was full back on that team with Hugo Keenan and Cian Kelleher on the wings. My target was to survive and a little more, to show myself as still being comfortable in this environment, still available and ready. I wasn't unusual in this. The bibs team doing our best impression of Munster all had two objectives. Help prepare the team as well as possible. Train well and show up as available and ready. Let the coaches know you are in a good place.

There's work to be done and I'm not sentimental but early on I get a ferocious shoulder in a tackle from my brother Dave. I can't remember the last time that myself and Dave were opposite each other in a full contact game. Jesus, I think, it is a long, long time if ever that he has done that to me.

A few minutes into the match there is a breakdown and one of the opposition finds himself stuck on our side of the ruck. I smack him on the back telling him to get out of the way. I shout at the ref that this is a penalty. My protests are punctuated by a shoulder come in from the side of the ruck and hitting me in the back.

I turn and square up. It's Johnny. He's pissed with me and I am pissed with him and the two of us get into a little bit of pushing which accelerates into a few swings, that are more than smacks but less than punches.

Johnny knows it too and behind the swinging when we look at each other there is a shared amusement. Aren't we a pair of gobshites throwing slaps in an empty stadium when we're going for a bit of food together in Johnny's house afterwards! We're both half laughing, half serious when Scott Fardy and Sean Cronin comes in and breaks the two of us up. No damage done.

When the game finished they had two tries to our one. As they were preparing for the game the following week they were given a little bit more ball than us. These things are coach-influenced sometimes.

I felt fine. I felt good. The big thing was that I didn't feel out of place. Just fitted in, which was all I wanted to do. Johnny and I sought each other out, the two of us grinning sheepishly. There was a hug and a laugh. Like two good friends.

No trace of the incident. By four in the afternoon our little group for the day; myself, James Lowe, Cian Kelleher, Jamison Gibson Park, Fergus McFadden were in Johnny's house eating sausage sandwiches and steak and trying to finish a discussion on what rogue elements could affect our preparations in the run up to the Munster game.

We drove to UCD to see Christy Moore at six o'clock. Leo Cullen stood up and said a few words and then for the second time in the day Johnny sideswiped me. Leo said the team wanted to honour two servants of Leinster rugby who had been a part of so much down through the years. I sussed straight away that he was talking about myself and Fergus. Johnny got up.

Johnny didn't say much. When Johnny speaks to Leinster or Ireland, emotion is always close to the surface. Those groups are second family to him and in that second family there would be nobody closer to him than myself and Ferg. Along with Devin Toner, Sean Cronin and Cian Healy we all played either as schoolboys together or we have come through the ranks almost as a package in the last fifteen years.

When the emotion rises in him Johnny loses control of his words. I have a strange feeling. I know that if I was watching this scene with any two other players being honoured, I would be feeling very emotional myself but because I am involved I instinctively detach myself so that I can speak and shake hands and do what needs to be done.

I can feel how emotional it is for us as friends, I know without bigging myself and Ferg up that Johnny will feel our absence when we are gone, as we will miss the days of laughing with him or bickering with him or occasionally being slightly in awe of him still. But for now, I am holding myself together.

Emmet Farrell pushes a button and we are shown two short films on the big TV, what reality shows might call our best bits. Brian O'Driscoll said some nice things about me, Isa did the same, and then there was a three-minute montage of my best moments in blue. Then Brian and Isa signed off and my dad popped up on the screen and said a few words. Johnny had Zoom called both my dad and Fergus's dad to put this together last week.

Myself and Ferg were both presented with framed collages of photos from our best days. It fell to Dave to present mine to me. I was still feeling the shoulder he'd put into me earlier in the day but Dave got a little emotional too. It was another short speech. Sean Cronin did the honours for Ferg.

I said a few words to the squad. I told them that I was grateful to have the chance to close out the next three months with them all and to be in the position to go and win some trophies. I was going to give it everything I had to get the best version of myself out there and available if needed. I told them that the best memories of the previous fifteen years were made on the days when we were winning trophies.

The collage I carry in my head is of trophy winning days. The other days are less enjoyable. As a group, I said, we are in an incredibly privileged position now to be able to win more trophies. Let's go and do that.

I was calm and said what I wanted to say but in my heart I could feel what a perfect rugby day this was. The timing was just right. Everything unfolded perfectly. Johnny and myself still more warriors than old codgers had gone at each other but then came the easy resumption of our old friendship, the eating together, and then this evening.

I've played rugby with Fergus since fifth year in school. We couldn't count the days or measure the fun. Hearing Johnny and Dave speak, watching Sean and Fergus, who are so close, everything was right. And the intimacy of the occasion made it more special than any handshake and slap on the back that you might get in Lansdowne Road with fifty thousand people clapping.

Christy took the stage and entertained as much as ever. His songs are his but they feel like they belong to any audience he has, and for us in that small gathering the music sealed our togetherness on the edge of the resumed season.

We beat Munster on August 22nd. Jordan struggled under a few high balls. Dave picked up a hamstring injury. If it was raining soup the poor man would have a fork in his hand. I played full back in our next game against Ulster. Neither Jordan's struggles nor Dave's injury were as serious as feared.

The story of the rest of the season will be set in the new normal. Then my life will shift to another 'new normal'.

The future in general is both scary and exciting. Rugby is all that I have known. It is what I have been good at and the prospect of finishing up and reintegrating myself into the real world is scary.

It will be hard to find a new purpose but it is something that every player has to go through and after fifteen years and all that came with them I can hardly complain. I have wrung every last drop out of the game.

I remind myself often that back around early 2016 I didn't know that I would even have these extra few years. As such I am very conscious this year to commit to everything exactly as I have done over the span of my career. How I behave this season is going to determine how so many people in the organisation will view me. The last impression is the strongest. I want my attitude to be exactly the same this year as it has always been.

It's a bit harder because I am a little on the outside but I don't think my relationship with the coaches has diminished. When I am told that I am not playing it doesn't sting as much as it would have a few years ago but it still takes a conscious effort not to let it visibly bother me. I have to remind myself to just enjoy this year for what it is. I still have a job where I am doing something that I love. I'm still enjoying my team-mates' company. It's still enjoyable and it still beats the hell out of an office job.

In fact, it beats the hell out of any other job I can imagine doing. Some days I am optimistic enough to think that I am adequately equipped for real life. I have been the chairman of the Players Association for the last seven years. I sit on a handful of boards. I have the recruitment firm with my friend Andrew, a few of us are involved together in two successful (pre-lockdown anyway) pubs in Dublin and I have an out-of-left-field investment in a company called Oslo Health in Dublin.

I have the economics degree and the MBA in business that I completed when my knee was crocked. I know that I would like to do a little bit more with all those things but none of them pull me towards doing a whole lot more. There is interest there but not the love or passion.

I have a decent insight into how sport works and about managing sport. I think that is where the passion lies, the business area of sport. What the job that would completely suit me looks like I still don't know but I will listen to ideas.

I don't want to coach because I don't think I'd be very good at it. Anyway, I look forward to what other people call 'weekends', spending time with family, starting my own family and not having to live according to a fixture schedule.

I don't want to be a pundit, except maybe to dabble occasionally. Everybody at this juncture wants to go into the media. It feels like an enjoyable job and it keeps you involved in sport. We all have the impression too that it is easy. You don't have to go to an office, you go to games. I see the attraction, there is something very convenient about it.

For now, though, I want the difficult challenge of finding a new purpose for myself and a new identity. I don't want to be forever trapped in who I used to be and what I used to do.

After fifteen years as a pro and a lifetime where I could never think of anything except being a pro, I expected that the outline of the next chapter would be clearer. I know that I am coming to the end of my lease on boyhood dreams but there are days when I wake up and think if given the option of playing for another year or two, I'd take that option because my body still feels good and I believe I still have a lot to offer.

That's how lucky I have been. I'm potentially dragging myself away from something I truly loved doing. Not many people ever get to live their dream life when they are young and fit and innocent enough to enjoy it for what it is.

It's not as if other passions aren't there. Lockdowns situations dictate that Jess and I won't be having a wedding until next year, 2021. My mind already swings towards that, the day and all the days beyond it as the next thing to go into with commitment and joy.

Maybe I have been wrong. There can be a fairy tale ending without a fifteen written on my back and fourteen guys in front of me. I can be more than the number. I can be half of one team and part of lots of others.

Next thing.

A LETTER
TO YOU

Where to begin?

Maybe I'll start at the end. My 219th and final cap against Ulster a few weeks ago in the Aviva Stadium. Nearly 15 years to the day from my debut against Ospreys in 2005.

I hoped it wouldn't be my last involvement in a Leinster jersey, but the reality is that in sport and professional sport especially, you just never know when you will get a chance again, so you treasure each chance you get in that jersey.

It wasn't my last involvement with the team and Ferg and I were granted the unbelievable honour of lifting a trophy on behalf of the 53 players two weeks later.

You always want one more as a player. The next one becomes the most important. The next match, the next trophy, the next training session even. That is the process, that is the drive within us.

It wasn't to be, but I am so very grateful for every run out that I did get in a Leinster and an Ireland jersey.

Losing to Saracens brought my time in a Leinster jersey and by extension an Irish jersey to an end.

I spoke to the players in the dressing room after the game and I spoke about living a dream, because that is what I have done.

I have lived the dream of every five-year-old boy or girl out there that dreams of pulling on a Leinster jersey, an Ireland jersey, a Lions jersey.

I consider myself very fortunate to have done the greatest thing that I could have done with my life and I have lived the dreams that I first had as a young lad in Dundalk RFC with the minis.

I also consider myself very fortunate because I have parents that supported and facilitated that dream and still do to this day.

To my mum and dad, thank you both so much.

You gave me the opportunity to make the most of my talents and to fulfil the ambitions that I had as a young boy.

To Richard and Sara, my older and younger siblings. We have shared some brilliant days together but your support away from the big days and the bright lights meant even more. Thank you.

To Dave. So many memories of watching you playing a few years behind me and watching you progress and such an overwhelming sense of pride to see you selected for the Academy, then make your debut and putting on an Ireland shirt alongside me. You have made the last 11 years all the better for having you by my side every day and I'll miss that the most.

To Jess. Thanks for your support. It's time to start our next adventure and I can't wait to do it with you by my side.

You never get to write the script, but if I could, it would go as far as a packed RDS or Aviva in front of thousands of Leinster and Irish Rugby supporters where I would have had the opportunity to thank you all.

The Leinster and Ireland supporters' role in this journey has been special and running out in front of full stadia is what gives the greatest buzz and we have all missed that over the last few months and you appreciate it all the more now playing in empty arenas.

I remember when we played away in Toulouse in the European quarter-final in 2006. Nobody gave us a chance but we came away with a win and played some unbelievable rugby along the way. It was the first time that I could sense the belief in the support as well. That trip home to Dublin and looking into the eyes of the supporters that had made the trip. Belief.

You all felt the same as us. That this club could become a mainstay of European rugby, a firepower to be reckoned with and you've stayed with us for every step since.

For Ireland, the sea of green in Chicago and in Twickenham on St. Patrick's Day for our Grand Slam decider are images that will be ingrained in me for life.

To get to that point, though, you need good coaches, good doctors, S&C and physios, good players and team-mates and I have been very fortunate to have been surrounded by them in Dundalk, in Clongowes Wood College, in UCD and, of course, in Leinster and Ireland.

Michael Cheika who gave me my first Leinster cap and did

so much for the club, Joe, Matt, Leo and Stuart. Each in their own way contributing to the journey and to the stars on the jersey and the trophies back at UCD.

I have also been very fortunate to have worked alongside some world class strength and conditioning coaches and medics. They have helped me through some tough periods in my career and I am forever grateful to them.

The medals and what you achieve are great but they are just by-products of good culture, good people and a relentless drive to do better. And we had that in spades in the teams I played with in Leinster and with Ireland.

There have been so many others that have played their part in my journey to this point and if I start a list now I will never stop but suffice to say you know who you are and over the next few weeks and months I'll catch up and thank you in person.

I would, though, like to mention David McHugh and his team in Line Up Sports. David has been my manager but he has been more than that and is a very close friend and has provided personal support over many years.

Thank you all once more and I look forward to being a supporter again, like I was in Dundalk all those years ago.

Rob, September 24th, 2020

A note of thanks and appreciation to all those who have supported me throughout my career as valued partners who I have built long standing and personal relationships with, which will continue long beyond the end of my playing career:

Audi Ireland – Thorsten Godulla, Richard Molloy, Aine Smyth
Nike – Barney Keeler and Jennifer O'Reilly
National Dairy Council – Zoe Kavanagh, Cathy Curran &
Jeanne Spillane
Aer Lingus – Mary Kate Lavin & Roz Duff
Newbridge Silverware – William & Oonagh Doyle
Bank of Ireland – Gemma Bell, Sharon Wood and all the team
Vodafone – Anne O'Leary, Gerry Nixon & Caroline
Hutchinson and the team at Vodafone
Optimum Nutrition – Hugh McGuire